CW01661485

THE DIVORCE DILEMMA

By the same author

THE COMFORT OF SIN
PROSTITUTES AND PROSTTUTION IN THE 1990s

The Divorce Dilemma

Richard Goodall

RENAISSANCE BOOKS

THE DIVORCE DILEMMA
by Richard Goodall

First published 2000 by Renaissance Books

Renaissance Books is an imprint of
Global Books Ltd
PO Box 219, Folkestone, Kent CT20 3LZ

© 2000 Richard Goodall

ISBN 1–898823–45–6

All rights reserved. No part of this publication may be reproduced or transmitted in any form or by any means without prior permission in writing from the Publishers.

British Library Cataloguing in Publication Data
A CIP catalogue entry for this book is available from the British Library

Set in Bembo roman 12 on 12 point
by Bookman, Hayes, Middlesex
Printed in England by Bookcraft Ltd., Midsomer Norton, Avon

Contents

Preface

In fairness, the reader should be made aware from the outset that my own personal credo supports the view that the unrestricted availability of divorce is, both from a personal and a social standpoint, a grave mistake; that the majority of those who divorce and remarry are, on a statistical basis, no happier than they were; that people who have remarried may be tempted to divorce and marry for the third or more times, thus on the one hand endorsing the general acceptability of divorce as a normal occurrence and, on the other, creating a self-perpetuating circle of 'divorce-prone people'; that the consequences of divorce are always exceptionally grave for the children of marriages that have failed, quite apart from having a negative and expensive impact on society as a whole; that divorce has already gone a long way to destroying the family as a socio-economic unit, and if unrestrained, will cause the family, even as it is normally understood in the twenty-first century, to disappear completely; and that the disappearance of the family is a major, if not the most important, factor in the increase in crime, juvenile violence, failure of moral sense and general judgement about people and events, social instability, lack of shame, of pride in one's traditions, absence of standards, and corruption of that moral sense, which alone can ensure the survival of a civilization and protect the individual from the all-embracing and ever increasing powers of the State.

These are the views of what I consider to be a moderate,

middle-class professional, one who is extrememly concerned about the unrestrained exercise of personal passions and whims and who believes that old-fashioned virtues such as honesty, trust, honour, manliness, self-respect, dignity, integrity, discipline, self-control, patriotism, and pride in one's family and country should not be allowed to be overtaken by selfishness, moral consumerism, unreasonableness, intolerance, and the outpourings of sick minds intent on exploiting the sexual weaknesses and foibles of a society which has lost its sense of direction and has become totally devoid of common sense.

Indeed, I invite anyone, from whatever walk of life, to challenge my premise that the ever-increasing rate of teenage pregnancies, violence against women and children, abortions, illegitimacy, venereal diseases, openly displayed pornography and of extraordinary violence in crimes are a disgrace to the Anglo-American cultures and ethos.

One of the problems is that we have a tendency, especially in the UK and US perhaps, to listen to preachers who are standing in the wrong pulpit. Thus we get agony aunts, whose marriage/s have failed, pontificating on how to keep a husband happy; women who have had no children advising on breast-feeding; non-drivers on traffic schemes; drug addicts on decriminalization of certain drugs; politicians with vested interests of one kind or the other, especially financial, on what certain laws should be; writers and politicians who have themselves been divorced, on the merits of the family unit; people who have forgotten to pray, on the value of the Christian, or indeed any, religion. Their views are as valueless as those of a vegetarian judging the quality of an Aberdeen Angus steak.

Whilst it is all too clear to my friends and family that I do not keep company with angels, I would beg for a hearing of what I see as a common-sense remedy for the damage caused to the family by divorce. It is a remedy which will, almost certainly, be unpopular and will, almost certainly, hurt. My proposal is that where there are children, there cannot be divorce. Where there is no divorce, the family bond will surely be strengthened. Where the family becomes once again a strong social and economic unit, the individual will gain protection, vis-à-vis the State, and the family itself will represent a haven of discipline and stability for the youngsters who will have to become the pillars of tomorrow's social structure.

To keep it within its narrowest confines, the essential family consists of father, mother, children and grandparents. Any other version of it or attempt to change it is misguided and corrupt and, in my view, doomed to produce consequences, the ill-effects of which we experience daily in our lives and which will become much more serious as time passes. To preserve such a family, where there are children, divorce must be eliminated.

Where the family bonds are strengthened, the family itself will be widened. In that way, children will have the benefit of the love and care not only of two parents, but of grandparents, uncles and aunts, cousins, and so on. Kinship and companionships will be revived. I cannot accept that these are old-fashioned notions: surely, it is quite the reverse. To me, it is without question that their validity transcends unbridled self-assertion, individualism, selfishness, moral feebleness, feminism, and both female and male homosexuality.

□

The reader will find that not too much attention has been dedicated in these pages to the concept of love. A simple explanation is that in every language 'love' is probably the most abused word, utilized to express a range of emotions and tendencies which are either unnatural, illegal or illicit. Accordingly, I have endeavoured to avoid referring too often to it since I subscribe to the view that as a component of a stable and successful marital relationship within which children can be protected and develop at the same time, it is less important than many other aspects of family life or relationships which are not so frequently recognized or praised. One may be forgiven for believing that love weighs less on the scale of a successful marriage than affection, care, consideration, companionship, devotion, loyalty, tolerance, mutual support and respect.

These virtues are not advocated in our society, nor, for the most part, in Western society generally. Some might say that such virtues are no longer understood. But it is they that hold a marriage together, particularly when the passions of youth give way to the tolerance of maturity and the gratitude of old age or, indeed, senility.

It is these unsung virtues that require rehabilitation. The hymn of glory sung daily in our press and on television to so-called individual freedoms, moral relativism, perversions and deviations proffered as normal, if not more praiseworthy aims than a stable and lasting family relationship, should give way to the realization that our society will not survive unless the family is restored to the status it has always held in those societies and organizations which have proved productive and successful.

The self-degradation and intellectual onanism of divorce at will, illegitimacy, single motherhood, pornography, lesbianism and homosexuality are infinitely less important, in the final outcome, than a strong, stable, traditional, family which, apart from any moral consideration, is the most powerful economic unit that has ever existed.

Instead, we seem to have decided that common sense and conventional wisdom no longer have any meaning and that they should be replaced by hysteria, perversion and dogma. As to these two latter features, the reader will be able to form his/her own view in the fullness of time.

As to hysteria, some very convincing evidence emerged in the last two months of 1999 when the number of divorce petitions in the UK escalated in a manner which can only be described as extraordinary. People decided, no doubt, that they wanted to start the Third Millennium with a clean sheet, and, accordingly, rushed to give effect to their decision, so thereby staking a claim, as it were, to a new life. Such an action is reminiscent of the same determination that currently guides around half the residents of Great Britain to the lottery, prompted by the forlorn hope that they might become millionaires.

And on the subject of money, consider, for example, the overall cost arising from the ever-increasing splintering of families, with the disruption that it causes to individuals, to the property market, and so on. No proper calculation has ever been made of such costs.

□

It is interesting to point out that the British situation is but an echo of the American experience. It is of course well known that there is an ongoing debate in the United States about 'family values' and that a number of objections have been raised to the concept of 'no fault' divorce, with its calamitous result as far as children are concerned. In the course of this discussion, I draw attention to the fundamental studies by Judith Wallerstein and Sandra Blakeslee. They are American authors who, in my view, have done more than anybody else to show what a damaging effect divorce has on children. In fact, the Americans themselves were so shocked by this particular study that some termed it a 'bombshell'.

However, it is a bomb which does not appear to have caused very much damage, although it did achieve one result. It raised the consciousness of Americans to the consequences of divorce vis-à-vis the children so much so that studies by the Family Research Council (September 1993) showed conclusively that 77% of Americans agreed with the proposition that children suffer when their parents divorce. But that is as far as they were prepared to go, because when asked whether, when there are children in the family, parents should stay together even if they do not get along, 65% disagreed with the questioner, and when further questioned about whether when there are no children a married couple should stay together regardless of whether or not they get along, an even greater percentage (80%) disagreed.

Put differently, it is clear that the American public accepts that divorce is damaging to the children, but is not prepared to do much about it. (See 'The American Enterprise' (July/August 1995) and 'National Opinion Research Center' (January/May 1994).) Or perhaps, this statement is not entirely fair because at least in Michigan they want to do something about it, since it has been suggested there that the old requirement of proving fault in cases where only one spouse is seeking a divorce, should be restored to the divorce book. Put differently, in order to get a divorce unless both parties agree, one of the spouses will have to show that the other is 'at fault'; and the faults mentioned include desertion, drug or alcohol abuse, physical or mental abuse, infidelity, or a prison sentence of three or more years.

It will not do. The clock can never be put back in this sense. To argue that the concept of fault should be reinstated because no-fault divorce damages the health of the children is no different from maintaining that smoking is bad but we can continue our puffing provided we use a cigarette with a filter. The problem in America is no different from the British one. The 1970s saw the advent of no-fault divorce at the same time as new sexual and living patterns were established that resulted in a confusion of the roles of men and women, let alone in an extraordinary increase in the divorce rate.

The USA already has the second highest divorce rate in the world after Russia, as well as the highest rate of cohabitation of couples before marriage (respectively 4.1 per 1000 and 50%). Indeed, the jump in the rate of cohabitation before marriage is even greater than that of divorce because it is recorded that in the 1960s only 8% of American couples cohabited before tying the knot. It is interesting to observe that only 1 in 16 marriages was at that time ending in divorce and even though then that was the highest rate of divorce in the world, it makes almost quaint reading compared to the present rate of more than 1 in 2.

Of course, we can try and say many things that will make us feel better. Like Constance Ahrons, a sociologist at the University of Southern California, we might even say that there are such things as 'The Good Divorce' (that's the title of a book she wrote in 1994). I suppose you could also argue that there is such a thing as a good cigarette.

The reader will forgive my cynicism. In the West, it could be said that we are following in the footsteps of Tom Paine, the political pamphleteer who in the 1770s, having separated from his wife, was rather outspoken regarding the need of divorce reform. We have got that reform but the question of whether we are any happier as a result has still not been answered.

□

The position in the United States is examined at greater length as an Appendix at the end of the book. Meanwhile, it may not be entirely a coincidence that a number of people, both in England and the United States, are gradually coming round to the view that one ought to challenge the notion that divorce should be blindly accepted as an inevitable fact of life. It must be more than a truism that in a society with a very high rate of divorce, not only is it a fact that more unhappy marriages end up that way, but the inevitable consequence of the free availability of divorce is that many more marriages are likely to become unhappy, whether divorce follows or not. And that is the gravest indictment of our Anglo-American society, namely that we are all becoming much less happy.

The reader may be tempted to believe that the style adopted in this book, and more especially some of the recommendations that are made in an attempt to remedy the present situation, appear to show a certain lack of compassion for my fellow human beings, demonstrating almost a 'holier than thou' attitude. If such an impression is created, allow me to apologize now. My own flaws aside, however, the only claim I would make in my defence is, through my experience of the law, the fact that I have acquired a degree of practicality and good sense in dealing with problems generated by my fellow human beings.

More particularly, I feel for all those whose marriages are unhappy, or who end up by divorcing: there, but for the grace of God... Apart from the loss of a loved one and serious illness, I cannot think of anything worse than an unhappy marriage, especially where it has to come to an end. Indeed, more than half my friends have experienced failed marriages. What has not befallen me is purely the result of luck, for which I thank God, almost daily.

In addition to luck, however, it is conceivable that my wife and I managed not to divorce for a number of reasons which must be part of our psychological make-up. For example, we may have taken a more cautious approach to the choice of a spouse; perhaps our innate cynicism has prevented us from believing that we might be happier after divorce, or upon remarriage, since human beings are all more or less alike; possibly, we lack imagination, and are thus unable to see that the grass is greener on the other side of the fence (assuming without conceding that such be the case); perhaps a lack of initiative prevented us from wishing to experience the excitement and novelty – some might say, the irritation and monotony – of getting used to the personality, habits, whims, foibles and, perhaps, on occasions, the virtues of a second, third or fourth spouse; maybe in the case of one of us the decision to stay at home, have children and rear a family resulted in the deprivation of seeing and conceivably being attracted to or preferring another person; more probably, our Christian (Catholic) upbringing induced us to believe our marriage vows and as a result, to work hard to ensure that marriage would be a success. I actually cannot tell, for in truth I do not know.

But that ignorance should not disqualify this writer from expressing a view, in particular because all he seeks to achieve is to project a different point of view and to engender a debate over a most important social issue.

RICHARD GOODALL
Spring 2000

THE THREE 'Cs' OF THE MARRIAGE LIFELINE

Once upon a time, society insisted that young children should be taught at least the three 'Rs': reading writing and arithmetic ('math' in the US). This was considered fundamental for their future job prospects, enrichment and for ensuring that they would become useful members of the community. Nowadays, I would strongly urge that our youngsters, having learned the three 'Rs' (albeit in many cases, with a struggle, and in some cases not at all), receive education in the three 'Cs', for the purpose of ensuring that they understand what the marital relationship is all about. These are: **Commitment** (to each other and the children, for life), **Consideration** (to each other and the children) and **Care** (for each other and the children). If modern trends are anything to go by, such an education is sorely needed since the youth of today steers clear of commitment in any shape or form.

Indeed, adventurous though they may be in other respects (travelling the world, experimenting with drugs, and otherwise) our youngsters appear terrified of the risks of enduring emotional involvement. Whether this is because sexual relations have become much easier and personal independence more convenient, is not easy to determine. It is a fact, however, that youngsters no longer marry: they merely cohabit. Even when they marry, they do not mean the relationship to be lifelong, since they start off from the premise that, should the relationship not work, they would divorce.

When in fact they do marry, it tends to be at a later age than previously; but the number of marriages continues to fall, as indeed they do elsewhere in the industrial world, including Japan, and in the UK marriage is at its lowest ebb. Furthermore, youngsters tend to live alone, even though they may share flats. Loneliness seems to have become a major component in the life of many people today, a condition reinforced by the increase in the suicide rate.

Consideration is another word for companionship. It is interesting to note that the latter word is hardly used nowadays. Consideration does not seem to come very high on the list of priorities for people who get married today. One wonders what ideas of consideration and companionship prompt those couples who ever more frequently decide to live apart as from day one of their married life.

And what can one say about the concept of the care of children at the beginning of the twenty-first century? The statistics we shall be looking at in more detail later, beyond any doubt demonstrate that a great number of them are illegitimate, more than two million live with a single parent (one in four families is now headed by a single parent), and an even greater number will suffer the trauma of a home broken by divorce. Moreover, if their parents in fact were married, the children will have been born to mothers in their late 20s or, more likely, 30s, and even sometimes 40s and, by their parents' choice, will be single children. The parents themselves, in 51% of all marriages in the United Kingdom, will have divorced, paying little or no attention to the well-being of their children.

Put another way, in Tony Blair's Britain, according to a BBC *Newsnight* report on 8 February 2000, out of a classroom of 30 children, 12 will be born outside marriage, 7 will be from one-parent families, and at least 2 will be living with step-parents. That leaves less than a third of the children coming from the once conventional two- (natural) parent family home.

This is no rosy picture.

Introduction

Divorce, together with abortion, is a sphere of human activity where the individual (man or woman) is allowed to avoid the consequences of his action (other than those who pursue criminal or fraudulent action which is not detected). For example, if we exceed the speed limit, or are caught with alcohol in our bloodstream, even slightly in excess of what the law decrees, or are responsible for dangerous driving, or for causing loss of life or limb through our driving, we cannot be heard to say, by the laws of Great Britain at any rate, that we did not intend to do any harm. Our motives become totally irrelevant. Indeed, it does not matter how carefully and responsibly we may be when driving on the motorway at a hundred miles per hour. If caught, we shall almost certainly get fined and maybe disqualified. We might be in a hurry for an appointment or rushing to hospital to see a parent who is dying: our motive is irrelevant to our conviction, though possibly not to the punishment meted out to us.

But in the case of divorce, if we make a mistake by marrying the wrong partner, we do not have to pay the damages that we would pay if we broke a contract, nor do we get prosecuted, because it is not believed that we have committed any offence. We are allowed to break up the marriage and indeed, if we wish, we are free to remarry and escape completely, as far as any escape is possible but certainly, escape as far as the law is concerned, from the consequences of our mistake and, above all, of the promises made when we entered into the marriage to love, cherish and live together, forever. In the case of a woman, until recently, British law also provided for capital or income payments; now, either spouse is entitled to them. In other words, we may even profit, financially speaking, from our own error of judgement, regardless of our duty to our spouse and our children, if any.

In fact, since 1 November 1998, we may continue to profit, regardless of the divorce. On that day, three paragraphs of Schedule 8 of the Family Law Act 1996 came into force. Their effect is to reverse the position which had stood for thirty years, namely that anyone who had agreed a divorce financial settlement was safe in terms of capital. Put differently, an ex-wife could only have one bite at the cherry in terms of capital, and she got it either by way of a transfer of the matrimonial home or some other asset, and/or a lump sum.

This position is no longer true. It is now possible for any ex-spouse (wife or husband) who is receiving maintenance to come back for more capital regardless of how long ago the divorce took place, and regardless also of the fact that at the time of the divorce it might have been clearly understood, either because of the agreement reached between the parties, or because the Court so ordered, that they could never come back for more of the family cash. All this is happening without any consideration of the damage done to the children, and is all the more significant because that damage is substantial.

The primary duty of marriage, which arises when children are procreated, is recognized by the law in many ways: a duty to maintain, support, feed, educate; and corresponding rights are afforded by the law to the parties vis-à-vis each other, and in their relations with the outside world (third parties and the State). But these duties do not include an obligation to consider the well-being of the children when taking decisions which, affecting as they do the family unit, have consequences for the youngsters. When they decide to divorce, provided they pay out money to feed, clothe and educate their offspring, parents need not bother unduly about the children's spiritual well-being.

Indeed, we as a society, along with the rest of the industrialized world, have come to take divorce so much for granted that we have ceased to consider what it entails for the parties, and above all, for their children. People say that they have divorced once or twice and/or remarried, in the same way as they say that they have been on holiday to Spain or Turkey or Florida or elsewhere; or that they have had a toothache or a filling. Speech is so casual: but the casualness of the words cannot hide the tragedy in terms of personal relations, even allowing for the laxity of current social mores. But above all, it cannot hide the damage done to the children, which is very great indeed. The reality is that the children are the only people who are not consulted about divorce and in all likelihood are not told about it until the very last moment. Their views seem to be discounted.

It is true that over the past few years society has, somewhat reluctantly, come round to acknowledging the fact that children may suffer when their parents divorce; but even in those studies where the authors have taken the trouble of considering the effect of divorce on the children – and regrettably there are not many – no stand is taken on the issue of whether divorce is a good or bad thing. It is merely taken for granted, almost as though there was concern that if the morality of divorce were tackled, one might be going against the current fashion.

□

We live in an increasingly fragmented society where, for whatever reason, views are polarized and turn constantly to extremism, of one kind or the other. Britain has been called the hooligan nation of Europe. It is not a flattering definition, but is quite apt. It is fortunately outside the scope of this book to consider the aberration of football hooliganism: but I make the point now, and shall stand by it throughout this discussion, that the fragmentation of our society and our country is purely and simply a reflection of the fragmentation of our family life and is a form of moral hooliganism. In the same way as we split up the family, we split up society; just as we quarrel within the family, so we argue amongst ourselves; in exactly the same manner as the child without two parents loses its sense of direction, so our society has lost its own.

Any reader who may be left in doubt as to the validity of the above statements may wish to consider the following facts:

1) More than 51% of marriages that take place in the United Kingdom end up in divorce (John Haskey in *Population Trends*, Volume 91, Spring 1998. ISBN 11-6209690).
2) There are 1.8 million single mothers in the UK, the highest percentage in the world (1.6 million in 1996 – op. cit., page 6).
3) There are now in the United Kingdom over 2.7 million illegitimate children (op. cit., page 13), in a population of 58 million.
4) 1 in 100 girls under the age of 15 are now pregnant and more than half have abortions. In 1997 there were 8,800 such pregnancies. In January and February 2000 Marie Stopes clinics (seven of them) arranged 6900 abortions (*The Times*, 2 March 2000).
5) 37% of all children born in the UK at the moment (40% in Scotland) are born out of wedlock; the equivalent figure for 1997 was 23%.
6) In Britain, 23% of families with dependent children are headed by a lone parent, the highest percentage in Europe (*The Times*, 30 September 1998). In Britain, one child in ten is living in poverty. (Rowntree Foundation Report, October 1998)
7) The cost of benefits to them in 1997 was £10 billion, the result of a system which treats single parents more favourably than married couples with children. (*Daily Mail*, 21 November 1997)
8) Britain has the highest number of teenage mothers in Europe, with more than 17 out of 20 in England and Wales being unmarried. (Policy Studies Institute Report 3 November 1998)
9) Women from divorced families are nearly twice as likely to become teenage mothers as those who grew up with both parents. (A study by Kathleen Kiernan for the Centre for the Analysis of Social Exclusion, LSE, 29 September 1997.)
10) The cost of divorce and family breakdown to the taxpayer has been calculated as £5 billion each year (Research Paper 96/42, page 74), such cost taking no account whatever of hidden items such as the enormous expenditure on extra housing, the cost of failure at work and school, and of the criminal activity which, as will be reviewed later, is very often a direct result of divorce. The cost of divorce to the Legal Aid fund alone amounted to £1.7 billion in 1998.
11) According to Patrick Tobin in his address as Chairman to the Headmasters' and Headmistresses' Conference (5 October 1998) the danger to children posed by divorce is greater than that of either drugs or alcohol.
12) The proportion of 'families' where there is only one parent is now (March 2000) 25% (Office for National Statistics).
13) Nine out of every 100 families is headed by a mother who has never married and has no 'steady' partner of the male sex (*ibid*).

In my view, it is impossible to deny the casual connection between divorce and the other manifestations of social instability that are evidenced by these figures. In fact, one could be forgiven for viewing divorce as just another manifestation of popular fashion. There are fashions in clothes, politics, food, music, and so on, but this particular divorcing mood is lasting a worryingly long time and, indeed, may well be with us for the foreseeable future; its ever-increasing acquisition of respectability in the social sense as well as, to some limited extent, in the religious one, gives cause for concern.

I hasten to make clear, however, one important point. What follows is not to be taken as having been prompted by religious fervour since neither God, religion or morality have much to do with the present approach. It is a fact that all Western religions display a great deal of hypocrisy when it comes to divorce. Whether, choosing at random, we think of the Bible (Ezra 8 *et passim*); – see also Deuteronomy 24.1-4, and Genesis 2.24) –, of the Protestant Church's acceptance of divorce or of the sophistry used by the Catholic Church in its Canon Law, there are not many creeds that come out well when addressing the question of the sanctity of marriage. Writing in 1971 (*The Churchman* – Church Bookroom Press), J.R.W. Stott was hard put to reconcile what the Old Testament has to say about marriage and divorce. In order to keep in touch with present thinking, despite the unequivocal terminology of Corinthians 7.10-16 and Romans 7.1-3, and despite his stated willingness to acknowledge that one should have the courage to resist the prevailing tide of permissiveness and to set ourselves against divorce and remarriage, Scott had to accept that divorce was permitted on the two grounds allowed by the Bible, whatever they might be.

There definitely seems to be some difficulty in reconciling religious dicta on divorce, since both the Old and New Testaments, as is common knowledge, take fairly opposite views. Under Jewish law, a man was quite free to write out divorce papers and send his wife away from her home (Deuteronomy 24). A wife was to be respected, but did not, obviously, have the same rights as a man. In addition, it was fatal to marry foreign women. When Ezra learned of the intermarriages with non-Jews, he knelt in prayer to the Lord and asked forgiveness for this disgrace (Ezra 9). Arrangements were made for the foreign women to be sent away (Ezra 9 and 10). The rather cavalier fashion in which these foreign wives were dealt with does seem to contrast with the passionate feeling for woman contained in the *Song of Songs*. Yet, when Zechariah's angel saw the lid of the basket being raised and a woman appear, he said: 'This woman represents wickedness' and pushed her down into the basket and put the lid back down (Zechariah 5.8).

One does not know, of course, how far those who recorded the words of God are to be trusted. One is left wondering because it is unlikely that a Supreme Being would be inconsistent in matters of such importance as the relationship between man and woman, and divorce; but if we are to believe Malachi (v. Malachi 2.16), the Lord God of Israel is also recorded as saying: 'I hate divorce. I hate it when one of you does such a cruel thing to his wife. Make sure that you do not break a promise to be faithful to your wife.' Which perhaps goes some way to redressing the balance between Ezra's and Zechariah's statements and anticipates the New Testament, but is of little comfort to those who seek consistency.

Matthew, Mark and Luke are unanimous in stating and supporting the sanctity and indissolubility of marriage (Matthew 5.31, 19.3, Mark 10.2, Luke 16.18). The message is clear: 'If a man divorces his wife even though she has not been unfaithful, then he is guilty of making her commit adultery if she marries again.' Indeed, Jesus is recorded by Matthew (Matthew 19.8) as observing to the Jews that 'Moses gave you permission to divorce your wives because you are so hard to teach'. The concept is repeatedly established that man should not divorce his wife and that marriages are supposed to last forever. Those whom God has joined together should not be cast asunder.

The Catholic faith, derived directly from the New Testament, has maintained this concept fairly consistently, despite the vagaries of its Canon Law. The layman finds it difficult to understand how Jackie Onassis could be divorced simply because she did not *intend* the marriage to have effectively the aims of a Catholic marriage and looks suspiciously at those situations where Canon lawyers manage to achieve, even for Catholics, an annulment of marriage. But the number of Catholic annulments is small. Despite them, the Catholic Church is the only one that rigidly maintains the indissoluble nature of a marriage, not only in theory, but also in practice.

The words used in some marriage ceremonies are significant. If we take, for instance, the rite of marriage as used in the Catholic dioceses of England and Wales, we find that on the occasion of the marriage ceremony the priest first addresses the parties by reminding them that marriage is a 'special sacrament' which allows them to assume the duties of marriage 'in mutual and lasting fidelity', then asks both bride and bridegroom to recite the hallowed formula whereby they take each other as lawfully wedded spouse '... to have and to hold from this day forward, for better, for worse, for richer, for poorer, in sickness and in health, to love and to cherish till death do us part'.

The marriage service of the Church of England is not quite so specific as to the marriage being a sacrament. Perhaps some dilution of the concept has already taken place here, but there is no doubt that in this service, too, the spouses are called upon to repeat the hallowed formula. There is a gentle variation by changing the second half of it which now reads '... in sickness and in health, to love, cherish and worship till death us do part according to God's holy law; and this is my solemn vow'. The terminological nuances are insignificant, since the concept in this case, too, is quite clear. Marriage is for life.

The Methodists vary it slightly, again. The Minister first reminds the intending spouses that '... marriage is given by God. It is not to be entered upon or thought of lightly or selfishly; but responsibly and in the love of God. According to the teaching of Christ, marriage is the lifelong union in body, mind and spirit...' The hallowed formula which is now used in Methodist marriage ceremonies is in line with that of the

Church of England save that the concluding sentence is changed to '... and to this I pledge myself'. A blessed unanimity of concepts is evident in all the three marriage rites just referred to.

The Jewish marriage ceremony is, by comparison to that of other religions, quite refreshing. The spouses do not bind themselves for life, so at least the hypocrisy of making a statement of that kind at a time when divorce is freely available and indulged in by many members of society regardless of their religious beliefs, is eliminated. It is true that the Jewish religion does look upon marriage as an important occurrence and as strengthenmg the family; it also looks upon the marriage bond as absolute but it does envisage, in line with Biblical teaching that, apart from death, it may also be dissolved by divorce. This is not a recognition of modern tendencies, rather an endorsement of what was written in the Bible.

Clearly, the 'Christian' religions are in no doubt about the nature of matrimony, although the Jewish tradition acknowledges divorce. Moreover, the truth is that one has to take what both the Old Testament and the New Testament say on the matter with more than a pinch of salt, since there are concepts, particularly in the Old Testament, which by modern standards appear somewhat repugnant. One instance will suffice, namely the destruction of Jericho; then, the city and everything in it was destroyed by being burnt to the ground, saving only things made of gold, silver, bronze and iron, a useful booty. It is quite clear, too, that the only person who was spared because of the help she had provided to Joshua's spies was Rahab, together with her household. Rahab was a prostitute. (Joshua 6). But does that matter? The point really is that it is not in religion that one has to find a solution to the problem of divorce, for there seem to be as many answers to the problem of a failed marriage as there are perceptions of God. Jews, Muslims, Hindus, Protestants, Baptists and Catholics, to choose but a few, all have a different view of the matter. If there is only one God, as most people would suppose, His spokesmen have been taking liberties with His doctrine. One must assume that they have done so to suit their convenience, rather than please the Almighty.

The current hypocrisy of most Churches on the divorce issue arises from the fact that they are more interested, like political parties, in counting the number of heads who could be said to subscribe to their creed rather than in maintaining logical consistency. It would be tiresome to trace the different developments and the changes in direction which religions have undergone as regards the question of divorce, but one thing is clear; feminism and selfishness have meant more than the revealed tenets. And that is why it is not considered here that any answer to the ever-increasing rate in the breakdown of the family and the spread of divorce can be found by listening to priests. It must be found in humanity and good sense. Apart from the present comments, therefore, any benefit that any expressed view might derive by being related back to one or the other form of religious teaching will hereafter be totally discounted. In this study the approach taken is rational, rather than religious.

THE UK DIVORCE RATE

The UK divorce rate, that is to say the rate of divorce per 1,000 members of the population, rose from 2.6 in 1985 to 2.9 in 1990, and finally to 3 in 1998. (*Encyclopaedia Britannica*). The divorce rate is the highest in the European Union, and the second highest in Europe, where the UK is beaten to it only by the Czech Republic (3.2). Furthermore, the UK rate is the fourth highest in the world, Russia being the leader with 4.5, followed closely by the United States with 4.3. These rates compare quite unfavourably with those for Mexico, Macedonia, and Pakistan, all of which have a rate of 0.3, Italy, with 0.5 and Greece with 0.7.

1

How did we get here?

The word 'marriage' has more than one meaning. In its concrete form, it identifies the ceremony that takes place when a man and a woman decide to take each other into an intimate and stable union, sanctified by religion, recognized by the State, or both. In its abstract sense, it means the union itself between man and woman which, theoretically, is aimed at a physical and spiritual integration of the two personalities resulting, if the parties so require, in some kind of satisfaction of their sexual instincts.

In the Christian, and more particularly in the Roman Catholic marriage service, it is all these things; but marriage also has as its primary object the procreation of children for whom the parents must undertake responsibility. For Catholics, marriage is a Sacrament; for Christians, it ought to be; for some it is a game; and for others, it is a state that is entered into simply because it is expected of them.

For those who consider that marriages are made in heaven, it is indissoluble and thus, in the already quoted words of the marriage service, the parties are united for better or for worse, whether or not they get rich, are or are not fit, until their mortal spoils are abandoned. Or, nowadays, as a rather cynical

American lawyer put it, 'Until death or the laws of the domicile us do part'. Another way of looking at marriage is to say that it is no more than a simple contractual relationship between the parties, who can get into and out of it at will. But things were not always so.

In Roman law, marriage was a situation of fact from which certain legal relations flowed. In the legal sense, it was equivalent to possession of a chattel. Man and woman decided that they wished to live together and, once they actually did that (and bred children), they were looked upon as man and wife. But it was their intention to live together that determined the relationship so that, once they had decided to part company – that is to say, once their living together and their mutual love and affection had gone – they could divorce either by mutual consent or for specific reasons that were considered as adequate 'just cause' – such as the wife's adultery, her prostitution, the public co-habitation of the husband with another woman, a long term of imprisonment, impotence and so on.

The availability of divorce should not be taken as meaning that the Romans had no interest in marriage as an institution. Quite the reverse. For them, it was of religious and almost sacred value in the same way as they respected the family, which Cicero had considered the principal force of the State. But, as a practical people, the Romans accepted that husband and wife need not live together if they had ceased to love each other, without stopping to consider the consequences that would follow from the availability of divorce. The Romans boasted that in the five hundred years of the Republic, no husband had taken advantage of the bias of the law in his favour to get rid of a troublesome wife. 'Roman wives were serious and devoted and constant like Lucretia and Pauline. Pliny even believed that women demonstrated their inherently superior purity when they were drowned by floating modestly face down, whereas drowned men were supposed to float on their backs.'[1]

Casual divorce was discouraged by financial penalties and by limiting the power of remarriage for the sake of the children; Seneca spoke with distaste of those noble women who counted their age not by the number of consuls, but by the number of their husbands.

As soon as Constantine had acknowledged the Catholic religion as an acceptable form of worship, that is to say, from the beginning of the fourth century up to the time of Justinian (early sixth century), a formal reaction set in against divorce. This was partly due to the influence of the Catholic Church, but mainly the result of abuses of the system which coincided with ever-increasing corruption in Roman society. Although Justinian deplored and punished divorce, he could not help remarking that he thought it was natural and inevitable because, since husband and wife had themselves established the relationship, they could just as easily dis-establish it. Clearly, as a lawyer, he was looking at it from the contractual point of view. It was only a little later, as a result of the preaching of Ambrose (c340-97) and Augustine (354-430), that the Catholic concept of the indissolubility of marriage became firmly established. Yet some time later Thomas Aquinas reinforced the idea and laid down Catholic theories and beliefs in systematic form.

As we all know, Henry VIII (1491-1547) was not happy with the Church's teaching on the subject of divorce and the consequences of his dissatisfaction are well recorded. Nevertheless, the Christian view of marriage as made in heaven continued to prevail throughout the Western world, despite the not-too-many decrees of nullity issued by the Catholic Court (the 'Sacra Romana Rota').

In England, the basic approach of the old Canon Law was to adopt only the concept of nullity of marriage and to reject divorce. Put differently, nullity of marriage was easier to obtain whereas divorce was exceptionally difficult. Even so, this did not represent such a great problem because decrees of judicial separation were available in the English Ecclesiastical Courts from about the thirteenth century onwards, mainly for desertion, cruelty and what were then termed unnatural offences. Inevitably, there were anomalies and it was these that were subject to stringent criticisms by the Protestant Reformers of the sixteenth century, whom one could term the forerunners of present-day feminists, at least as far as divorce is concerned.

Whatever the principle may have been, economics determined which way the parties' future would develop, since the cost of proceedings in the Ecclesiastical Courts was considerable. Time, amongst other factors, contributed to the cost. It has been calculated that an undefended decree of judicial separation would take between six and eight weeks to obtain; but a defended one, two or three years, at a cost of thousands of pounds.

There was a let-out for some. Those powerful and wealthy enough could promote a private Act of Parliament and get a divorce that way. This was not only an expensive procedure but it was also a comparatively rare one. Ten private Acts of Parliament were passed before 1714; and from 1714 to 1856, a significant date for divorce in England, as we shall see, there were only 307 private Acts of Parliament dealing with divorce.

Our American cousins, on the other hand, had got their legislative act in order earlier than we did. The first judicial divorce law in New York's history was pushed through the New York Assembly by Alexander Hamilton in 1787 but it was not until 1846, when legislative divorce was abolished by New York's Constitution, that the legislature passed special Acts granting divorces on such grounds as desertion, drunkenness, etc. Adultery itself remained the sole ground for judicial divorce until April 1976 when the Divorce Reform Law came into force.

In England, the dissatisfaction with such a hybrid system must have been substantial. Today, England is mainly a Protestant country and the Protestant approach to life and morality is somewhat different from the Catholic one. The Protestant, on the whole, rejects natural law and instead of proceeding from abstract rules of conduct, wishes to draw the dividing line between good and evil from his view of what practical problems need by way of resolution. Essentially, the Protestant/Calvinist tradition upholds the individual's freedom of choice and of self-determination: man is master of his own destiny. There are no basic, fundamental concepts of 'morality' which are entitled to be upheld if they clash with practical reality.

This kind of belief is totally irreconcilable with the concept of the sanctity of marriage; accordingly, pressure for reform was great, so much so that in 1850 a Royal Commission was appointed to consider matrimonial offences. It reported in 1853 and the Matrimonial Causes Act 1857 was based on that Report. Since it was 'expedient to amend the law relating to divorce' and to set up an exclusive jurisdiction court,[2] divorce law was reformed substantially and the structure so laid down lasted well over a century, that is to say until the Divorce Reform Act 1969 superseded it.

One of the features of the 1857 legislation was the establishment of fault or guilt as the basis for divorce. Accordingly, and subject to a substantial number of limitations (like passage of time from date of marriage, connivance, condonation and collusion, and so on) the parties, whilst not entirely free to bring their marriage to an end, could achieve the same result if either was guilty (or could be made to appear to the Court to have been guilty) of adultery, cruelty, desertion, unsoundness of mind, sodomy, bestiality and rape. The door to unrestricted divorce, which the Christian tradition had kept more or less shut and bolted, was opened halfway, to the great joy of divorce lawyers and private detectives.

In 1951 there was another Royal Commission on Divorce to make that step somewhat easier (see the Matrimonial Causes Act 1957) and in 1969 the Divorce Reform Act turned the whole situation round. Whilst the hypocrisy of the legislature was insufficient to enable it clearly to state that just as the parties had decided to marry so they would have to be free, if so minded, to terminate the marriage, 'irretrievable breakdown' of the marital relationship resulted in the institution of marriage being essentially demolished: the 1969 Act was the death-knell of marriage as it had always been understood. To all intents and purposes, we now have divorce by consent.

Let no-one tell you that the practical situation is any different from what has just been stated: those who practise law or have any association with agencies involved in matrimonial matters will confirm that, in substance, the position is exactly as has just been stated, whatever it may have been formerly. It is true that the Court still has to endorse what the parties have achieved: but that is mere rubber-stamping. The intervention of the Courts to provide a decree of divorce is no different from that which takes place in the Probate Division on a death in order to 'prove' a will. The factual situation of either the breakdown of the marriage or the demise of the deceased cannot be changed. It must be repeated: the divorce courts merely rubber-stamp what husband and wife have already decided about their future. It must also be repeated, *ad nauseam*: divorce can now be obtained formally because of what the law terms the 'irretrievable breakdown of the marriage' but the formulation is quite clear: it is the parties who decide whether the marriage has irretrievably broken down. No-one else is in the position of being able to determine such a subjective matter.

In earlier times, we at least had the face-saving device of the Court being asked to determine whether one or other of the parties had been guilty of a matrimonial offence (adultery, cruelty, desertion, etc.). The theory was that one had to preserve a balance between the sanctity of marriage and the considerations of public policy which determined that whenever a marriage had come to an end, this ought to be officially stated. The Court could find that none of the factors that amounted to a matrimonial offence had been proved, so that the parties were not entitled to divorce. This happened rarely, but the possibility was there.

Now it is up to the parties to decide whether the marriage has or has not irretrievably broken down. From this it follows that the motivation for saving the marriage has gone. Given that the marriage can in fact be dissolved, it will never be retrieved.

The conclusion of this short historical exploration is that whereas, say, in the case of Henry VIII (which is a classic), divorce was used for dynastic and political reasons, in present-day society divorce has become a social tool. The State has in reality actively encouraged divorce and when one hears politicians speaking of the binding sanctity of marriage or of the need to uphold family traditions and values, one is forced to the conclusion that they are all either stupid or liars, or both.

* * *

HOW WE VIEW MARRIAGE

We go from one extreme to the other when considering the institution of marriage, depending on how we assess the role of woman. If we consider that the role of woman is to give birth and look after children, then the strength of the family as a result of the marriage is great and the concern about the indissolubility of the marriage is equally important, because otherwise it is difficult to determine which is the real family that one has to protect. If, on the other hand, one considers that the role of woman is not to produce children but to perform in society on an equal footing with man, which is the other extreme view, then we must come to the conclusion that there is no need whatsoever for people to marry and, if they do marry, there is no reason why they should not divorce at whim, which prompted H. G. Wells to propound the view that women's part in life was to be the petrol of the world; but most of them wanted to be the engine.

Nowadays, however, the difficulty our society has to face (and Western societies generally), is that we have consistently refused to come to grips with the problems that arise as soon as the role of woman is altered. It is obviously true that no-one can insist that a woman should give birth to children. With ever-increasingly reliable methods of contraception, woman can effectively live her life without having to procreate. It is also true, however, that the moment woman decides to procreate, she puts it out of her control to be, as the expression goes, 'mistress of her own destiny' because her natural role now is to look after the children.

It is said today that this definition of woman as having to care for the children to which she gives birth is out of fashion. Children can quite happily and, indeed, successfully and without any emotional trauma whatsoever, be entrusted either to other individuals, or to their fathers, or to the State, or to different organizations entirely, or to one or two lesbians, or to one or two homosexual males. In the 1930s we had the Oneida community type of marriage in New York. We now have the communes, where it is said that children can grow up freely and psychologically independent. But if one analyses the concept, one reaches the conclusion that the establishment of communes did not come about for the benefit of children but merely for the benefit of wives or mothers who had to go out to work and who therefore had to find somewhere to park their babies, or to satisfy other needs of the State. It seems to me that there is no inherent benefit in a commune other than the practical convenience where the wife is at work.

We also have the example of the 'kibbutzim' which are often put forward as the best proof that woman can leave the children in the care of someone else and go and be like a man, whether at work or in the Army. Too great a significance ought not to be attached to the concept of the 'kibbutz' which is typical of Israel. It is believed that, even in Israel, only a very small percentage of families live according to the 'kibbutz' concept. There, no doubt, it is more a political and religious concept than a truly social one. But even if we do consider the 'kibbutz' as an option, its establishment is of benefit to the mother/wife who does not wish to stay at home. If the mother stays at home, she does not need 'kibbutzim'.

When these alternative solutions to the problem of the working mother are put forward by sociologists or reformers, they are always justified on the basis that it is better for the children that things should be organized in this way, proceeding from the obvious premise that because so many spouses divorce, there must be something wrong with marriage. Indeed, in his book, *Is Marriage Necessary?*, published in 1974, Eustace Chesser (a psychiatrist, an abortionist and one of the few who in his day felt able to state openly that pornography is good for you) maintains that nowadays marriage is a luxury, and is totally unnecessary.

As a matter of fact, from his standpoint, what he says is perfectly logical. On the other hand, one is forced to wonder about the validity of certain theories when they are put forward together with statements which sound fairly absolute and which with the passage of time are found to be somewhat inaccurate. For example, even such a sympathetic writer as Chesser is found at fault in this context. At page 87 of *Is*

Marriage Necessary?, we find the following statement: 'Contraception and legalized abortion will in time reduce the number of unwanted children to negligible proportions. They are unlikely to be so numerous that adoption presents a difficulty.' Anyone reading his book at the time it was published would have accepted this statement, as reasonable and logical. The statistics I quote (p.xx) concerning the increase in illegitimate children since 1974, however, would appear to cast considerable doubt on the validity of Chesser's thinking.

The trouble is that marriage is in such a state of flux that it is very difficult to be proved accurate at any given time. Statements which may have been valid twenty years ago have lost their significance today and, by parity of reasoning, anything that one says nowadays may equally be proved wrong and out of fashion in twenty years' time. What is forgotten is that the legal institution of marriage reflects the nature of the relationship between the two individuals who are parties to that contract and, by extension, the nature of the society in which they live. If one proceeds from the premise that the male is necessary for the protection of the children, then a certain solidarity is created in the husband/wife and parent/children relationship which is conducive to permanence. One finds a close parallel in the animal kingdom: apes are monogamous, as are most primitive people, and both apes and primitive people operate on the basis that the female of the species looks after the children and the male looks after the survival of all members of the family.

So it was until recently in Western society; the State endorsed this concept while it was seen as convenient to do so. With the extension of progress in every sphere, the pressures upon marriage and upon the State with regard to marriage, have increased enormously. The more progressive we are, the more difficult, or so it appears, we find staying married. The more progressive we are, the more elusive our search for happiness becomes. The more progressive we are, the more difficult we find monogamy.

This has nothing to do with civilization because civilization and progress are by no means coincident. But just as we have too much variety in the choices around us, whether they relate to food, motor cars, holidays or whatever, so we have too much variety in our choice of partners, we have too many opportunities for comparing our partners with others, and all too often we become dissatisfied with what we have. On the basis that the more you see, the more you want to have, particularly at a time when woman is freer in every respect than she ever was, it is very difficult to maintain the concept of marriage as something normal in society, although we keep expressing the view that we should be concerned about its existence. At the same time, however, we have complicated the situation by our insistence that marriage is a partnership where the spouses are quite equal. This concept reflects an ambition, but not a reality, and contributes to the parties having misconceived expectations of the relationship and its outcomes.

It used to be said that marriages were often unhappy because the parties were sexually ignorant when they got married. This myth is certainly exploded in our days. The problems of modern marriage mostly stem from the sexual freedom and the control of conception granted to women. It is said that women were bored when they were not free and thus they had greater temptations to commit adultery; once they were freer, they would be less bored and more faithful. But this does not seem to be borne out by statistics. Havelock Ellis had himself identified the problem nearly a hundred years ago, for he claimed that with the growth of civilization, the concept of marriage as a contract had fallen into discredit. According to him, by transferring marriage from Church to State, as a result of Protestantism and especially of Puritanism, we had caused the unfortunate result of secularizing the sexual relationship and, by so doing, ignored the transcendental element in life. Interestingly, he maintained that the Catholic view of marriage as a sacrament, fantastic and impossible though it has become in many of its developments, has at least insisted on the natural and actual fact of marriage as something above the purely sexual relationship. He pointed out that even in his time we were taking a much more romantic view of marriage, inasmuch as we no longer considered it a contract but more of a union and that was the reason why we are unhappy when it fails and we go seeking other partners.

It is true to say that this attitude stems from a very false idea of individual liberty, particularly of democratic ideas which have been taken out of the political context (for example, by Mary Wollstonecraft[3]) and applied to personal relationships. But when applied to family life, the net result is that the spouses become impatient with the duties that the individual has agreed to accept. In our opinion, what the modern trend fails completely to realize is how quickly women are changing. In earlier times – let us say, a century ago – women used to believe that their work in life was to marry and have children. Now women believe that they are primarily individuals who can pick and choose what they are going to do with life. In so doing, however, they have lost woman's greatest asset – the spontaneous capacity of giving.

There is a marked contradiction in thought here as far as women are concerned. They seem to be torn between two views. On the one hand, there is what could be termed the romantic view of marriage. This has been inherited by present-day woman and inculcated into her by custom, tradition and all those persons who have a vested interest in maintaining expenditure at a particular level. Hence, the glorification of the concept of love, the abuse of this noun in the press and elsewhere, short engagements, and, most contradictorily of all, white weddings. This view hardly lives up to modern expectations and makes no sense whatsoever in circumstances where the parties have already been physically close before the marriage. Romance and the various forms of contraception do not mix very readily.

The second view is what one could term the practical one. It stems from the premise that if the intending spouses cohabit before marriage, they will then get to know each other. They may also be able to balance the budget. They will understand each other's requirements and their subsequent marriage will accordingly be a success. This view, too, is contradicted in practice by the fact that 51% at least of all marriages celebrated in any one year end up in divorce: so the premise must be false. It is an illusion to maintain that the relationship established between a man and woman who are not married will remain the same once in fact they do bind themselves in holy matrimony.

But the more damaging feature of the practical view which preaches co-habitation before marriage is that it ignores a fundamental psychological fact; that is to say, that the human mind attaches no value to what is not fought for. What is freely given, neither man nor woman gives any value to. At the end of the day, the two views clash dramatically for there can be no romantic love for woman after a long series of cheap and quick affairs. Romance comes from struggling, from adventure, from being conquered. What is not achieved through effort is no longer precious. It is just something that can be picked up and dropped easily. It may be lust, if may be passion, it may be perversion, but is certainly not romantic love. The difficulty is that our society has decided that there is no longer any symbolism attached to woman and to her conquest by man. A spouse is but a chattel which one wishes to own or discard in the same way as a motor car.

Difficulties arise from the belief that marriage is made for the spouses and is of interest only to them. This is untrue: marriage is part of the texture of society. The personality of the spouses is irrelevant as far as society is concerned and so, in a strange sense, is love. Romance does not help much either because it causes people to look at matters through rose-tinted glasses, whereas very often marriage is a mist and in a mist one needs much light and great magnification.

The growth in either actual or envisaged equality in the marriage partners has also resulted in a marked increase in the sexual, if not psychological, impotence of the male of the species. In Sweden, for example, children are taught sewing, knitting, home economics and child care; girls learn handicrafts and masculine skills. This process of education is said to make the spouses interchangeable. But there is no evidence that as a result marriage is stronger in Sweden that it is in those countries where such 'advanced' educational notions have not yet been attained. Furthermore, once it is accepted that marriage is no longer the kind of bond which is solid because it is meant to last forever, it is difficult to determine to whom the children of the marriage 'belong'. One does not wish to go back to Roman days when the powers of the *pater familias* were of life and death, nor would it be right nowadays to differentiate in the degree of culpability, at least as far as the law is concerned, in the sexual deviations of man and woman. But if we pause merely to consider the position of the children in a marriage which is a lukewarm relationship, we must reach the conclusion that the children do not belong to the parents. In fact, by modern standards it could be argued that children do not belong at all: they are individuals. The difficulty is that until a child has grown up, that child itself wants to belong either to a family or to a group. It is not easy to determine to whom the child, in fact, does belong if it does not belong to the parents. Does it belong to that State? The mere thought is abhorrent but it may well be that that is the correct answer in today's society. So much has this concept been extended, that children are now allowed to sue their parents in circumstances which seem to run counter to common sense.

★ ★ ★

There is a school of thought that the psychological integrity of the children dictates that they have two parents to whom they belong until they grow up. Certain findings by Israeli sociologists have shown that children who have been brought up in 'kibbutzim' have been imbued with politics and religion and, as a result, are lacking both in critical sense and in self-awareness; in the former, because of the solidarity of the group and in the latter, because their individuality has had to be subjugated to that of the community which controlled them.

The greatest failing, however, in our present-day approach to marriage as an institution is that all sense of security in it has gone. It has gone for the spouses but, above all, it has gone for the children. The weakening of the marriage tie has had as its inevitable consequence the destruction of the family. This was bound to happen the moment marriage became dissoluble at will. The family is a unit which transcends the spouses: it has a solidity and a continuity which cannot be interfered with by one or more divorces. If I marry Joan and have two children and then we both divorce and remarry and have more children, which is my family? The one I started with Joan or that of my second or even third remarriage? Which is Joan's? How can anybody be expected to 'run' or to be part of two or more families? It is difficult enough to manage and/or be part of one.

Furthermore, there is ample evidence that marriage rates have fallen as cohabitation has increased. This is a trend which has been going on since 1981, when it became apparent that the rate of first marriage (for bachelors and spinsters) had begun to decline. When people divorce, cohabiting between the various marriages is virtually the norm. A study by Kathleen Kiernan,[4] found that about seven out of ten marriages were preceded by a period of cohabitation. For this reason the family is becoming obsolete. The word is almost quaint and may explain the excessive interest in those civilizations or sections of society where the family still carries social weight and status.

Nowadays, we emphasize the rights of the individual and are less concerned either about the family or the effect that the exercise of those rights has on society as a whole. If we start from the premise that the State has an interest in the success of the family as a unit, we then without difficulty go on to reach the conclusion that divorce ought only to be allowed where it could be proved to be of benefit to society. The proponents of divorce argue that because it is of benefit to the individuals, it must be of benefit to society. But this proposition begs two questions, namely (1) whether, in fact, divorce is of benefit to individuals and (2) whether, assuming that it is, it is also of benefit to society. On the scale of benefit/detriment to society, the proponents of divorce seldom, if ever, put the effect that divorce has on the children which is the principal area where the greatest disbenefit to society occurs.

More than one writer has perceived divorce as a form of surgery. The patients are unwell and the only way to cure them is to operate on the marital bond. But this analogy ignores the fact that there are many types of illness which can be cured without recourse to surgery and therefore one has to be highly selective regarding the use and benefits of the knife.

The truth is that so many people nowadays have a vested interest, of a clear monetary nature, in the maintenance of divorce that they can only be equated with surgeons who are keen to operate, whether it be on haemorrhoids, kidneys or hearts, because, if they did not, they would be out of business. This is not to suggest, of course, that in no situation can surgery be of benefit to the body. But the considerations that apply to the removal of a cancerous growth, assuming surgery to be the only remedy left, on the one hand, and the kind of surgical intervention which affects the psyche and the personality of divorcing spouses, on the other, are completely different.

A further consideration is that divorce by definition implies change and change, of itself, carries with it, whether on a temporary or on a permanent basis, chaos, disorganization, crisis and trauma. The surgeon's knife may remove the marital bond but has no effect whatsoever on the psychological heritage of the individual, which, in Western society, is tied to marriage.

NOTES

1. A. Alvarez, *Life After Marriage*, (Macmillan, 1982).
2. The Family Division of the High Court nowadays, but then called the Probate Divorce and Admiralty Division of the High Court; cynics might find the association of divorce jurisdiction with death and navigation at sea somewhat humorous.
3. M. Wolstonecraft, *A Vindication of the Rights of Woman*, (Penguin Books, London, 1981).
4. *Family Change and Future Policy, 1990*

2

Why did we get here?

One should analyse the principal reasons why society has decided that divorce is an acceptable and, indeed, normal feature of its structure. They can be classified as follows:

a) Feminism, contraception and sexual emancipation
b) Search for happiness
c) Spiritual (or moral) consumerism

These are convenient headings which embrace a multitude of concepts and are in no sense meant to be exhaustive. But they represent the cardinal points which govern the attitudes of both men and women when it comes to divorce, and they all, in some form or other, interact.

Feminism, contraception and sexual emancipation

The title of this section identifies three psychological, physical and social developments which are so closely inter-related as to be almost incapable of separate definition. The sexual emancipation of woman could only come about once contraception enabled her to escape from the slavery of unwanted pregnancies. When that stage was reached, the theory which is known as 'feminism' was developed. The noun conveys different meanings to different people and, indeed, has different meanings in varying contexts. To define it is not easy because any definition automatically amounts to a restriction and that of itself is not acceptable to a true feminist.

It is a little trite to say as D. Spender[1] does that '... a feminist is a woman who does not accept man's socially sanctioned view of himself .....': the statement is meaningless. There are millions of women who do not sing man's praises, either discordantly or in unison, who nevertheless do not argue that there is no difference between man and woman.

I believe one can propose a very simple definition of feminism: namely, it is a view of nature and life which argues that men and women are exactly the same not only by reference to their equality before the law but also in the physical sense. Whenever therefore either that noun or its derivative adjective 'feminist' is used in this discussion, it does not refer to those women who maintain that they are entitled to equal rights or job opportunities but merely to those members of the female sex who effectively decry their physical and psychological traits, tendencies and peculiarities and equate themselves to men and who, inevitably, argue that women are in fact better than men. After all, it is hardly a coincidence that Lady Mary Wortley Montagu in her work *Woman Not Inferior to Man* (1734) claimed that the female sex was the better one on the basis that '..... no-one will deny but that at least, upon the most modest computation, there are a thousand bad men to one bad woman'. It is this kind of hyperbole, both thematically and linguistically, which is identified with feminism. In seeking to argue that women were the equals of men, feminists ended up by contending that women were better than men.

As Bertrand Russell so pithily puts it:[2] 'The rights of women did not, of course, depend upon any belief that women were morally or in any other way superior to men; they depended solely on their rights as human beings, or rather upon the general argument in favour of democracy. But as always happens when an oppressed class or nation is claiming its rights, advocates sought to strengthen the general argument by the contention that women had peculiar merits, and these merits were generally represented as belonging to the moral order.' As far as I can see, however, there is no better or worse between the sexes. If we take the male and female of any species (ignoring the homosexual variations in both) we find that, like their genitalia, the sexes are complementary in the sense that each contributes to the other, to nature, to society, to humanity, something different. The feminist's argument is analogous to the political dichotomy existing between opposing political parties: one must be better than the other and all ideas of the other must be worse than one's own. That is logically nonsensical, socially meaningless and practically damaging. If an idea is good, it should be put into practice no matter from which political party it originates; if a woman is better at one thing than a man, then she should be allowed to do that thing rather than usurping the function of the man; and vice versa. That, I remark in passing, is the basis of a successful marriage. The feminist's creed is its antithesis; and that is why this writer attributes such importance to feminism (coupled with contraception and with the inevitable sexual emancipation of woman) as a breeding ground for divorce.

There is an old saying that when two people have to ride a horse, inevitably one of them will have to ride in front. On this basis, whatever relationship or structure is established, someone has to be in charge.

Human beings are quite content to accept that this is so in practically every aspect of their life in society. There are governments who tell us what to do, policemen who arrest us for what we do do, teachers who tell us what we ought to do, priests and doctors who try and cure us, judges and courts who endeavour to punish or reward us; and so on. There are always those whose word or command we are prepared to take or obey or to whom is entrusted power to suggest or enforce, because we are afraid of the consequences of failing to comply.

These hierarchical arrangements on the whole do not seem to give rise to many problems. It is only when one comes to marriage that the battle-lines become more marked. The battle has always raged. The Roman matron cannot have been too happy when her husband went off on his campaigns for months and even years, and there can be no doubt about woman's unhappiness at having between her teeth the bit of presumed male superiority and lordship. The speed of change in women's status has, however, been impressive.

We must start with the proposition that one cannot dispute the claims by women to equal treatment with men in society and in the market-place: they follow inevitably from the fact that we are all equal before God. Observers of society will look back at the twentieth century with astonishment regarding women's battles for the vote, equal pay, better career prospects, maternity leave, etc., and wonder how primitive and selfish our society was in the 'bad old days' when women's rights to equal treatment were not recognized.

It is perfectly proper and useful that woman should be allowed and be entitled to do the same jobs as men. The only qualification must be that there are some jobs that women find more difficult to do; but this must be a practical and not a legal disqualification. There seems to be no sphere of remunerated work, where women should not be allowed to prove that they can perform as well as men. All this ought to be axiomatic, and one can find no fault whatsoever in those women who claim that it should be so.

There are, however, certain consequences that at the practical level flow from the claimed equality. It is obvious, for example, that if a woman performs the same job as a man, and therefore has the same responsibilities, remuneration and career prospects as a man, it is because she has been found capable of doing just that. Natural selection in the market-place will soon eliminate those women who are incapable of attaining certain standards or the same standards as men attain, at least in theory. But the price to be paid for the attainment of those standards, performing the same job, to the same specifications, with equal responsibilities, remuneration, career prospects, etc., must be the development by woman of those very traits that made it easier for men to succeed in their jobs. It is only by developing those traits that woman will be able to compete effectively with man. If she wishes to be a weightlifter, for example, she will have to develop strong muscles. By becoming more like man, she will inevitably suffer from all the ailments that have eluded her so far.

It is too easy to maintain that the reason why women have so far lived longer and appeared tougher than men is because they are in fact stronger than men. That is true only to a very limited extent, namely, that they have led a different life from men. They have had different pressures and varied requirements which were consistent with different results. The moment woman starts behaving like a man and attaining his same performance, she must develop not only his characteristics but also his very same ailments.

All this is done avowedly in the name of equality. Equality of rights is presumed to derive from equality in everything else. But equality of rights and of opportunity also carries with it equality of duties. The equation, rights/duties, opportunity is the sum total of equality. Equality starts and stops there. Apart from that equation, equality is a myth. No two human beings really are alike (except possibly certain types of twins), no two races are any more alike than the two sexes. Some people are stupid, others are intelligent, some have an artistic bent and others will never learn to paint or play the piano.

The extreme conceptualization of equality is pursued with great determination both by the individual and the State. Hence we have co-educational schools, despite teachers very often indicating that there are so many differences and tensions between boys and girls that perhaps there is no need for both sexes to study together; there are women trying to be miners, or boxers or rugby players, or fighter pilots, or front-line troops despite the obvious physical difficulties inherent in the work, never mind the inherent problems of functioning emotionally.

This equality is claimed for the woman, but our society has not yet come to terms with it as far as men are concerned. For instance, a woman may dab her tears in public and be considered an object of gentility and tenderness; but if a man cries, he is considered either effeminate or a weakling, or both. The trouble arises when the concept of equality is transposed onto the sexual plane: for there, equality cannot exist, simply because of the different physical components of male and female genitalia.

It is conceivable that, a hundred years from now, we shall have tampered so much with the genetic make-up of both the male and the female that they will be indistinguishable or at least interchangeable. But until we reach that stage, that is to say, until the physical characteristics of the sexes are so altered beyond recognition that there is no point in having any differentiation between the two, we must proceed from the premise that woman is different from man and cannot, and indeed ought not to, be his equal, save in the legal sense.

For present purposes it will suffice to observe that as things progress, woman is herself becoming more critical of certain features normally attributable to her or with which she tends to be associated. This defeminization is not confined to woman's place in business or on the career ladder. Women are now looking at the way they are allowing themselves to be portrayed much more critically than in the past. Hence the long-lived campaign about sexist advertising. The Advertising Standards Authority in Britain has gone so far as to publish on 28 February 1990 a report where it considers the views of the public on the way in which women are treated in advertising.

The way women are so treated has been a bone of contention for some time. In 1963 Betty Friedan's book, *The Feminine Mystique*, sparked off a lengthy debate on whether advertisers were doing women an injustice when they created models that women aspired to attain, whether it be in clothing or body smells or otherwise, which were in fact over-flattering to woman simply because they showed her principally as a sex object.

It is not quite clear what the net result of the campaign and the findings of the ASA is. From nude women to Pirelli-type calendars, the choice is great; but it is difficult to draw firm conclusions as to the effect on the relationship between the sexes, of depicting women as objects of lust. It is really a matter of taste and of representation. Certain female images, not necessarily in the nude, are pleasant to the eye both of men and women; others are objectionable to both. But the clamour for eliminating any representation of woman which shows her as an object of beauty or of design goes beyond a mere concern for parity of treatment and equality of rights. Some men, the real ones, might complain that the representation of scantily clad 'men' with extraordinary physiques or overgrown muscles is an offence to the dignity of manhood. Should we therefore campaign for the prohibition of the publication of certain types of photographs?

It is not believed that any benefit can be derived by either men or women prohibiting the representation of either the male or the female body in postures which are not obviously pornographic. Bad taste will continue to reign supreme and it will not avail either sex to complain of exploitation. The real exploitation of woman or man is not photographic, but psychological.

At the same time, one hears that fatherhood is no longer fashionable, at least in the sense that once upon a time a father was expected to financially support a woman and his children; nowadays men seem to be endeavouring to escape this responsibility in droves.

These anomalies in behaviour are recalled at this point for the sake of completeness; some of them are analysed later on. As far as woman is concerned, however, it will become increasingly more difficult for her to remain unaffected in her feminine role. Furthermore, she will find herself less and less fit to carry out her primary function of being a mother. Her function of being the breadwinner or of doing exactly the same job as a man is, as far as nature is concerned, very much a secondary one. The primary function of woman, until her bodily structure is altered beyond any recognition from what it still is, is that of procreation. Whether that primary function reaches its avowed purpose in the course of a woman's life is a totally different issue.

Thanks, in part, to the Americans and the Second World War, the British woman has come into her own. The contributory factors are well known: war marriages, working in factories, the more sensible exercise of the right to vote so strenuously fought for by the suffragettes, and so on. Woman has become more assertive of her rights and her personality, more critical of her male partners, whether stable or occasional, more determined to have it her own way, and at an earlier age than her mother.

It should come as no surprise to learn, therefore, that 72% of the divorce decrees awarded in 1987 to one partner were granted to the wife, 52% of them on the grounds of the husband's adultery.[3] (See p. 42 for further analysis of these data.) The question of adultery is dealt with in some detail later on, but statistics are usually symptomatic.

Woman's newly-established freedom gives her the edge in taking the initiative and her dissatisfaction with her partner is obvious. On the other hand, she is not terribly fussed about his adultery, possibly, though not necessarily, on the grounds that she herself might have indulged in it. The paramount consideration is asserting her newly-found power.

The following are said to be some of the reasons why more wives than husbands sue for divorce:

1) Women have more at stake in marriage than men and therefore are more inclined to feel the sting of failure.
2) The husband lets the wife sue for divorce because he is a gentleman: chivalry is not dead.
3) Courts are on the whole more sympathetic to women.
4) If the couple agree upon financial matters, the Court appears to be more inclined to have the woman as Claimant.
5) It is easier for a man to face public opinion.
6) Women nowadays have greater freedom in any event.

There is some validity in all of the above, though no single one is conclusive. Above all, I question reason 2: I do believe that chivalry died with romance, and romance died when woman become easily accessible. But be that as it may.

If one looks at the matter logically, however, there is no connection whatsoever between women's rights and divorce. After all, women exercise their rights just as well by not marrying; particularly nowadays, when they also have the ability to determine whether they should get pregnant or not, they are under no compulsion whatsoever to embark upon marriage. It is an oddity of the present situation that modern women who, generally speaking, are more socially aware, have acquired, in law at least, equal rights with men and inevitably are much more experienced (at least physically, if not emotionally) at an earlier age than they were 150 years ago, should find a greater need to divorce than men. In a strange sense, one would have better understood woman's keenness to divorce 150 years ago rather than now. At present, women develop sexually at a much earlier age, have many more partners before marriage and therefore ought to be much more capable of understanding what the marital relationship is about. This is unassailable in logic and also in psychology, but is not borne out by the figures. The rate of divorce is consistently increasing.

The first conclusion that one can derive from such an increase is probably a very obvious one, namely that there is a lot more to a marital relationship than sex because, if marriage were only a matter of sex, one would be forgiven for thinking that today's woman ought to be quite successful at it. The oddity, for such it is, has puzzled more than one commentator.

It seems clear, therefore, that whilst feminism is one of the principal reasons why divorce is increasing, it is of itself no sound basis for a successful marriage. In a strange sense, the more feminist the female partner, the more likely a marriage is to end in divorce. And the negative experience of marriage cannot fail to colour the attitude of the spouses in their future relations with the opposite sex. The second conclusion to be drawn is that feminism, on the whole, is counter-productive.

I do not disagree for a moment with those writers who have maintained that the emancipation of women is the result of the technological advances made by mankind (see, for example, Jessie Shirley Bernard in *The Future of Motherhood*; the same point is made by Elizabeth Hardwick when she says that 'technology annihilates consequence'). This is, of course, quite true by reference to contraception, but what is even truer is that industrialization has dramatically transformed the functions of marriage and of family life from the situation where the wife used to be the producer of goods and the performer of essential services, and got married to the husband who was the provider of food or money, the defender and the ruler of the wife and of the children; to the context of today, when this is no longer happening.

The examples quoted by these writers are not necessarily conclusive but the theory is correct in this sense: once man offered to woman, so to say, on a salver, control over her own body by providing reliable methods of contraception operated by the woman and no longer by her male partner, her emancipation was ineluctable.

There is, of course, an inherent justice in the concept of equal rights for women but an unfortunate consequence flows from the fact that they have been acquired all too quickly. One should consider, for instance, that from Emmeline Pankhurst to, say, Margaret Thatcher, the time lag is not too long and is measurable quite easily in decades. Like a pauper who suddenly becomes wealthy, woman has developed a certain vulgarity in her displays. Just as the newly-found rich flaunt their wealth, so the new woman displays traits which are hardly flattering to her sex. Even a capable and sensitive writer like Jessie Bernard refers to the work done by mothers as 'shit work'. It is true, of course, that nappies have to be changed, but to degrade the work of a mother to the level of excrement seems excessive.

Jessie Bernard was saying nothing new. The same observation, namely that housework is not worth doing and that effectively it is 'shit work' which only women are required to perform, was stated quite clearly in 1790 by one of the early feminists, – Judith Sargeant Murray. It is hoped that this is only a short-lived phase, but the matter must remain uncertain, since one does not know to what extent the sensitivity, consideration and understanding of women can survive feminist pressures.

At the risk of appearing repetitive, this writer needs to underline the fact that he discounts, entirely, the suggestion that is made, and repeated, that women are just like men. Apart from the differences which are obvious even to the most ignorant student of anatomy and human biology, it is an undoubted fact that the physical, anatomical, physiological, psychological, temperamental and teleological differences between man and woman are so great that only fanaticism can lead anyone to maintain that they do not exist.

The reader who, whether inspired by an innate sense of justice or indoctrinated by feminist dogma, is in any doubt as to the above statement, is reminded that in 1894 Havelock Ellis published his 'Study of Human Secondary Sexual Characters' under the title *Man and Woman* (London: Walter Scott Publishing Co.). In this study he dedicates considerable effort and scientific knowledge to a very detailed consideration of the less obvious differences between the sexes. It is interesting to observe in passing that woman comes out of it much better than man, but for different reasons. The power factor is significant and is not at all related to the consideration that women have been kept in slavery because men exercised political and economic power.

No-one denies the strength of the female sex, but the nature of the strength that is exercised by woman is totally different from that of man. Ultimately, this explains why, instinctively, a woman prefers a strong, energetic man to a weak, delicate one. The Italian scientists Lombroso and Ferrero[4] have pointed out almost conclusively that because in some respects woman is physically weaker than man, she has to resort to obtaining results by ruses. They argued that in women deception is 'almost physiological' and the analysis made at pages 133 and 139 should be compulsory reading for all those who believe that there is nothing in the point that women differ from men.

If it is true that women are now less emotional than they were say, fifty years ago, and that they have to be so in order to compete with men, it is equally true that they may be eliciting from men less understanding, less consideration, less response. The moment their tenderness and their compassion goes, their charm goes too.

It is interesting to observe that feminists are determined to argue that women should have the same freedom as men in matters sexual. I would suggest that whilst there is no doubt whatsoever as to the strength of woman's sexual emotions, the way and the intensity by which it is manifested, is clearly different from man's. It is, in a strange sense, wider and more diffused through the body than in man and yet, it is less energetic. It is sedate, whilst man's is restless; it is diffused whilst man's is concentrated; ultimately, it is passive rather than active.

Feminists object to this type of definition of woman's sexuality. And yet, to criticize it is tantamount to a failure to recognize what occurs in nature. It was Professor Sash who remarked that wherever we are able to observe an external difference between the male and the female reproductive cells of plants, the male cell behaves actively in the union and the female passively. From this observation he draws an analogy with plants and animals. Personally, I have never understood the objection that feminists raise to the differentiation between man and woman based on the 'passivity' (actual or alleged) of the latter; but perhaps I attach too much importance to physical conformation.

The almost obsessive desire for official recognition of equal treatment of woman with man coincides, as we have already observed, with woman's present intention, if not ambition, to be allowed to perform all the jobs normally done by her male counterpart. Such intention and ambition are part and parcel of the otherwise wholly laudable striving for a full, legally acknowledged recognition of equality which is irreproachable and indeed inevitable as a matter of principle. Its exasperation in matters of detail and practice, however, is a different thing entirely. The concern, however, in this discussion is not with the state of woman *per se*, but with the effect the pursuit of parity with men in all spheres has on marital relations as a whole.

A case in point is woman's increasing lack of feeling for being a mother. This is evidenced also by the ever-increasing number of sterilizations that women undergo nowadays. One can understand, if not necessarily condone, those instances of sterilization performed on mature women for health, economic or psychological reasons; but it is much more difficult to appreciate why an otherwise physically healthy young woman would wish to be sterilized at an early age, especially if the avowed object of the exercise is to eliminate the risk of pregnancy.

The psychological motivation, and above all, the consequences for both body and mind of sterilizing woman at an early age, have not so far been the subject of adequate study. Again, the interest here is not in sterilization for its own sake, but merely because one of its consequences in the marital relationship is to create disharmony, especially where the husband may not have been aware before the marriage of what the wife had already done to herself.

The Search for Happiness

In this search, both man and woman are in full agreement. Man is conscious of the scientific advances that enable him to shorten distances between continents and that appear to be giving him ever-increasing prosperity. His trust in his ability to mould destiny no longer stems from spiritual considerations prompted by a Protestant background, but rather from unbounded confidence in his ability to control and, ultimately, to conquer nature. His confidence is shaken every now and then by major disasters such as earthquakes and hurricanes, but is not easily shattered.

Woman, at last liberated from her function as a 'stay-at-home mother', feels that her assertiveness would be meaningless if at the same time she did not seek the satisfaction that had eluded her when she was not 'free'.

The search for happiness is a concomitant of unrestrained determination in sexual activity. Put differently, one would not feel entirely happy unless one were totally liberated, as the expression goes, in matters sexual. All this is perceived both by men and women with clarity; but even more clearly by women than by men because the picture is, for them at least, more novel and because they have had to struggle much harder than men to reach this stage of independence. What is not seen as clearly by either men or women is that the exasperation of individuality in fact results in the destruction of individual freedom. One need only consider for example the restraints that the spread of Aids has imposed upon sexual conduct: clearly the result of a form of exasperation of freedom to act in the sexual sphere without regard to consequences.

But the mere fact that these manifestations are so intense also shows that they are to some extent aberrant. The continuous search for pleasure by taking on different partners highlights the constant dissatisfaction with one's current partner.

To the question that is often heard, sometimes uttered in despair: 'Have I not a right to happiness too?', the answer is not an easy one, of course. But there is an inherent misconception in the use of the noun 'right' by reference to happiness. Nobody has any right to happiness any more than they have a duty to be happy. Rights and duties are socio/legal concepts that have no application whatsoever to what human beings want to achieve, at least in the personal sphere. You have a right not to be detained by the police for longer than a stated period of time and the police have a duty to pursue and arrest criminals; but it is surely an abuse not only of language but above all of concepts to talk about a right to happiness. The most that human beings can claim is an expectation of happiness. I get married expecting that I shall be happy; I may or may not be. But I should be naïve if I complained to my partner that I had a right to be happy, for that partner would then be under a duty to make me happy: and the reverse applies.

But even if it were true that I have a right to happiness, then I should also put on the same line, before I drew any balance between the two, my duties to my spouse. And it is on the score sheet of duties that modern marriage seems to collapse. There are many reasons for this, of course; some have already been mentioned or hinted at and others will be considered in greater detail later; but the principal one is to be found in what can be fairly termed 'spiritual (or moral) consumerism'.

Spiritual (or Moral) Consumerism

We all know that we live in a consumer-orientated society. This is a much abused expression that has several not entirely coincident meanings. The use itself of such an expression is interesting.

By consumer-orientated society we can mean society which tends to consume more than it should; perfectly true of us, because we are the most wasteful civilization that has ever existed on this planet. We may also mean a society where the consumer is protected so that his rights are safeguarded by law, vis-à-vis those who manufacture the products which are consumed. A third meaning is slightly derogatory: it is that of a society where nothing is required or expected to last.

The use of the language is very significant and is almost indiscriminate. Unfortunately, Sir Francis Bacon reminds us, it is not we who control language; very often words control our minds. One need only think of Orwell's *1984* and of the effect of the imposed jargon 'newspeak' to see how right Sir Francis was. The indiscriminate use of the word 'consumer' or 'consumerism' is imbuing our Western society, or at least the English-speaking one, with concepts which are futile, lax, and of short duration, like everything else we use nowadays. We are always after new cars, televisions, hi-fi, new job, home, foods, music or mobile phone; or obsessed with something different. Such an attitude is perfectly consequential, since we have adopted the profit motive as our sole criterion for determining the success of our lives. There would not be more new cars, tv sets, hi-fi equipment etc. unless there were a profit to be made in manufacturing them. It is a vicious circle, but it does create a fashion and, if there is a fashion in human relations, there is one in divorce. If I can change my car, television, mobile phone etc., why should I not be able to change my partner? Hence one, two or three spouses in one's lifetime as one acquires more than a single car over the same time-scale.

The utilitarianism of the concepts woman/man is universal but the primary consequence of such a utilitarian approach, certainly as far as women are concerned, is that they are reduced to the state of chattels. Put differently, at the very moment when the assertion of their equal rights and of their personality should cause them to take a jump upwards, if not to reach the same pedestal on which men have stood for centuries, women find themselves the object of violence, rape and pornographic abuse. The surprise expressed by feminists when these abuses occur seems a little ingenuous but the tendency is difficult to resist and the ever-increasing rate of divorce proves this point.

Moral Consumerism is but a manifestation of short-term thinking or put differently, of grabbing what is available and acceptable today without a thought for what might happen in the future. We have all become tacticians rather than strategists of life. This mind-set developed particularly after the Second World War, perhaps prompted by the consideration that the atom bomb will destroy us all tomorrow. Horace's *carpe diem* ('exploit the day') has become topical. Long-term policy and strategy are out. Short-term tactics are all that count.

The constant variability of the social and physical environment in which we live, brought about by the ever-increasing pace of technological advancement, creates a mood of change for the sake of change which is transmuted on to the psychological plane. Gone are the immutability of the seasons and the natural cycles of weather, plants and animals; forgotten or neglected are the inflexible laws of nature which man is hell-bent on controlling, altering or, as is inappropriately if not vulgarly put – as though nature were a wild animal – to 'tame'. We may remember his *carpe diem* but we have forgotten Horace's *Epistola* I, x, 24: 'You may pitch nature out with a fork, yet she'll always come back again.'

We *must* change the things that we possess; we must be with it, at the forefront of so-called progress. In this environment, disposing of one spouse for another is no different from changing a punctured tyre; or so it appears at first blush. The truth, however, is otherwise. It is a well-established fact that our hankering after material things is out of step with our own inner development and that makes our acquisitions lose all significance. As Jung so aptly put it (*The wise men of India* – 1944 – in volume II of his collected works under the heading

'Psychology and Religions: West and East'): '... the externalization of life turns to incurable suffering because no-one can understand why he should suffer from himself. No-one wonders at his insatiability, but regards it as his lawful right, never thinking that the onesidedness of the psychic diet leads in the end to the gravest disturbances of equilibrium. That is the sickness of Western man and he will not rest until he has infected the whole world with his own greedy restlessness.'

The reader may consider Jung's remarks far removed from matters of divorce. Not so: they are totally apposite, once the attitude is fostered that a spouse or a child is looked upon as a chattel, something that one must have at all costs, and change it when it is no longer needed or in fashion. This approach inspires tunnel vision and, in marriage situations, it encourages hasty decisions. The old saying 'marry in haste, repent at leisure' is not only forgotten: nowadays it is also meaningless, because there is nothing to repent. If you fail, you divorce. A marriage does not work: very well, it will be brought to an end. There is no need to consider why it has not worked out. This sloppiness, however, also extends to ignoring the consequences of what is being done. Nobody wants to stop and consider what the by-products are, for our consumer-orientated society, of so many divorces coming about.

Incidentally, the same consumer-orientated approach is evident in the case of those single, or even married, women, who obtain a child by donor artificial insemination (AID). When challenged as to why they have decided to procreate in such an artificial manner, without the contact – spiritual and physical – with man and without ensuring that the child-to-be has a father who will join in caring for it, they usually reply that they 'want a child'. Leaving on one side the many problems that AID might bring in any event – for instance, children born to lesbians – in the absence of an acknowledgement of parenthood by the natural father – could intermarry with brothers and sisters – it seems to this writer that people now want children as they want a new car, or TV set, or mobile phone: they want them, therefore they should have them. And have them they will, without stopping to consider whether it is fair to the child to grow up not knowing its father.

One may have some sympathy for those teenagers who, married at eighteen, are divorced at twenty, but they should not have got married in the first place. In their case, it is not the spiritual consumerism that this chapter is analysing which has caused the divorce: it is sheer ignorance of what marriage entails, and utter irresponsibility. But one hears of divorce after twenty-five or more years of marriage. If one enquires, one finds out that the parties were determined to seek out for themselves a new life. This idea of a 'new life' after twenty-five years of marriage is a misconception; it is the sublimation of a hope which in most situations will be frustrated; it is the fruit of a reluctance to admit the failure of a particular relationship which stems from some personality fault and which will undoubtedly affect any association newly to be formed.

But the most negative trait of it is the disposability of human beings. There is no question here of suggesting that woman is any worse than man on the moral consumerism scale; in theory, they both start at the same level and achieve the same results. However, as we have seen, the statistics show that woman is more likely to take the initiative in divorce and this seems to support the contention that in a desperate search to assert her freedom, independence and personality, woman may have lost sight of her duties to herself and her offspring.

Regrettably, in the consumer-orientated society, few pay much attention to the wellbeing of the youngsters. It is they who most of the time suffer as a result of what the grown-ups are doing. One need only consider how they are manipulated by 'adult' mass operators whether it be in the field of pop concerts, acid parties, hot telephone lines, drug-taking, child abuse, sexual abuse. Nobody asks the youngsters for their opinion or their wishes. This is the gravest fault for which all grown-ups have to carry responsibility.

NOTES

1. *Women of Ideas* – Pandora 1982 page 8, 1989
2. *Marriage and Morals*, Unwin Paperbacks – London 1976 p.59.
3. Government publication FM2, No. 14 at page 10, 1989
4. See *La Donna Deliquente, la Prostituta e la Donna Normale* (Turin 1893)
5. *Op. Cit.* page 363.

3

Why do people divorce?

When one speaks to people who have divorced or are about to do so, or wish to remarry, the usual explanation given by them for the failure of the first relationship runs along the lines: 'I made a mistake', 'I was inexperienced', 'I was too young', and they add: 'It will not happen again'. These statements may well be genuine and the relative beliefs sincerely held; however, they highlight both a *naïveté* in terms of the value judgements they have brought to their situation, as well as a degree of conceit, and possibly arrogance.

It is disingenuous to attribute failure to youth or inexperience, for such justification could easily be countered by the consideration that the particular party ought to have waited until he/she was older and more experienced. It is conceit to assume that, because one has made a mistake, that mistake will not be repeated: and it is downright arrogant to embark upon the same relationship with such confidence.

Of course, this is not to say that second or third marriages may not be more successful than the first. Examples can be found of people who marry young or inexperienced or both, divorce after a short period and remarry and die still married to the same second partner, and quite happy at that. But these are exceptions that merely serve to prove the rule: one cannot ground a philosophy of life in situations that are of an exceptional character. As will become apparent later on, the statistics do not bear out the contention that, because one has made one mistake, one can remedy that in a future set-up. Quite the reverse, in fact. But in order to understand the despair that lies at the heart of these reasonings one has to consider somewhat carefully the kind of mistakes that people make. The following observations are generalizations, because each individual relationship must be looked at within its own context: but they are useful for a consideration of the problem in its broad outline.

The mistakes that occur in the relationship of marriage are broadly of two kinds. They are objective mistakes, that is to say wrong views as to certain qualities or traits that one believes exist in one's partner; and subjective failings, that is to say, faults that are part and parcel of the make-up of the partner/s. Let us consider the objective faults first.

A spouse may be found at fault for all sorts of reasons. A male may believe that his female partner and wife-to-be has particular qualities: for example, she is a good cook, is a virgin, is honest, trustworthy, can manage money, loves children; a woman may believe that she is marrying a man who will provide for herself and the family, who is a good lover, a kindly father, a hard worker, etc. For those who got married in the Victorian era it would have been very easy to say that they did not have a clue as to the objective qualities of their spouse until they started cohabiting, by which time it was too late, so it was nobody's fault that a marriage failed. In 2000, this theory can no longer be maintained.

Youngsters start developing, sexually at any rate, at a much earlier age than before; today, there are few girls who reach the marital chamber inviolate and most people who get married have had some prior sexual experience. In all probability, they also have cohabited. It seems, therefore, that any lack of appreciation of the absence of certain qualities that were considered essential to the success of the marriage is due to a lack of perception or of understanding on the part of the offended or disappointed spouse. Put differently, and crudely, the goods could and should have been inspected earlier: the buyer should beware and only has himself to blame. This may sound harsh, but nowadays it is perfectly true.

If this analysis is correct – and an exception must be made only for the situation where faults emerge during marriage which have not arisen during cohabitation; there cannot be that many because the changes that take place in the relationship are psychological and are not related to one's ability to provide for children or to one's sexual prowess etc. – then it follows that it is an inherent defect of analysis or failure of comprehension in the particular party, which has led to the failure to appreciate that, for example, the wife was not a good housekeeper or the husband was a bad provider, or whatever. It is a personality fault or problem, something within rather than outside the spouse, that is causing difficulty.

If one then looks at the subjective faults, one starts from the premise that, like the leopard, a human being does not change his spots. There are, of course, some animals that have the ability to blend into the landscape: the chameleon, some insects, butterflies, etc: but the changes are of a physical and cosmetic kind. The nature, the instincts, the feelings, the reality, the entity of the particular animal do not change.

If you are born mean, violent and lacking artistic sense, you may live to be a hundred and twenty like Moses, but you will not become generous, kind and of an artistic bent. Certain things cannot be taught and certain traits cannot be altered. Our society has learnt to control and repress them, but has not yet developed the ability to change them in the absence of extreme courses of indoctrination and drug-taking which cannot yet be made universally applicable.

It can be stated with conviction, therefore, that human beings seldom change their spots during the course of a lifetime. They *have* evolved over millennia, but it has taken tens of thousands of years: there is no change in the basic instincts and feelings of human beings over the span of a single life. One learns to control oneself – but basically we remain as we are born. If this be a correct analysis, then there is no certainty whatsoever that a human being, guided by certain views and certain instincts when first entering into a second marriage, will have learnt from the mistakes that have occurred and will be able to deal with remarriage in a totally different way. It is a misconception to assume that human beings learn anything in personal relations for the simple reason that personal relations are not governed, on the whole, by the mind, but by the heart. Or so, at least, they should be. Take, for example, the question of remarrying males, and what I call the 'mirror image' syndrome. It is hardly a coincidence that most men marry women who either look like the man's mother, or like the woman or even young girl who first stimulated his sexual interest. The affective memory of the mother derived from his upbringing close to her and the image of the girl after whom he hankered in his youth stay with him forever.

And it is for this very reason that the second, or even third, relationship is not likely to be more successful than the first. A mistake was made in choosing the first wife; the mistake was prompted by the man's psychological make-up and emotional needs: the second wife will be no different from the first, and therefore the mistake will be repeated. The same situation can be said to apply to a woman's choice of a second spouse.

This is, of course, an over simplification because there is more to marriage than just the tendencies of the individual spouses and the analysis that each of them has made of the counterpart. If it were not so, marriage would be a much easier institution to cope with. The difficulty is that in the gilded cage of marriage, human beings move about in ways that are not entirely governed, at any one point in time, exclusively by either their mind or hearts.

But as a starting point it must be accepted that a failure to appreciate one's partner's faults combined with one's own basic temperament and character, lies at the root of all matrimonial trouble. It is often said that there are other reasons why marriages break down, and we shall be looking at some of them.

But when all is said and done, it is the nature of the personality of the human beings involved, their education and, above all, their background (factual and psychological) that determine whether they will make successful marriage partners and how they decide to react when problems occur. Their reactions, however, are not really their own: they are prompted, if not dictated, by the prevailing mood. In the days when divorce was not permitted, the reaction may well have been to put up with what had 'gone wrong'; now that divorce is freely available, the reaction, first and foremost, is to escape. This is understandable, because any animal wishes to get out of a cage, no matter how beautiful and well furbished that cage may have been. The tragedy inherent in the situation is that one may leave a modern, clean and convenient type of prison and end up in a dungeon. But that, too, is a different story. The psychological mechanism which causes the aggravation in a relationship and ends in divorce has been analysed in great detail in *The Old Love and The New* by Willard Waller.[1] Although written seventy years ago, the psychological observations remain valid. Waller stresses the notion of circular reaction mechanisms in emotionally-charged behaviour. In this circular interaction, the responses of one person evoke more decided responses from the other. Once people are involved in this process, it keeps snowballing until it culminates in some sort of climax or break. Put differently, the spouses start quarrelling and cannot stop until it is too late.

He also suggests that, when people have begun to shift apart, the group enters as a wedge between them and makes the healing process extremely difficult, if not impossible. As a result, divorced people frequently break completely with the friendship group to which they belonged before and during the marriage. (It should be noted, however, that in a later work, another American author, William J. Goode, found that this was not true. He found instead that the wife retains most of her friends, certainly about half the divorced women do, whereas the men tend to lose more; but it really depends on the circles in which they move.)

To put the problem in its proper perspective, however, we must consider the significance that the parties attach to the reasons for a breakdown in marriage. In the 'good old days' (that is to say, before the latest batch of liberating legislation) – shall we say, from the Second World War up to the late 1970s – a party who was not happy with marriage had to go and prove a specific deficiency, failure or betrayal of the spouse. Divorce lawyers and private detectives enjoyed themselves in finding evidence of even one act of adultery by either the husband or the wife, doctors and psychiatrists had great fun analysing examples of cruelty, unsoundness of mind and other less appealing manifestations of the degradation of human beings. All this has now gone: nowadays, the parties have only to say that they find it intolerable to live with each other, and their marriage is dissolved. Tidier, cleaner but, at the end of the day, equally damaging, if not more so, to the institution of marriage. The parties no longer have to rationalize why they cannot live together, as they had to do in the past, at least for the benefit of the courts. As we have seen, their decision that the marriage has come to an end is for practical purposes final, conclusive and not open to appeal by anyone if they themselves are in agreement that the marriage should cease to exist.

On the other hand, no amount of court work can eliminate the fact of the former marital relationship from the psyche of the divorced spouses. One finds that in numerous cases where parties divorce, they remain psychologically tied to their former partner. It is an odd relationship that persists: often one of increasing contempt and rancour, at times, or even unexpected tolerance and understanding on other occasions. But the memory of the former marriage will not easily be erased. Nevertheless, the parting has come, the vows are broken, and hatred/contempt/dislike, or whatever, the precipitating factor of the divorce, has set in.

But why have they got that far? Why has the marriage broken down? Why has it become intolerable for the two of them to live together? Why have the roses on the bed become thorns? Every writer on divorce, from whichever standpoint (scientific, psychological, social, remedial and so on) has in one form or another tried to analyse in detail the causes of divorce. This is not an easy task because although one usually identified with some degree of success the precipitating cause, that can only be seen as the last drop that caused the cup to overflow. But what went into the cup prior to this point is much more important.

Thus, when a spouse rushes to see solicitors because the adultery of the other spouse has come to light, we know that the reason for the separation or divorce is the adultery but we do not know what went on long before the adultery took place, which in turn may have been the precipitating factor of the extra-marital adventure.

ADULTERY

Adultery is the first cause of divorce alphabetically and, probably, also in practice, and is very fashionable indeed.

As usual, the statistics are interesting. When a husband sues for divorce, in at least half of the cases, he alleges adultery by his wife. This is not to say that adultery was the only ground for divorce, because even in those cases where the facts of separation or desertion have been proved by the husband, it is probable that there was adultery by the wife as well. Indeed, in today's world, it is most unlikely that where the wife is living apart from the husband, or is separated from him by consent, she has not herself committed adultery: the modern ethos and the independence of woman dictate that this should be so. In situations of marital conflict woman asserts her independence from her husband principally by sleeping with another man: this is an understandable psychological reaction in a tit-for-tat situation.

One does not hear very often the conclusion being drawn from this, namely that in all such situations the wife cannot possibly have been satisfied with the husband's behaviour, generally; and specifically, with his sexual performance. One is not merely considering what could be termed 'casual' adultery. For example, even in those situations where it is the wife who alleges adultery by the man (a quarter of the divorce petitions, the remainder complaining of the husband's behaviour generally), there may have been a wrong appreciation of the nature of the matrimonial offence.

The statistics show that more men sue for divorce on the

grounds of their wives' adultery than women in respect of their husbands' infidelity.[2] In other words, most husbands who sued for divorce alleged that the wife had committed adultery. As previously noted, this is not to say that adultery was the only ground for divorce. What this means in effect is that in about 40% of divorce cases in 1987, the wife was not satisfied with the husband's behaviour, generally: and specifically, with his sexual performance.

One is not merely considering what could be termed 'casual' adultery, since even in those situations where the wife alleges adultery by the man (out of 107,556 divorce petitions by the wife in 1987, 26,944 so alleged and 55,844 complained of the husband's behaviour generally; the remaining near 19,000 are on the grounds of separation: there are others but are less significant), there may have been a wrong appreciation of the nature of the matrimonial offence. It is worth recalling at this point that 72% of all divorce decrees awarded in 1988 went to wives, a situation which *Marriage and Divorce Statistics 1988* HMSO, series FM 2, number 15, termed 'a record level historically'.

There is little doubt that feminists see no difference between adultery by a husband and adultery by a wife. One can understand why, before the spread of reliable contraception, adultery by the woman was always considered by the law as more serious than adultery by the man: the obvious reason was that it could leave the man legally responsible, as father, for a child that was not his.

Even in this day and age where the risk of a man being held responsible for a child that was not his has, to all intents and purposes, almost completely disappeared, it is far too trite an argument to put forward that man and woman are the same when it comes to sexual relations. Anyone with experience of the real world knows that this simply is not true, for reasons which are not far to seek.

Man is essentially a hunter. The hunting instinct has been dulled almost into insensitivity by the great freedom that is being enjoyed by woman in matters sexual, but it is still there, in the background of the psyche. Man loves the chase and perhaps that is why he is so disappointed (and, it is believed by some, this writer included, also potentially impotent) when the prey is offered to him without resistance, so to say, 'on a plate'. Man is also essentially 'polygamous' and certain civilizations and religions have acknowledged this fact.

It follows that insofar as *some* men commit adultery, they are merely being guided by their natural instinct. This is not to say that their conduct is any the more forgivable: but one must try and understand it in order to criticize it. There are few men who wake up in the morning saying to themselves: 'Today, I feel like sleeping with another woman.' They may, however, be walking down the street and something nice attracts their attention. It may be a pretty ankle, a shapely bosom, a sensuous walk, or a friendly smile; it may be something indefinable like a look. The male's instinct, however, is aroused.

The same does not happen to a woman, no matter what you may hear or read about. There is a lot to be said for the theory that, on the whole, a woman who is happy in a relationship with her male partner (whether married to him or not) does not develop any wish to interfere with that relationship on a sexual plane or, indeed, at all; and in all likelihood – but who knows for certain what goes on in the minds of women . . . – is not even remotely tempted to look at another man in sexual terms. There is an inherent sexual stability in woman which, generally speaking, man lacks and which is directly attributable to her procreation function (one discounts for the purposes of this discussion the aberrant manifestations of nymphomaniacs and of men affected by satyriasis: one is considering the norm, whatever that expression may mean).

The difficulty is that whereas, whether we wish to acknowledge the fact or not, men are instinctively and essentially drawn to more than one woman, society has decided that all men ought to be monogamous and, for the sake of the children, that is the rule by which men live. But the basic roving instinct is there and now that woman is freer to act and to do, she, too, has greater opportunity for infidelity than at any previous moment in history. It is, as has often been observed, very difficult to commit adultery in an isolated rural community, which has to protect itself by maintaining clear-cut relations: it is so much easier for a woman who goes out to work to find the same opportunities for infidelity that her husband has had for many a year.

As Alex Comfort has pointed out[3] '... evidence is accumulating that marital stability under present conditions is higher after a long courtship, within limits, than when marriage is undertaken on impulse. The increases in psychological overtones in civilized communities probably demand a longer period of adjustment than the purely physical and a more gradual process of mate selection is possibly in keeping with the relative slowness of growth into adulthood which often seems to be a characteristic of cultures that reach a high intellectual level.'

You start thinking about adultery and you end up by committing it. Indeed, it is hard to avoid making the point that the situation is quite amusing. One can understand the difficulties that would arise in a situation of the kind that must have been fairly common in Victorian days when girls were either forced into marriage or married merely to escape the slavery of the family, a termagant mother, or an overpowering father, in circumstances where society ensured that the betrothed knew not very much of each other and whose physical contact may have been limited to a quick squeeze of a hand, the view of a couple of inches of calf, or both.

It must have been a very difficult process of adaptation for both parties but particularly for the woman, who perforce had to adjust, since that was expected of her at the time. A similar distance between intending spouses, though perhaps not quite so marked, may well have occurred, for all we know, in the country and in the villages, although there, then as now, people knew more about one another than in the towns. Even so, the trauma of the coming together of the spouses must have been very substantial. Our sympathy goes out to those poor girls or women who, with no direct experience of intimacy whether of a physical or an intellectual kind, were thrown into the arms of bullies of some sort or other. The clamour for divorce, if it could have been heard on the part of these sad cases, would have been very great, understandable and in fact, irresistible.

Compare that situation with what happens in England at the beginning of the twenty-first century. Very few women reach the altar or the registry office without having had some kind of experience of the opposite sex. Certainly, they will have learnt at school the so-called facts of life (as though life were a series of facts rather than of experiences and emotions), in all likelihood they will have made a free choice of partner and, as we all know, may have co-habited for longer or shorter periods of time with their 'intended'. They might have been left with some virginity of mind, but their hymeneal, oral and possibly anal virginity is, if the many media reports and commentaries of present-day society are to be relied upon, practically non-existent by the time the marriage ceremony takes place.

These individuals, male or female, can no longer claim failure of understanding or compatibility quite so easily and justifiably as their counterparts of a hundred years ago might have done, if they had been allowed. And yet, in present-day society, where youngsters have the opportunity of learning practically everything about everything, except of course about their emotions, for the system steers clear of even trying to provide any help at that level, the rate of divorce is staggering. This would appear to demonstrate beyond any shadow of doubt that divorce is not the result of lack of physical knowledge or of understanding, of incompatibility, insensitivity, change of personality over the years, or whatever other reason is normally put forward for this breach of the marital vows. Quite the contrary: divorce is the result of our desperate, self-defeating search for self-assertion and selfishness.

It shows, furthermore, the extent to which modern spouses are inclined to neuroticism, simply because they live in a world of make-believe, a world of images which are forced on them by films, television, advertising 'literature', a world the temptation of which they find all the more difficult to resist, the further removed they are, as they must be in our cities, from the realities of natural life. It would surely profit a youngster much more to spend a fortnight on a farm, watching the behaviour of animals, than a year at school being taught the so-called facts of life.

What is surprising is that woman does not appear to have considered that the greater her emancipation, the less likely her success in marriage. Formerly, the wife fell in with the husband's needs and personality; now she feels she has her own rights and her own personality and the husband should fall in with her. Tensions arise, quarrels develop. It is clear beyond any shadow of a doubt that the present format of the institution of marriage is incapable of coping with these types of stresses.

The analyses that have been made of adultery, of the circumstances in which it occurs or the reasons that bring it about, are legion. Depending on whether the analyst is man or woman, one finds that it is easy to pin blame on the other sex. For instances, in *Divorce Won't Help*, Edmund Bergler maintains that very often husbands complain that women are unreasonable in the sense that they expect mental and physical intimacy to be maintained on the same level as it was during the weeks just before and after the marriage, and that they seem incapable of making allowances for the passage of time, once early dreams of love have evaporated. The observation is clearly true, although one is tempted to observe in passing that every marriage goes through this kind of phase. In the marriage that is solid, either doctrinally or practically, this conflict is absorbed inasmuch as the lowering standard is taken for granted: it is only in neurotic marriages that the conflicts become insuperable because the parties think that they should go back to the idea of the 'great love' that prompted them to get married in the first place.

Bergler goes further and makes a point (which this writer does not share) that frigidity accounts for 90% of *female* infidelity. I think that is carrying misogynism a little too far and am much more inclined to believe that marital infidelity on the part of the woman is brought about by a lack of imagination and sexual prowess by the husband rather than by her own frigidity.

He is also very hard on women when he criticizes them for

not making allowances for their age and diminished attractiveness. He claims that women seem to live in a fantasy of timelessness, as evidenced by the fact, which he terms 'ridiculous', that women in late middle-age often continue to dress as young girls. He considers that this is a most glaring example of neuroticism and argues that there would be fewer adulteries and indeed divorces if women were more prepared to come to terms with reality. At the same time, he does not seem too bothered about temporary transgressions into the forbidden, maintaining – and here I would agree with him – that it is the basic attitude to the marriage that counts.

Bergler's misogynism is not complete, however, for he acknowledges fully that the success of marriage is shaped by the wife because she is, generally speaking, more mature than the husband and more capable of succeeding in managing him with invisible diplomacy.

Other writers blame the man's adultery on the woman's bossiness, or her loss of sexual drive. Most writers blame it on the widening gap between the spouses as physical attraction is reduced. Some writers consider that society has made it too easy for woman to have extra-marital affairs because she knows that, if she is found out, she can divorce and that such a divorce, even though it may be traumatic, will not create the same kind of tragedies that it did, say, fifty or more years ago inasmuch as the woman would be able to keep the matrimonial house in any case and can rely, particularly where there are children, on being awarded maintenance.

The belief of modern woman that she can encompass all emotions and be everything to her man when coupled with a rather unforgiving nature, which we are all developing as we begin the twenty-first century, the further away we move from religious beliefs, has resulted in more and more divorces being caused by the husband's infidelity. There is no better example of this than an interview that was given recently to one of the major daily newspapers by a female television presenter who, having been married for nearly seven years, and having two children aged four and five, discovered one day that her husband had committed adultery with a family friend. When confronted with the fact the husband admitted the adultery, and put an end to the relationship but, as far as the wife was concerned, that was the end of the marriage.

The reasons given by the wife I shall transcribe, with my comments, for I consider them to be an unwitting classic exposition of the attitude that modern woman adopts to life, marriage, relationships and divorce.

Here she is, giving the interviewer her feelings upon discovering the betrayal:

> At first, I didn't think it could possibly be true. When you marry somebody, you think it is because you are the perfect people for each other. So it comes as a big shock to discover that maybe somebody is more perfect than you. It was just horrid.

Of course one must sympathize with any woman who discovers that her husband has been sleeping around; the shock is great. But the rationalization is wrong. What this lady discovered was not that there was someone more perfect than she, but surely that her husband had a roving eye and was not prepared to be faithful. The majority of men are that way inclined anyhow.

'I never thought it would happen to me.' Undoubtedly true, but naïve. What was so special about her?

The first thing she did was to remove her wedding ring which 'meant so much to me when it was bought, but everything it meant has gone now'. Understandable: but removing a wedding ring does not erase seven years' relationship, especially where there are two young children.

'We have separated and divorce is the next step.' Why is that, one might ask?

'There are no reasons for us to get back together.' Really? What about two children, aged four and five?

'I believe in monogamy and I couldn't continue in a relationship that was anything other than monogamous.' Here, emotion must have taken over, unless the woman is ignorant. What has happened is not that their relationship has ceased to be monogamous, but merely that it has become adulterous or promiscuous. You can believe in monogamy and be promiscuous, whilst at the same time you can be polygamous without being promiscuous. Monogamy is the marriage of one spouse only; polygamy is the marriage to several spouses.

Of course she thought about the children:

> I used to think that whatever happens, the best thing for children is to have a mother and a father all the time. . . . ., but if things aren't right then you have to go for the next best . . . . . Luckily the children are young enough not to be adversely affected by it.

It is surprising how we, all of us, wish to believe only what we wish to believe, and not necessarily the truth. The rationalization of the belief that the children will not be affected is quite humorous.

'In many ways, they think of it all as quite fun, because they now have two houses to go to and two bedrooms to sleep in.' If this poor woman really believes that it is better for her children to lose contact with their natural father simply because they can enjoy the fun of two houses and two beds, then she is in for a shock.

But she may survive.

'I think marriage is a great institution and I can envisage getting married again.'

So much so that she admitted having begun a relationship with a long-standing family friend, and recited her delight that 'it is lovely to discover that someone who you have always been a good friend to can become something more to you, and I'm very lucky in that respect. It is nice for the children to have somebody who's a friend to the family and a constant in their lives.'

The reader will no doubt see some confusion of thought in what could be described as a very typical reaction. But this is the same person who is on record as saying that:

'After I got married and had children, my friends all told me that it was the best thing I had ever done. They would tell me what a perfect life I had. And it did seem so idyllic and marvellous.' Has the love that must have existed and that gave her seven years of idyllic and marvellous marriage disappeared so suddenly and completely? Why is she rushing to divorce? If she is thinking of remarrying perhaps she will remarry the long-standing family friend who has been so good to her at the moment. He is a man too, after all; what guarantees does she have that he will not stray? And if and when he does, will she also divorce him? Where will it stop?

This hankering after perfection is naïve and irresponsible at the same time. Perfection is not of this world and many marriages survive the occasional straying of either spouse. One presumes it cannot possibly have occurred to this woman that she herself might, in some way, have caused her husband to commit adultery.

It would really be invidious to be dogmatic as to the reasons which cause any particular spouse to commit adultery. It must be true, that the reasons and effects vary from spouse to spouse and from marriage to marriage. However, on the whole, – and this is an unfortunate generalization and one of the few that I shall indulge in for the purposes of this discussion – adultery committed by the man may indeed be a consequence of his wife's behaviour but is more often the result of his promiscuous tendencies; whereas adultery committed by the woman is, in most cases, a direct consequence of her husband's failures (whether sexual, physical, emotional or intellectual).

DISILLUSIONMENT (WITH EACH OTHER)

This is brought about partly by familiarity, but essentially it is the result of a change of pace. We cannot keep going throughout our married life with the same energy and spirit we brought to the relationship during the first year or so, when everything is new. Newly-marrieds are excited, and thrilled, discovering each other sexually and otherwise. But human beings slow down, and the honeymoon is soon over. The number of revolutions of the human motor vehicle cannot be kept constantly close to the red. It reduces, and the engine ends up by barely ticking over; people find it difficult to come to terms with this fact because on the whole they expect too much of marriage.

It is this high expectation which should be worked on by educationalists. People should be taught that marriage is not a bed of roses but something that one must work at constantly throughout one's life. Unfortunately, books, manuals, magazines, newspapers and television programmes all tend to overemphasize the technical aspect of love-making and to glorify the attainment of the greatest possible pleasure. With the excuse of teaching people the basic facts of anatomy and physiology our society has inculcated into its youngsters a mechanical approach to love-making.

What has been ignored is that the mere fact that one has been shown how to play the piano does not make one a good pianist. There is more to playing the piano than just moving hands across the keyboard, no matter how accurately the notes may be reproduced: there is understanding, intuition, feeling, artistry, love and genius. In the same way, to concentrate merely on sexual arousal and orgasm is to rob the marital relationship of compassion, mutuality, spontaneity, good taste, love and, above all, fun. People should smile at each other and not grimace, when indulging their sexual fancies.

The constant objective of sexual performance designed to conform to theoretical standards laid down in textbooks is no different from the purchase of a car that will travel at 155 miles per hour. It cannot be used on our roads.

LACK OF COMMUNICATION

This is ironical in an era where communications are supposed to be so good. According to Kinsey[4] the percentage of college-level American women who have had extra-marital relationships reaches 31% by the time they are aged 40. There is other American research to the effect that college students who have experienced pre-marital sex appear to think that they will have extra-marital sex at a later date. The irony cannot be wasted on the reader that it is exactly in those marriages between educated parties, where the spouses should be most capable of talking to each other, that non-communication must develop at least in the sexual area, if one or even both of them go looking for outlets outside the marriage.

The difficulty is that when parties get married they presume, as a matter of course, that they will understand one another. The wife is confident that the husband will be sympathetic and know instinctively what her needs and whims are now and how to satisfy them; and the husband knows that at last he has joined his twin soul, the woman who will appreciate what he really wants out of life.

They soon find out that it is not quite so easy as that, since they may even have a psychological inability to communicate with each other. One spouse or the other may be of the kind that is reluctant to give in or to admit to being wrong or to say sorry. There is very often a psychological barrier which is aggravated by cohabitation and, as a result, the spouses curl up inwards, psychologically, like hedgehogs when prodded. Psychological estrangement is soon followed by physical rejection. That is the first phase.

In the second phase one spouse starts thinking that although this particular partner does not understand, someone else certainly will. It is so easy to blame the other spouse and to proceed from the premise that the inability to communicate, even assuming that it is identified as such, is caused by the other spouse. In most cases the failure is inbred in whichever spouse does not wish to communicate. The lack of communication is a personality defect and that will continue no matter with whom one associates.

This is not to say that a more amenable partner may not be found the second or third or umpteenth time around. Indeed, it may happen that what is a cause of mental rejection in one person, is insignificant for another; but if there is always a personality fault that causes or encourages a failure to communicate, that will not easily be cured by a second marriage.

LOOKING AT THE RELATIONSHIP THROUGH ROSE-TINTED GLASSES

For instance, I may quarrel with all and sundry but I am never going to quarrel with my wife, whereas exactly that happens. The honeymoon (the sexual excitement, the novelty of the new relationship, etc.) is expected to last throughout married life. But, of course, it does not and cannot, because that kind of level of excitement simply cannot be kept up by human beings. People get used to each other, so accustomed to living together, to the extent that their rate of intercourse reduces, they may even get bored with each other. Marriage is based on more than a honeymoon, as we have just observed when dealing with the subject of disillusionment.

THE SEXUAL EXPERIENCE OF THE SPOUSES

The woman who has either not had any previous sexual experience or very little, is less capable of analysing correctly the sexual ability, or otherwise of her partner. The same goes for the man. In the case of the woman, such a situation not only makes it easier for the man, because his performance is subject to less stringent standards and criticism, but it also provides greater peace of mind for her, since she cannot miss what she has never had. And again, the same applies to the man. The difficulty nowadays is that either because of the accelerating effect of sexual education or because of greater freedom in 'mores' or a combination of both, it is almost certain that one of the parties to a marriage, if not both, will get there having had some premarital sexual experience. The standards expected of the other spouse will be higher. Indeed, they will almost be unattainable if one listens to what is broadcast or written in books and women's magazines. The result will engender dissatisfaction for the man or for the woman or for both.

This is a very odd feature because if one believes what is commonly stated, then woman ought to reach the state of marriage having had such experience and knowledge that she can adjust more easily. But the reverse is happening in our society and indeed one can go so far as to say that if a careful analysis were made of the couples who divorce, one would find that the greater the sexual experience of the parties before marriage, the greater their dissatisfaction within marriage, because it is statistically likely that the performance of the male at least will be much more capable of criticism. (One is taking the performance of the male because the adaptability of woman – where there are no neuroses – is sufficiently great to compensate for inexperience.)

In any event, such pre-marital experience is less important than the sexual behaviour within the marriage.

When difficulties arise in pre-marital relations because of the refusal of the female, or sometimes the male partner, to accept particular techniques, the relationship may be broken up; whilst that may seem unfortunate, it is not so disastrous as breaking up a marriage. Furthermore, pre-marital petting experience provides an opportunity for the female to learn to adjust emotionally to various types of males. Despite petting, however, it is a fact that some marriages get into difficulties because they are based on sexual interests alone.

The females who married at earlier ages had had pre-marital coitus when they were younger; the females who married at later ages had not begun coitus until much later. There is an obvious correlation between these two phenomena and it is a question whether early experience in coitus leads to early marriage or whether the possibility of a forthcoming marriage leads to an acceptance of coitus just before marriage.

A further consideration is the different approach to sexual relations as a result of age. When the man is younger, he is more keen; when the woman is younger, she is less keen. As the woman gets older, she is keener, but the man becomes less so. Woman becomes less inhibited at the time when the responses of the average male have dropped considerably. All this has to be taken into account when considering the divorce rate, but it should be borne in mind that divorces by people of older years are less frequent than among younger ones.

MODERN FREEDOM

This hardly needs discussing. The reaction to Victorian values is so great – and nowadays no longer dramatic – as to be well known to everyone. As a consequence there is a certain lack of parameters. Hypocritical Victorian society may have been but, for it, things were clear-cut. There was a structure to work within and, where appropriate, and no doubt with great hypocrisy, without. But it is far too easy to accuse the Victorians of being hypocritical. It could be said that we are too because we take the trouble to shave when we are due to meet people at home or in public. The reverse of the coin is probably the argument that we are merely being polite; but every form of good manners is, to some extent, a form of hypocrisy.

Today, we look in a somewhat derogatory fashion upon the term 'assortative mating', which is taken to mean that people make a biased choice. In other words, quite apart from whatever opportunities for contact that they may have within geographical areas and within social groupings, they tend to choose their marriage partners in their own image or, at least, in the image of their parents. This has a lot to be said for it. Marriage is a difficult enough institution without importing into the relationship concepts that are wholly foreign, both practically and psychologically, to the spouses.

Personally, I think there is much to be said for the theory of assortative mating. There are sayings in some Continental countries to the effect that one should choose a spouse from the same place where one buys livestock. This is an inelegant concept, but a highly practical one. If I am a non-smoker, I shall court disaster if I marry a tobacco addict. If I love food, I will not get on with a wife who struggles to open a can of baked beans.

It is surely self-evident from the historical records that our forefathers were much more prudent in such matters. In Victorian times, for example, there was a place and a time for everything: just as we had a time for our history and our empire, we had a time for meals and for sexual relations. All these rules are gone. Our society cannot countenance any longer that kind of structure and there is no doubt that the clock cannot be turned back. But at least as far as the children themselves are concerned, the lack of parameters within our society is damaging.

A contributing factor has also been the greater mobility of the workforce. Nowadays, people stay for shorter periods of time in the same place; their friendships almost automatically become of shorter duration than they were when they lived the whole of their life in a village or a small town, and the whole range of human relations acquires a degree of impermanence which militates against the stability of marriage. In the same way as some of our more common so-called durable goods are made to be short-lived, so those qualities which were rocklike have become ephemeral and evanescent.

It is often said that this is a direct consequence of the discovery of the atom and hydrogen bombs in the sense that human beings have, since the Second World War, lived in the shadow of possible global war and destruction of the human race. There is some truth in such statements but it is surely unwise to accept them as an explanation for what is going on in today's society. Greater significance, surely, should be attached to the new role that woman is not without difficulty trying to carve out for herself.

WOMAN, THE BREADWINNER (REAL OR SUBSIDIARY)

In 1948, the American author, Henry Adelbert Bowman, published *Marriage for Moderns*.[5] His observations relate primarily to the post-Second World War society in the United States but he has a lot to say about the position of the working woman. In the first place, he considers the absurdity of comparing the knowledge and skills involved in a career carried out outside the home with those involved in homemaking. For example, he makes the point that if a woman teaches somebody else's children, she is accorded professional status, whereas if she teaches her own, she is simply being a mother.

If she follows interior decoration as a vocation, she has a career but if, like most housewives who are fond of their home, she applies the principles of interior decorating to it, she is simply being a competent housekeeper. If she studies dietetics or is in charge of a large kitchen in a restaurant or an institution, she has a worthwhile and well-remunerated profession; but if she applies dietetic facts and principles to the feeding of husband and children, particularly with the discriminating eye which is needed nowadays, she is just being a cook/housekeeper.

According to Bowman, the same regrettable incongruity exists with respect to all the skills and knowledge involved in home-making and, as a result, he claims that we have depreciated the value of the wife and mother and increased the value of woman as a breadwinner. Not that he is too much in favour of woman going out to work. At pages 81 to 89, for example, he deals at great length with the arguments against women's wage-earning capacity, essentially on the basis that nobody can pursue two careers simultaneously, or at least, only very few exceptional people can. The problem of combining marriage and housekeeping with another career is especially difficult, since they both require different qualities. The former requires self-negation, the latter, self-enhancement; the former demands cooperation, the latter competition.

The woman who attempts to combine the two has a problem of integrating the various elements of her personality and to ensure that the outside career elements do not impinge upon those demanded by home life. The consequence, as most of us who are involved with matters of personal relations well know, is often fatigue, irritation, illness, or even breakdown. In the case of the wage-earning wife, her sources of fatigue are simply duplicated.

Bowman also makes the point that many of the positions held by the married woman wage-earner do not keep her mentally alert, offer her no opportunity for self-expression or development and entail very little satisfaction except that derived from the pay cheque at the end of the week. Women very often do jobs which are crushingly boring and monotonous, and are the result of a very exhausting routine. Consequently, woman may neglect the home because she cannot cope with both sets of demands. She may have neither the time nor inclination and even, if she has both, she may lack the strength.

The employed wife may also neglect her husband. Bowman makes a further point which has much validity: 'Would society not consider it neglect of the wife if her husband worked for wages only part of the time and spent the rest of his time doing something he wanted to do because for some reason or other he did not derive sufficient satisfaction from his occupation?'

As regards making contacts, for instance, Bowman claims that a woman who works outside the home may make contacts that are directly to her advantage but not necessarily to the advantage of the husband. The homemaker in many instances has the opportunity of making contacts which are advantageous to the husband and thus the two functions are complementary.

The gainfully-employed woman may also neglect the children, since children require a great deal of time, effort, interest and information and any kind of child-care service does not provide these. He differentiates with older children where the amount of time spent may be less; but when children are at school for part of the day, the mother cannot be with them anyway and therefore it balances out. This is debatable.

Since children do not ask to be born, if a woman has children she must have a responsibility to them, no matter what her other interests may be. She may hire someone to care for them, but will they have the same interest in them and the same cultural background and ability or a personality as attractive as her own?; in any event, she would not be the mother. There are changes in people who care for children, the long history of continuity in domestic staff no longer prevails.

There are also financial considerations, namely that when the spouses are working they will get so accustomed to a higher standard of living made possible by the joint income, that it becomes difficult for them to lower their standards if one stays at home and has a family. This may well pre-empt them to postpone having a family, thus causing readjustments when finally they do have a family: the woman is then sufficiently old that she is not prepared to have more than one child. Wage earning by the married woman, he claims, is often the result of marital adjustment in the first place and is a contributory factor to domestic problems. Some husbands do not like it, they may be concerned about the image that is projected and, especially where the wife is more successful, the husband may feel inferior. He may also resent her being away from home or he may resent what he considers to be neglect, in whole or in part, of her domestic duties.

This need not be just but, as Bowman puts it, the question that a woman has to face is not whether the husband's attitude is right or wrong, justifiable or unjustifiable, but rather whether they can be happy together when his attitude is what it is; which is a practical question and not a theoretical one. He claims that these are points that should be decided before people get married. There is also the problem of deciding how the income is to be used.

One cannot theorize, it is not a question of whether married women should work for wages, but rather a question of whether being a particular married woman with no skills, personality, opportunity, interests and taste, a particular husband and a home situation, with children or without, is not a special occupation; and that has to be solved from time to time. He continues by saying that in all probability there has been no stage of human development where marriage has not existed and when the father has not been the protector of the family. It is clear that human marriage appears to be an inheritance from some ape-like progenitor.

But how can the father be the protector of the family in the twenty-first century where the wife is the bread-winner? After all, in present-day society the protection by the father is primarily of an economic nature and if woman takes over the role of seeing to the economic wellbeing of the family, the need for the father disappears proportionately. Perhaps the father-figure ought to disappear in its entirety. Also because the bread-winning ability of the wife is a very powerful cause of disagreement within the family. The points made by Bowman more than half a century ago, appear well-founded.

The point still needs to be made, however, that often escapes the notice of commentators. There is an enormous difference between a working woman and a career woman. The former usually works out of necessity, the latter out of ambition; the former may cease to work when her economic position improves, the latter will persevere until she has the strength to realize her dreams.

There is no equivalence in the situations of working mothers and career mothers, since motherhood is in fact both a full-time job *and* a career. Agreed, it is no longer correct to say, even assuming that it was ever appropriate to do so, that 'a woman's place is in the home'; but is it not sensible to insist that a mother's place be in the home at least whilst the children are of school age?

Sociologists, psychologists and politicians, occasionally review, with varying degrees of clarity of analysis and success, the balance of benefits to the State and to the family of the working wife. This discussion is not concerned with such aspect of the matter save insofar as we have already referred to the 'risks', as far as the stability of the marital bond goes; but it is hard to refrain from commenting that there is a very immediate consequence of a wife working which clearly affects our environment: it is the enormous increase in the consumption of packaging material and in the use of chemicals in food.

Formerly, when the wife stayed at home, she had time to go shopping, if she was so minded, almost on a daily basis. She could purchase anything she wanted, from bread to vegetables, from meat to fish, in a comparatively fresh state. Packaging hardly existed, save for particular products of a more durable nature. Chemicals were not needed: in the majority of cases nowadays, the addition of chemicals to food is the result of the need to ensure a longer shelf-life or to make the food itself more pleasant to the eye. Put differently, the pre-packaged, pre-sliced, frozen, fast-food industry would be less active and much less profitable if wives did not go out to work. The convenience of buying things ready-made or ready-cooked, off the shelf, is enormous (and cannot be underestimated) when both spouses have spent eight hours in an office, plus the time spent travelling.

At the same time, however, whilst we are clamouring for a cleaner, greener country, we never stop to consider that one of the principal reasons why we have a surplus of plastic film, containers, packaging and a never-ending list of 'E numbers' associated with foods is directly attributable to the fact that the 'housekeeper' is not at home during the day. And yet, if there are children of school age, woman really *ought* to be at home to see to their safety and well-being. It is surely doubtful that a working wife is as 'fulfilled' psychologically as a mother is.

The impact of divorce on housing and housebuilding requirements results in further damage to the environment. It is only in procreation that woman finds the fulfilment of her personality and the justification of her existence. It should be noted at this stage that whenever a firm statement of this nature is formulated, especially by a man, a chorus of protest is usually heard from women, especially feminists, to the effect that man has no right to make such an assertion, for he cannot know what is entailed; that such a view perpetuates the submission of woman to him through pregnancy; that it is time that men realized that women are more than mere wombs destined to ensure the survival of the species; and so on, in the same vein. What utter cant. It is obviously true that no man can ever aspire to understand what woman experiences in being a mother, from impregnation through to childbirth, weaning and caring throughout her life. That appreciation is her undoubted privilege and is something of which she can truly be proud, even boastful, for it places her on a totally different, and higher plane, from man; but it is naïve to assume that men cannot understand the finality and destination of women's activity, even without direct physical and psychological experience of the inner feelings developed by woman in performing them.

Men are fathers and men are lovers; men talk to women. Some men spend considerable time, both in a personal and in a professional capacity, with women. Some have frequented prostitutes and brothels and, also by chatting to women of that ilk, have been able to form views as to woman's general feelings and reactions. Not all men go through life blindfolded by the so-called mysteries of the female body and mind. A sense of humility is certainly called for when trying to understand human relations of any kind; but the line has to be drawn somewhere and to assume that, merely because woman's development through the centuries has been impeded by man, man is therefore deprived of the ability and opportunity of commenting on and understanding her, seems unwarranted. Furthermore, it seems to me that woman is neither so simple as man would wish her to be, nor so complicated as she would like to believe herself to be.

At this stage, perhaps it is opportune to restate a concept that is frequently lost sight of, namely, the primary destination of woman is motherhood; her secondary destination may well be up to her to determine, but her primary one has been predetermined by nature. Nature never does anything in vain. If it had intended women to be miners, it would not have endowed them unnecessarily with a complicated reproductive system and, merely because the last one-and-a-half centuries has seen a steady decline in the birth-rate, the primary function is not eliminated: reduced yes, terminated no. It is entirely understandable that there are many women who are disposed to have either no children at all or only one or, as the statistics say, 1.8. But it is a basic part of woman's psychological make-up that she should be a mother and where, for whatever reason, that expectation is frustrated, woman is apt to become either neurotic or unhappy or, usually, both.

Of course, one must accept that an increasing number of women nowadays find it no longer convenient or practical to have children. What is not acceptable is to argue that a decision of this kind, once taken, has no effect upon the woman's psychology. As Ruth Brandon has observed,[6] 'once a woman has made a conscious decision not to have a child, the way she looks at the rest of her life is changed, because she attaches importance to everything she does'.

If a woman ceases to have children, she will have no incentive whatsoever to remain married to one man, for it is children who strengthen the bond between man and wife. If she ceases to be essentially 'faithful' to one man, she will compound the destruction of the family brought about by the laxity of our laws on divorce. The fabric of society is at risk.

Let us go back to Ruth Brandon's observation above, which is very perceptive and deserves a great deal of attention. We have all seen in practice how correct the observation is and how successful this particular kind of woman is in whatever she turns her hand to. I am not for one moment decrying the advantages to society of this outlook on work; but one is bound to question whether it results in giving the correct importance and priority to the right things.

Being deprived of her primary aims and functions, woman is perfectly capable of concentrating all her energies single-mindedly on one object (as successfully in fact as unmarried priests and nuns are said to be about their educational functions), though not necessarily on the right one.

Nevertheless, it remains a fact that the primary function of woman is procreation and that when that particular finality is *purposely* frustrated, there is an element of incompleteness in the personality of the woman concerned.

GETTING MARRIED TOO YOUNG

This is the result of the fact that our children mature, at least in the physical sense, more quickly. Consequently, there are more marriages at a much younger age, and inevitably, as statistics now show, more divorces occur at a still tender age. The rate of failure in personal relations is self-perpetuating and the younger the spouses marry, the more likely they are to divorce. It should be noted, however, that nowadays fewer youngsters marry. Marriage has ceased to be fashionable.

HAVING MOST THINGS FAR TOO SOON

We have all suffered from this. Our children, (ours, by the standards of this writer, who is over 60) are thoroughly spoilt. Just as we spoil our children with material things (television sets, video tape-recorders, motor cars, expensive holidays etc.) so they in turn spoil themselves when they get married.

Some of us hardly had a roof over our head and maybe only a cooker and a bed when we got married. Modern married couples, on the whole, have a lot more. The absence of joint achievement, the struggle slowly to buy one thing more to beautify the home, the feeling that one is building for the future, is almost non-existent as far as modern couples are concerned. That, in turn, dilutes the intensity and the strength of the bond between them because only those who have struggled together, and won, feel truly close to one another. There is no doubt whatsoever that what could be termed the absence of joint achievement in young married couples is a potent contributory factor to divorce.

THE SOCIAL AND SEXUAL CLIMATE

Human beings are clearly affected by the society in which they live. Indoctrination by dictators, totalitarian governments, advertising agencies, the press, the State, family planning agencies, the Churches and other organizations, good or bad, that aim to capture the attention, loyalty and money of the individual, all proceed from the premise that if a statement, no matter how false, or a doctrine, no matter how misguided, is made or disseminated often and persistently enough, it will be believed. This is how the masses are made to conform, how collective hysteria is whipped up, hatred generated, prejudice fostered. These are what Sir Francis Bacon so aptly described as 'the idols of the mind'.

Most individuals are unable to discriminate between the truth and what is convincingly and authoritatively proffered as such. This is particularly true if one analyses the shift in the average person's perception of the meaning of marriage. In the 'old' days, and in simple language, one got married for better or for worse. More liberal or more progressive people maintain that marriage is no different from any other contract with the consequence that, as the parties enter into it, so can they get out of it at will, or indeed on a whim. And from the logical point of view they are quite right: you either believe that a marriage is indissoluble or you must reach the conclusion that it is capable of being terminated at any time by either party and for whatever reason.

The attitude of the Anglo-American world in this connection is wholly hypocritical. From the historical standpoint it was firstly the Christian/Catholic approach that was adopted, namely that marriage was indissoluble. Then, in the middle of the nineteenth century, at least in England, the concept of the matrimonial offence (similarly in some States of the United States) was established, to the great joy of divorce lawyers and private detectives. More recently, no doubt as a result of feminist pressures, the United States have come to develop the concept of no-fault divorce and in Britain we have adopted the concept of the 'breakdown' of the marriage, without necessarily having to attach too much significance any longer to the reasons for the breakdown, except perhaps when it comes to financial considerations.

There appears to be a reluctance in Britain to go the whole way and to be logically consistent; accordingly, to say that once you accept that God has not joined two people in matrimony, they can get out of it any time. This reluctance is very difficult to follow: people and governments seem to be either shy or afraid of using logic. As Sir James Fitzjames Stephen said in 1873 in *Liberty, Equality and Fraternity*'[7]: 'If the parties to a contract of marriage are treated as equals it is impossible to avoid the inference that marriage, like other partnerships, may be dissolved at pleasure. The advocates of women's rights are exceedingly shy of stating this plainly.'

In any event, divorce by mutual consent has existed in China for many years as well as among the Eskimos, the ancient Welsh and the ancient Germans. Since Stephen wrote the above, the principle of divorce by consent has become established in countries of such disparate cultures and traditions as Luxembourg, Switzerland, Rumania and Japan. The logic of the argument that the parties who enter freely into a marriage ceremony can just as freely and easily themselves dissolve the marriage was underlined centuries ago by Milton and somewhat more recently by Shelley and Montesquieu.

It is a fact, however, that in most other countries the puritanical or Christian inheritance is causing people to sit on the fence and behave hypocritically. Apart from the Catholic Church, no-one has any longer the courage to say that a decision has to be made between the belief in the mystical nature of marriage and the acceptance that, just as we embark upon marriage, so we should be allowed to disembark from it when it suits us. At least the Catholic Church is consistent. It has stated repeatedly that man is quite incapable of separating what God has joined, that the spouses become a single flesh and that the purpose of their coming together is the procreation of children and the establishment of a family.

You either believe in this or you do not. But, if you do, you cannot have divorce.

The purpose of this discussion, however, is to show that even if you do not believe in it, you ought not to have divorce. Let us get back, therefore, to the marriage which has turned out to be unhappy. It is going to be difficult to put it right; that is fairly obvious, sometimes desperately so, otherwise there would never be divorce. The difficulty cannot be shirked, it is there, it is or may be a fundamental one and the parties have to come to grips with it. In the present social climate, the way in which the parties come to grips with the difficulty is to decide that they have made a mistake, that they will get out of the marriage, forgetting about the vows they made at the altar, or in the registry office, and that they will then start a new life. By starting a new life the parties do not think that they will abandon the old one; but they already know that sooner or later they may remarry.

Whether for reasons of convenience, or for sexual or economic considerations, for the sake of the children, if any, or of respectability or to save face, remarriage is a goal and divorcing parties very often think in terms of remarriage. The statistics show that they remarry very quickly: whether because they already had a relationship going, or whether for the reasons just mentioned, one cannot tell. In this way, the decision is taken to get out of the marriage. The rationalization of the decision to divorce varies depending on whether there are children or not. If there are no children, the decision is fairly easy. Indeed, it can be accepted that where there are no children, there is no family in the traditional sense that needs protection by society and divorce itself is, at most, a meaningless occurrence in the social sense. The neuroses of the spouses are of no great interest to society because they do not immediately result if any great problem, either social or criminal, although divorce costs the State a great deal of money.

It is a wholly different situation, however, where there are children. In such cases, the spouse who is not irresponsible must consider the duties he/she has which result from the existence of children, especially when they are young and highly dependent. The rationalization of the decision to divorce, therefore, proceeds from the premise that if one of the spouses is dissatisfied, then the children must also be unhappy in the marriage which is 'on the rocks'. So, they can only be happier outside it, or even better when the mother/father remarries. There is a very human and understandable weakness in this way of thinking, but it is nevertheless a fundamental one: and it is, that nobody knows.

Nobody has asked the children. The children are seldom, if ever, consulted about the divorce: they are merely presented with the *fait accompli* of the decision to divorce. There is no statistically reliable data of what the children of divorced parents think; 12,000 boys or 8,000 girls under the age of 18 (the numbers of the adult interviewees of the two Kinsey Reports) have never been asked whether they thought they would have been happier in the former marriage or whether the second/third remarriage was more successful as far as they are concerned. It is utter conceit on the part of the spouses, and of all the psychologists who support the theory that the individual must assert his ego at all costs lest he should develop a complex, to presume what the children might say.

As far as the children, particularly if under age, are concerned, the effect of their parents divorcing at any stage of the marriage is considered at some length later. Here, meanwhile, we should note that there are some who maintain that the ever-increasing rate of divorce will result in the decline and fall of Western civilization in the same way as certain practices towards the end of the Roman Empire resulted in its decline and fall. We are not concerned, for present purposes, with the decline and fall of anything so great. If our Western civilization were to decline, another would soon take its place.

In America, critics of divorce have raised the question of whether civilization as we know it can survive, or whether divorce is in conflict with the fundamental American way of life inherited from the days of the Far West; or of whether it represents a threat to moral values. All these complaints do not mean very much. As already noted, our civilization will survive. However, it is absurd to expect the American way of life in the year 2000 to be the same as that in the year 1850 or thereabouts. As to whether divorce represents a threat to moral values, is the wrong question. Surely, it is because moral values have declined that divorce has reached the level it has. If the matter stood otherwise, namely that moral values prevailed, divorce would not exist.

Quite simply, therefore, either you take a moral view of marriage or you take a contractual view of it: there is no way out. If you take the contractual view of marriage then you are entitled to say with consistency that you can resile from it at any time; if you take the moral view then you have no escape from the axiom that you cannot have divorce. We are not concerned here with morality, as has already been stated at the outset. We are concerned merely with the practical problems brought about by divorce so that, in considering them, we may be able to determine whether divorce is a good or a bad thing not in the moral sense, but merely in the practical one.

□

Let us look at some of the arguments that are put forward for justifying the non-maintenance of a marriage which appears to have broken down (not necessarily in order of importance):

1. We should not accept an unhappy marriage because by so doing we degrade marriage as an institution. Everyone ought to be happy, married or otherwise.
2. There is no point in living with a person whom one does not love.
3. It is inappropriate to indulge in sexual relations with a spouse who is no longer loved.
4. The marriage has ceased to be a source of satisfaction and/or security and/or happiness.
5. Children of unhappy marriages will suffer psychological damage.
6. By feminists, the thought that woman is not to be a slave of anyone whom she does not love.

There may be others. They are constantly cropping up and the mere frequency of their occurrence highlights the almost desperate psychological need of those who divorce to justify their actions. The fact that this need arises is indicative of a feeling that divorce is not the obvious choice; this is borne out by the further consideration that every time any person who is in favour of divorce and who divorces, is taken to task about it, that person indicates that the decision to divorce was not taken lightly. One could counter that by saying that if the decision to marry had not been taken lightly either, the difficulty might not have arisen.

The truth probably is that divorce is an attitude and a fashion which does in fact provide woman with certain advantages. In the first place, it gives her the initiative, and for this reason divorce tends to breed divorce. People who have divorced want to provide themselves with a justification of their behaviour. This is useful for their psychology and it is also useful as an explanation to their friends.

In the second place, once spouses have divorced, they are not likely to go around saying that they have made a mistake and that divorce is wrong. Quite the reverse; in order to maximise their success they will keep saying that they never did anything better. This in turn creates an atmosphere where people accept that divorce is a good thing. If you couple such a situation with what one sees on television, you inevitably feel that there is an aura in favour of divorce.

The children themselves, just as they copy their adults in terms of behaviour, honesty, cleanliness, smoking, promiscuity, etc., will copy them in terms of divorce. It is as certain as anything that the children of parents who have been divorced and/or remarried will be more prone to divorce than those of parents who have not been divorced.

There seems little doubt that divorce will continue to spread whilst married partners are dissatisfied with their marriage. Divorce will also continue to spread because there are no moral social or religious hindrances to it. Once upon a time, when people believed that marriage was indissoluble, they felt uneasy about divorce. Now that they believe in nothing, they do not feel concerned – such are the consequences of the society in which we live.

There is a negative side to all this. Whereas men have on the whole had power over women – which they lost as soon as woman took charge of the conception process – now a wife can turn round to the husband and blackmail him, ask him either to improve his behaviour or help with the washing-up or become more proficient in bed and, if not, she will leave him: and society will endorse what she has done.

It is not that human beings have changed, it is not that there are new problems within the marital relationships. The problems are exactly the same because human beings have always been and always will be exactly the same. What has changed is the breaking point in the tolerance by both spouses, but especially by woman, of behaviour which is unsatisfactory. In other words, people are no longer prepared to put up with behaviour that does not please them, whereas they might have been more prepared to acquiesce in it when there were greater restrictions on divorcing and remarriage, and society looked askance at the break-up of a marriage.

There is no doubt that the new approach to divorce is casual. This casual approach in turn breeds divorce because young people get married and they merely say: 'Well, we'll try and see; and if it doesn't work, we'll divorce.'

It used to be said that one of the great benefits of the sexual liberation of human beings, and especially of women, and of the new freedom in sexual morality, was that, having 'had sex' before marriage, the parties knew what they were letting themselves in for. This was one of the tenets of feminists behaviour and indeed one of the planks put forward by the Family Planning Association. It has proved to be a pious hope. Statistics now show conclusively that, at least in the United Kingdom, 50% of married couples have cohabited before they got married. The same statistics show that 43% of these same people who now get married, subsequently divorce within five years. Having lived together has obviously taught them nothing whatsoever about living together, or about marriage. It may have taught them something about their sexual proclivities, but even the value of that is debatable, since these may change with the passage of time.

A further cause for the increased rate of divorce is the spread of both male and female homosexuality. It is, of course, true to say that homosexuality *of itself* need not necessarily result in divorce proceedings being instituted by one or other of the spouses. But any increase in the frequency of the homosexual tendency, whether for man or for woman, must be a contributory factor to marital disharmony. Given that homosexual tendencies are on the increase, for both sexes, there can be no doubt that as a result there are, and will continue to be, more divorces. It is almost impossible to determine in such situations which is the party to blame. Indeed, when it comes to divorce, the apportionment of blame is not only notoriously difficult but, ultimately, totally irrelevant, save at present for the purposes of maintenance.

Centralized urban societies produce heightened emotional tension that leads to a state of persistent sexual excitement, persistent because it is often unsatisfied. The dissatisfactions of the public with their personal sexual experiences are expressed in art and entertainment as an intensive preoccupation with romantic love, sexual success and virility. This is proved in the growth of that form of advertising which depends on the promise of sexual success and virility rather than on any image of togetherness.

□

It may be appropriate at this moment to append a few short references to the work of Professor Kinsey. The first one is extracted from *Sexual Behaviour in the Human Female.*[8] This publication resulted from an enquiry into women's sexuality. The views of 8,000 females were sought (two-thirds of the number of males interviewed five years earlier). One passage (p.11) seems quite relevant:

> We have said that there seems to be no single factor which is more important for the maintenance of a marriage than the determination and the will that the marriage shall be maintained. Where there is that determination, differences between the spouses may be overlooked or forgotten and minor disturbances may be viewed in a perspective which

> emphasizes the importance of maintaining the marital union. Where there is no such will, trivial and minor disturbances may grow until they appear important enough to warrant the dissolution of a marriage.

One of the few comments that Kinsey allows himself to make appears at page 544 of the 1948 edition of *Sexual Behaviour in the Human Male*,[9] where, almost as a partial conclusion to their work, the researchers state that their research '... suggests that there may be nothing more important in a marriage than a determination that it shall persist. By such a determination, individuals force themselves to adjust and to accept situations which would seem sufficient grounds for break-up if the continuance of the marriage were not the prime objective.' This statement, which seems to be of the highest moral calibre, is both very trite and very old. The Catholic religion has adopted it throughout its history, as it has always preached resignation and acceptance of one's fate. Ultimately, marriage is part of fate, if one believes that marriages are made in heaven.

Divorce is rather like the death penalty. Once you have established it, you have got to use it; that is why, once the concept of divorce comes into being, it is used in preference to any other solution to marital problems, such as, for example, a separation, whether temporary or permanent, or, in the rare case, even murder.

It is hardly a coincidence that what we shall call the animal as opposed to the spiritual features of sexual relations are glorified by our society at the same time when family and home are disintegrating. This is a point which is particularly well made by David Mace in *Does Sex Morality Matter?*,[10] where he argues that the logical outcome of sexual freedom, so far as the relationships between men and women are concerned, is that the structure of society begins to creak for, as he puts it: '... the duties and responsibilities which are regarded as a burden are in fact the very means by which sexual desire is enabled to be called love and prevented from degenerating into lust'.

It certainly cannot be a coincidence that the disruption of

family life comes at the same time as woman asserts more loudly than ever her right to sexual promiscuity. As David Mace puts it:[11] '. . . if a woman is prepared to give to a man the greatest privilege she has to offer without asking any pledge of responsibility in return, the result is inevitable: namely that when she does desire his responsible co-operation she will be left no inducement to offer him in exchange for it'. At the same time, however, it is not clear that the issue can be reduced solely to one of virginity: there must be more to marriage than just that. Nevertheless, one is left wondering whether it may not be true that by concentrating on sexual attraction we are discounting temperamental compatibility. Pre-nuptial relations may make some contribution to the clarification of the former requirement of a happy marriage but comradeship is more important than sexual adjustment.

After all, if Robert Louis Stevenson was right when he said that marriage is more a field of battle than a bed of roses, then temperamental compatibility seems a much more important standard to apply to any long-lasting relationship than sexual attraction.

A much more negative feature, which has nothing to do with divorce directly but which is still relevant in this context, is the fact that the abuse of a particular man/woman relation does result in the depreciation of that particular commodity. Although one is hopeful that he was exaggerating, there is some justification for the statement made by Earl H. Brill at some time in 1966 that 'sex is dead'. It is dead in the sense that it has ceased to represent either the most interesting subject for discussion or the most exciting sphere of activity for pursuit on the part of youngsters. The reasons for this are manifold. It is conceivable that the old saying that one can have too much of a good thing does have a sound foundation in psychological theory. Certainly, there was more satisfaction in seeing a few inches of a woman's calf in the eighteenth century than there is in having her naked form transmitted on to one's home television screen. As every experienced philanderer well knows, nothing tempts more than temptation: and it is difficult to be tempted if something is flaunted at you.

Brill himself lists seven points in support of his statement as to the death of sex. They range from the fact that sex is no longer the most popular subject for discussion amongst students to the indifference provoked by nudity, mini-skirts and bikinis. He claims that the existence of magazines such as *Playboy* shows beyond doubt that there is a need to proclaim that sex is still alive, or at least that it has been resurrected by Mr Heffner. Brill's argument on this issue is somewhat questionable since such magazines, I would suggest, together with any other publication of a pornographic nature, do not prove, as he would have it, that sex is dead: they merely prove that human beings are becoming more impotent and depraved because of the kind of sexual 'mores' which society is endorsing, and consequently have need for titillation or substitutes.

There is, I believe, a much more fundamental reason for the obvious disinterest, at least by the male – whose correlation must be the increase in the manifested rate of homosexual tendencies – and it is this: whether we like it or not, we all live with an accumulated psychological heritage which goes back thousands of years and that heritage is being interfered with by present-day customs.

As part of this heritage, both man and woman are aware that at a certain point in time in the lives of their ancestors, man was the hunter and woman the hunted. What has happened in contemporary society is simply that the hunting instinct is gone: there is no need any longer for man to hunt woman, since woman is freely available to him. With the disappearance of the hunting instinct there has occurred a reduction in man's excitability in his dealings with woman. The concomitant of this reduction is the sexual disinterest which Brill has correctly identified and the consequence of such lack of interest and excitement is the reduction in the quality and duration of man's penile performance. Odd though it may sound, by her freedom and aggressiveness woman is effectively castrating man, or at least, causing him to be so little interested in her that his lack of excitement transfers itself to his sexual prowess.

As far as women are concerned, men's sexual requirements nowadays are very quickly and easily satisfied. There is not the joy and the excitement of the hunt; there is merely the convenience of the immediacy of the relationship brought about by the free availability of this particular commodity, and the spread of reliable contraception. This is highly damaging to the psyche. Youngsters ought to have little time left from their search for sexual satisfaction because it is only in that way that they will be kept apart from drugs, violence and other forms of anti-social behaviour. If you have spent all your time hunting, whether a woman or a beast, you will not turn to breaking windows or slashing car tyres because you will have neither the time nor the inclination to do so: what you will have to seek is rest from the hunt itself.

This is not in any sense to be taken as minimizing the part played by the woman; nor should it be interpreted as meaning that woman is merely an animal whom man hunts. But let us not forget that the same considerations apply in any event *mutatis mutandis* to a woman. It must be more exciting, one would think, to be wooed, courted and conquered than to offer oneself freely, carelessly, casually and drunkenly at the first opportunity.

FORCED OR UNNATURAL MOTHERHOOD

This seems a somewhat strange heading particularly in the twenty-first century when, as a result of the increasingly reliable methods of contraception, it is unlikely that any woman would actually be coerced into having a family; and yet, children can be a cause of divorce, particularly where they emerge as unwanted. This is not to suggest for a moment that parents who only have one child, because they find that one is too much to cope with, will have an unhappy marriage. Quite the contrary, in fact: it is conceivable that by concentrating all their efforts on one child only they may make each other happier than they would perhaps have been if they had had half a dozen.

It is becoming increasingly apparent in today's world that there are women who are not cut out to be mothers. These are the women who go and swell the figures that show that more women apply for divorces than men. For example, until recently, there has been around the myth that a woman will always make a last-ditch effort to save a marriage: her eleventh-hour attempts to rescue the relationship are fodder to those sociologists who believe that woman, deep down, accepts the sanctifying grace of a lifelong union. This is certainly not true and is not borne out by the statistics.

There can be no doubt that there is an increasing number of women who do not need motherhood, who do not wish to be mothers and who in all likelihood are unfit to have children. It is conceivable that, gradually, the instinct of procreation is being bred out of females in the same way in which, for example, a woman athlete acquires male characteristics. Her body reduces, if it does not eliminate entirely, certain hormones, or produces much less of them; this is shown in the reduction, if not total elimination, of menstrual flow: it is perfectly possible, therefore, that in the sociological, physical and psychological sense, modern woman may be reaching a stage when she is almost incapable of producing children.

For example, there is already scientific evidence that women are becoming less fertile. There is also ample scientific proof that some instincts can be bred in and out of animals, as any dog-breeder or farmer knows. Chickens can be 'trained' to lay eggs but not to sit on them. One would not wish to be so unkind as to compare woman to a hen, but the fact is that there are tendencies, trends, abilities, functions, which atrophy when the need for them comes to an end, rather like the wings of penguins.

From this it follows that, again in the fullness of time, a clear differentiation will have to be made between women workers and women mothers, between those women whose function in life is the secondary one of contributing to society in the same way as men do and whose primary function has become non-existent, on the one hand, and those who will procreate and care for children, on the other.

The difficulty is that our society still expects women to be mothers, since most of us are brought up to believe that it is only by having a child that woman completes the cycle for which she has been put on earth. In a strange sense, all feminists should be keen to procreate because it is only in that way that they can beat men to it: the experience of giving life is something that no man can have or ever expect to achieve.

Nevertheless, whatever feminists may say, our society almost insists that women have children. There are financial incentives for those who have children, although they are quite indiscriminate, in the sense that they do not distinguish between the good mother and the bad one; they are also insubstantial.

A rather more sinister development is the increasing number of very young girls, below the age of legal consent (in the UK 16), who get themselves pregnant, either because they feel that way they will gain more importance or because they may receive benefits from the State (allowances, accommodation, etc.) which would otherwise be denied to them.

The regrettable fact of life is that not only are there some women who should not have children but, for some women, children create problems which rub off on the husband and ultimately result in unhappy marriages. It is often said that a child is a bond between the parents. There are many cases to show that a child may be a source of conflict as well as a bond and there is ample evidence that the existence of children is no deterrent whatsoever to a divorce.

When women are interviewed about their grounds for divorce seldom, if ever, do they mention their having had a family whether of one or more children, as the actual reason for divorcing. There is a reluctance by woman to acknowledge that she has failed as a mother. She may be perfectly happy to accept that she has failed as a wife, but it is the ultimate sin, one supposes, for a woman to say that she failed as a mother. And yet, there must be women who are unfit to be mothers in the same way in which there are men who are unfit to be fathers. They are the men who beat or molest their wives or children, or fail to pay maintenance for their family.

The importance of the maternal instinct for the well-being of a marital relationship is not to be underrated in any event and is certainly not to be considered solely by reference to children. As Professor W. Thomas has observed in *Sex and*

Society: '. . . so-called happy marriages represent an equilibrium reached through an extension of the maternal interest of the woman to the man, whereby she looks after his personal needs as she does after those of the children – cherishing him, in fact, as a child – or in an extension to woman on the part of man of the nurture and affection which is in his nature to give to pets and all helpless (and preferably dumb) creatures'. This writer wholeheartedly endorses Professor Thomas's observation. It is surely self-evident that much that is wrong in the present relationship between the sexes can be ascribed to the failure or, at least, unwillingness of many wives to extend what Professor Thomas calls their maternal interest to their husband, even though they may retain it for their children; and vice versa, to a similar failure by the husband.

This failure or unwillingness, as the case may be, is self-evident in those situations where women actually give birth to children with the avowed intention of living on their own. That is to say, without the support, protection and companionship of a man. One can partly explain this development on the basis that inasmuch as man is no longer so necessary for the protection of either the wife or the family or both, he is becoming redundant. His functions, insofar as protection from third parties is concerned, have long ago been taken over by the police and the State.

But this explanation is valid only in part, for there is nothing to prevent anyone from looking to man for support and companionship rather than for protection. Put differently, if someone is knocking at the door menacingly, we no longer have to grab the shotgun and kill him: it is quicker, simpler and, ultimately, safer, to call the police. In a happy marriage, however, situations where the woman looks to the man to protect her in this way are few and far between because both spouses know that they would rather call in the State, acting through the police, than place themselves at risk by trying to protect the family or their home. But they still look to each other for company, support and, ultimately, for love.

The tendency of modern woman to do away with man goes beyond the consideration that he is no longer needed as protector. He is no longer needed as companion and lover and that is where the major difficulty in modern husband-and-wife relationships is to be found.

Of course, as noted earlier, we have always taken it for granted that women were born to be mothers. For example, Havelock Ellis saw motherhood as the culmination of woman's activities on earth. He claimed that nature had made women more like children in order that they might better understand and care for them. He also claimed that in the gift of children, nature had given woman '... a massive and sustained physiological joy to which there is nothing in men's lives to correspond'.[12]

Ellis himself did not have children out of his relationship with Edith Lees, whether because he was impotent or, as claimed by him, because they had decided that parenthood did not suit them. Accordingly, he called his marriage to her 'a semi-detached marriage'. Nevertheless, apart from idiosyncratic situations, women themselves are educated to believe that and, at least from the days of Queen Victoria, everything they see or hear about their future is inspired by this fairly simple and essential requirement. That women are so brought up cannot be denied. What must be disputed, however, is that all of them are fit for motherhood.

As there are variations in every human character, temperament, reactions, abilities and so on, so, as far as women are concerned, there are some in whom the motherly instinct is either thwarted or deficient or, indeed, non-existent. Whilst society imposed the requirement that in order to be fulfilled women ought to give birth and care for her children, it was easier to hide this particular deficiency. Now that woman is asserting loudly and successfully that she only wants to be what she thinks she ought to be, rather than what society or men expect her to be, it has become patently, if not painfully obvious, that there are some women who ought never to have children.

In those cases, therefore, where the woman, for whatever reason, is not capable of resisting the pressures that society imposes upon her to be a mother, and actually gives birth to children despite the availability of contraceptive devices that would ensure that she remained barren, there arise situations of conflict, tension and very often violence which psychologists have been so far unable to explain but which could really be resolved quite simply by arguing that that particular type of woman has missed her vocation. Any parent knows the pressures that children create and any mother who spends her time at home, – caring for her children for a much longer period than was ever necessary in the earlier days when, because of pressures of work and because of the different organization of the family, others (mothers, grandparents, in-laws etc.) could have cared for the children, – knows only too well how those 'little monsters' can drain the resources of even the strongest woman.

The pressures that arise, therefore, as far as the mother is concerned are reflected in the marriage. It is difficult for most men to understand what a mother has to go through, particularly if she is not one of those women who can go out to work and delegate the care of her youngsters to third parties.

These pressures cannot be minimized and not even the sharpest and keenest 'male-chauvinist' husband could deny that they exist and have an enormous impact on the wife. This impact is compounded by the present social structure and the organization of labour because, at the same time as society expects a woman to be a mother, it insists that she should also take responsibility for earning part of the family income, caring for her children at least up to the age of eighteen, for being in effect a slave to the family, when that woman may either not have really wished to be a mother, or be objectively incapable of performing the duties of a mother, or may finally have had her feelings for motherhood affected, reduced or even eliminated at an early age because of the way in which she was brought up. She may well have been brought up to believe that men were no different from women and that, therefore, since men could not give birth to children, there was no particular requirement that a woman should do so for their benefit. As many writers, particularly from America,[13] have amply demonstrated, the motherhood instinct is much less obvious and real than the procreating instinct; and there are some writers who have argued that motherhood is not at all necessary to fulfilment by woman of her role in life. This is not the place in which to deal with such contentions, even assuming that it were necessary to rebut them. But if they are correct – and there seems to be increasing evidence that they are – then it must be a source of great stress within a marriage for the woman to have to cope on a regular basis with children in circumstances where she may barely have wanted them and, even if she did want them, she certainly did not wish to care for them. These stresses must have a bearing on the relationship between the wife and the husband, come what may. And it is this kind of situation which, in a number of instances, adds to the problems that may already exist within the marriage and become a causative event as far as divorce is concerned.

It is not a question of maintaining the view that, because a wife gives birth to children in circumstances where she is unfit to care for them, then divorce must follow as night does day. But there can be no doubt whatsoever that the marital relationship is already under sufficient stress in the twenty-first century; if we superimpose upon it the further stresses that arise out of a total failure by a spouse to understand his/her role in life then one is asking for trouble.

According to Jessie Shirley Bernard,[14] in modern society the two basic roles of woman, those of mother and of productive worker, have been separated, with implications for both that we are just beginning to trace and hopefully to understand.

There are now different pressures on mothers. Before it was the scrubbing of clothes and now it is the fact that children, in cities for instance, have nowhere to go and play. All she says about the pressures put on modern mother is absolutely correct. But to develop the argument, that because of such pressures, there should be no motherhood, seems more debatable. Women's pressures and anxieties seem to weigh heavily with her. It is of course true, as she says, that the home was always looked upon as a sacred place and therefore this isolated the home whilst at the same time creating pressures within it.

She quotes on page 13 Ibsen's Nora[15] who, in reply to her husband's criticism that before all else she should be a wife and a mother, says: 'That I no longer believe, I believe that before all else I am a human being just as much as you are, or at least that I should try to become one.' Ibsen wrote this in 1897 and she takes it as her starting point for the whole of the book.

She states that affluence has brought more technological help to the mother but, as the same time, has provided less personal help to her, so that the role of mother generally has become more difficult. This is not because of technological help, I suggest, but because of the reduction in the extent of the family. Grandmothers, sisters, brothers, cousins, and so on, have disappeared from the picture. They used to help with the children and the housework and now that they have gone, all we have is a mother, a father who may be out at work, and perhaps an 'au pair': but in those cases where the mother has to cope with half a dozen children, obviously she cannot manage any longer.

She also refers to what is known in the trade as 'the prolongation of infancy', the point being that the amount of time that the mother dedicates to the children has increased substantially from what it was in the nineteenth century because the children stay much later at school and they need attention for longer. All this is perfectly true; but the answer is not to have children, surely, rather than to complain about them once you have got them. She quotes the Royal Commission on Population which in 1949 recommended that '. . . a deliberate effort should be made to devise adjustments that would render it easier for women to combine motherhood and the care of a home, with outside activities'.

Incidentally, dealing with the increase in the rate of marriage, she claims that since the late 1950s the trend of the first marriage rate has continued to decline whilst divorce and remarriage rates have risen sharply. It is the remarriage of divorced people that keeps the marriage rate going up.

She says that working mothers can no longer be termed 'deviant' because they have now developed a lifestyle which combines both work or career, and motherhood. However, it would seem that she does not differentiate too clearly between working mothers or women, and career women. The distinction however, is a fundamental one, as already observed, and it is hard to understand why she does not deal with it as a matter of principle.

One of her main points is that fashions have changed. In the past, a blue-collar worker's wife was proud of her status as a housewife. The fact that she stayed at home meant that her husband could afford her and there was enough food on the table, so that she did not have to go out to work. This is no longer so because, according to her, most of the time it is not the second income that the wife is after, but personal satisfaction, although a second income does provide a better car, two television sets, or a second home, or college for the children; and so on.

She says that the role of the working-class mother is being redefined in any event, since the work ethic has changed. I have to agree with her on this, but wonder why she fails to come to terms with the difficulty that women who are driven by an absolute compulsion to succeed as men do, and reach the top of their job or profession, women who are determined to win and to make it, at all costs, are not likely to have the qualities that make for successful motherhood. She identifies this difference but does not go the whole way to say that it is those very career-minded women who should *not* be mothers because they have not got the right approach to motherhood.

She quotes all sorts of writers who say that it is perfectly possible to combine profession and marriage, provided three conditions are satisfied:

> 1) That the man is not threatened by the woman's capabilities and achievements;
> 2) That he sees his wife's work as adding to his stature, rather than as diminishing it, and,
> 3) That the woman herself has identified her correct roles, either as a worker or as a mother, and is not ambivalent about them. But this is exactly the difficulty: if woman had the ability to do that, we would not have this type of problem.

In essence, however, one of her principal arguments is that we are looking at it wrongly. We say that man is aggressive and therefore woman should be passive: we say that man has certain particular qualities which are desirable in him, but woman cannot have the same qualities. She claims that we insist that each sex specialize in only one set of circumstances whereas we should be seeking the complete, wholesome, non-mutilated personalities that can have both masculine and feminine virtues, that can be just and merciful as the occasion demands or be stern and gentle, that can be both healer and disciplinarian. In other words, she expects woman to be more like a man, rather like Professor Higgins in *My Fair Lady*.

Quoting from experience in the USA,[16] on page 180 she makes an interesting point:

> In almost two-fifths of contested divorce cases, custody is given to fathers, for recent cultural changes in American society have weakened the stereotype of the woman as the home-maker and the man as the provider. Sociologists looking into the future of sex characteristics foresee a softening of gender identity lines which will have the effect of rendering men more capable of responding positively to changes in women's roles as they occur: it will therefore be easier and easier for professional women to find the kinds of husbands they need to help them integrate their mother and their worker roles and the husband will contribute more than mere financial support.

This a significant observation because it ignores the children. If man wants to stay at home or be subservient to woman, that may well work between the two of them. But what will be the effect on the children of such confusion of roles, if not functions? Indirectly, she is aware of the danger when she claims that girls are developing identity crises (that go unreported) in their relationship to men. They are basically dependent but they want to be independent, they are told they should be wives and mothers but they do not want to be and a sense of guilt develops.

She says it used to be respectable once upon a time for woman to work only if she needed the money, but now other reasons are making for respectability. She does not take at all seriously the point made in 1973 by George Gilder[17] that by earning more money than the men around her, woman tends to demoralize them, she undermines their usefulness as providers, she weakens men's connection with the community and promotes a reliance upon other anti-social ways of confirming their masculinity, namely hunting and fighting and chasing women to assert themselves. 'A society of relatively wealthy and independent women will be a society of sexually and economically predatory males or a society of narcotized drones who have abandoned sexuality entirely.' This is what Mr Gilder says and he may well be right.

Nor does Bernard deal with Gilder's claim that, when a male makes money, that is socially affirmative because if he is unmarried, a higher proportion of such earnings than a woman's will be spent on the opposite sex; accordingly, man's money gives him the wherewithall to undertake a long-term sexual initiative. It also gives him an incentive to submit to female sexual patterns without too much problem because he knows that he will retain the important role of provider. Accordingly, his sexual impulses can assume a civilizing rather than a subversive form.

It is worth drawing attention to this point because since traditionally woman has been psychologically trained as a housekeeper, and has learnt how to be careful with money, women on the whole can be said – and this is not meant to be offensive – to be much more cautious about the way they spend money than men. It follows, therefore, that there is a lot more in Gilder's observations than he actually spells out. On the whole – the danger of generalizations apart – men are more inclined to spend lavishly than women.

Bernard also maintains that women nowadays no longer have to worry that they have a loving husband who provides the money because they themselves can earn it. They want to worry about earning an income and they feel they want to be active in politics and they want to run the country. In fact, they wish to be onmipotent. But there are drawbacks to this. For example, there is an inevitable softening in the attitude of children as a result of women taking over their socialization. From manipulation by threat of force used by men, we are thrown upon the manipulation by seduction, enticement and guilt. Whipping and brutal physical punishment like spanking or slapping have gone, they are practically extinct. 'Mothers today shape the development of the child by assuming love and trust and demanding guilt.' The character formation of people in the highly industrialized countries has changed dramatically, the emphasis being shifted from external behaviour to internal motives.

Bernard certainly has a point with her claim that women who do not take up motherhood, are helping in the population explosion. But it seems that in this way she admits implicitly that a woman who pursues a career is not fit to be a mother. She is not at all worried about genetic engineering and about women just having children through an injection. She claims: 'I have enough confidence in women to answer that they will show good judgment in handling this question.'[18] Accordingly, she thinks it is doubtful that black mothers would order white children, or white women black ones, or that blue eyes would be ordered more than brown, or more boys rather than girls. She claims that the decisions will not be either trivial or frivolous. Her confidence in the innate wisdom and common-sense of women is impressive, but leaves this writer somewhat sceptical.

She quotes Jeanne Binstock as saying that '... instead of endurance, patience, fortitude and tenderness – the traditional virtues of women in all previous historical periods – we have contraception and penicillin, the former ensuring that children are not born, and the latter that mother doesn't stay up all night if the child is unwell'. Practical, of course; but healthy? It is hard to say.

She quotes Alice Rossi as stating the obvious, namely that young women who are active in the feminist movement today may be women with naturally high androgen levels. So also may career women be. She goes on to say that if this is right, then women who want to reduce their 'infant hunger', that is to say, to have no children and at the same time increase their career or work motivations, should be prescribed androgens. She concludes by saying that, essentially, motherwork is 'shit work' because the intrinsic significance and value of early maternal childcare is devalued.

The reader will readily understand why Jessie Bernard's

book has ben reviewed so extensively, viz., that it highlights, albeit for different reasons and with a feminine bias, the essential point of the present work.

Women's intentions and roles will adapt to the social policy of the times but it would be foolish in the extreme to allow feminist dogma to dictate what society should do simply because some women have no wish to be mothers. Either we believe in the family as a unit which society should safeguard in the interest of itself and the children, or we do not. If we do not, then there should be no problem. If the family is not worth preserving, then there is no point in having marriage because there is no scenario against which to set the marriage. In that event, there would be no need for divorce, because people will only need divorce if they have married. If, on the other hand, we believe in marriage, then we should not have divorce.

To those who decide to be mothers, the State should offer substantial assistance, especially in the form of tax allowances and financial contributions (see chapter 10). The idea that the State should contribute to the maintenance and upkeep of mothers is not new. It had already been hinted at by Aristotle and it was restated by H. G. Wells in *The New Machiavelli*.[19] (It was supported in the nineteenth century by H. Ellis and in the twentieth by Bertrand Russell.)

In arguing that the subordination of women to men should be reduced, Wells propounded the theory that the special function of woman within the State was, in fact, motherhood and that only by the State acknowledging the fact that women cease to be degraded by being subordinated to an individual man. As Ruth Brandon pointed out in *The New Women and the Old Men*,[20] both H. G. Wells and Havelock Ellis looked upon woman, the mother, as the supreme being; the former, as already noted, claiming that the raising of children was woman's highest duty to the State and the latter, expressing his view that motherhood was woman's supreme physical and emotional fulfilment whilst '. . . the primary end of marriage is to beget and bear children'.[21]

It is strange to see two Anglo-Saxon men expressing views that are more appropriate to a Catholic (Latin) society. Latins have a tendency to put the mother on a pedestal much more than Northerners, this arising out of the indissolubility of marriage which has prevailed in Latin countries until recently. The concept of indissolubility has created the kind of mentality whereby the mother has been glorified as the centre of the family, as indeed she is, and the father has accepted that his primary duties to the family prevailed over everything else, including any commitments he may have undertaken towards either the State or his mistresses. The correctness of this view is expressed by Catholic art, where woman reigns supreme. The Madonnas, the holy families, are all a glorification of the family as a unit and an extreme form of flattery to woman herself but essentially, only insofar as she is a mother (at the other end of the scale, if she is a prostitute, she was until recently organized in brothels). The position is changing throughout the Mediterranean, however.

VANISHING FATHERHOOD

We are no longer a patriarchal society. Emphasis has shifted from fatherhood to motherhood. As Bertrand Russell has observed,[22] fatherhood makes human society more competitive, more energetic, more dynamic and hustling than motherhood. It may well be that it is true that there is something on the whole rather flat about present-day Western society. Whether, however, this flatness follows from the fact that the significance of the father is reducing or from what one may term different moral considerations and outlooks, is hard to say, but there is no doubt whatsoever that the role of the father in our society is one of ever-diminishing importance.

As we have already seen, very often nowadays woman is a principal if not the real breadwinner. The primary function of the father, therefore – that of maintaining and supporting the family – has gone. His secondary function was that of protecting the family against outsiders. That, too, has gone, particularly in progressive Western societies, such as the UK and US. Also, gone are the days when the patriarch of the family could rely upon his grown-up sons to defend the family unit now that the State has clearly taken over most of his functions.

There is National Health, the Social Services, the police. Come to think about it, any father nowadays is at serious risk if he even spanks his children, or maybe caresses his daughter. As to any financial benefit accruing to the family from his presence, in most middle-class families, mother and children would be infinitely better off, because of the insurance payments, if the father were dead rather than alive.

It is true that, if he does earn a good income, then, particularly in certain strata of society, he can provide his children with special advantages, like public school education or equivalent benefits; but it is difficult to see that he has any real utility at present. So much is this so that the number of women who have children as a matter of choice without either marrying or co-habiting with men is increasing all the time.

In their folly, inspired by a desperate desire to master nature, men have brought about their own demise as fathers now that a woman can so easily be provided with a child without not only the physical presence of the father, but even without either knowing who the father is, or was, or selecting a particular father who has bequeathed his seed to posterity.

It is clear beyond a peradventure that the State is replacing the father, gradually but inevitably, in all his functions. Whatever may have been the intention of the State in eliminating the father, it found a very powerful ally in woman. The women with political clout hitherto tended to be mostly spinsters. It is only nowadays that more married women are going into politics. But modern woman having decided to be psychologically and, above all, economically independent of man, there was really no way in which the father could survive as a figure of strength.

We should be under no illusion that fatherhood is becoming more and more meaningless. It is necessary to make these rather pessimistic observations because by reducing, if not eliminating, the authority and significance of the father, we are all self-evidently contributing to the break-up of the family unit. Above all, we are creating stress in the relationship between man and woman and especially husband and wife. The increasing lack of meaning for the function of a father is one of the most powerful causative elements in divorce.

Where the father wields authority over the family with power and compassion, where the family is economically dependent upon him and where, either because of his temperament or character, his position in society and his outlook on life, he projects towards his wife and children the picture of someone upon whom they will always be able to rely, who will solve their problems, who will protect them from outsiders and, if necessary, from the State, then it goes without saying that it would not be so easy to establish those tensions within the family which may result in divorce.

Feminists will no doubt remark at this stage that it is exactly such a state of affairs that the emancipation of woman is aimed at eliminating but in fact, such an observation is hopelessly wrong. The emancipation of woman has not a jot to do with whether the father has the ability and the power to perform his function as head of the family. A woman can be emancipated in every possible respect and yet still look up to her husband as the father of her children and 'the protector' of the family. To believe that female emancipation must of itself result in emasculation of the function of the father is the same thing as arguing that because the sky is overcast today, the sun is not shining or is not there.

Apart from the effect on men of these obvious reductions in their importance, which are already visible now since quite a few of them shun women and prefer one another's company, inevitably sexual relations will lose a lot of their importance. After all, the primary importance of sexual relations is brought about by the possibility of procreation. And what can one say about the effect of the disappearance of the father upon woman? There is an intimacy in the relationship between a mother and father which stems from the cooperation needed in rearing children and which is totally unrelated to sexual relations in themselves. That will go.

Nowadays, it seems to be the men who want children, more than the women. If men have no say in bringing children about – and they have already lost a substantial part of their say as a result of reliable contraception – women will probably end up by not wishing to procreate anyhow.

There is a further and much more highly damaging consequence which flows directly from the diminution in man's position and it is that woman, whose status has already been diminished in the moral context by contraception, will find that she is more and more looked upon as an object of lust and pleasure, with serious consequences as far as increased violence towards her is concerned. Furthermore, as more women refuse to bear children, the State will have to give priority to those women willing to procreate: priority of care, concern and, above all, financial assistance. Whereas at the moment a woman may be paid to be a prostitute and render sexual services, in the not too distant future woman will be paid to be a mother. The signs are with us already and they flow directly from the combination of contraception, easy divorce and the break-up of the patriarchal family, of which every man worthy of that description was an exponent and a proud actor.

With the reducing incidence, frequency and duration of male potency, which the Kinsey reports have found, man's function is equally reducing. It is as though his pride and survival ability are in direct proportion to his importance as a male. And, if the Bible is to be believed, the role of woman was to tempt man and to give him children.

We all know that the Almighty did not quite put it that way, at least in the sense that He did not say to Eve that she should tempt Adam; but He did apparently say that both of them should grow and multiply and replenish the face of the earth, and this is essentially what man and woman had been doing until not too long ago when man abdicated his function. He handed over to the State absolute control over those who tried to interfere with himself and his family; he renounced his privilege of feeding and clothing his family when he enabled the State to establish welfare services ready to take over the moment he might fail; be became a non-entity as far as procreation was concerned at the point when his scientific advances enabled his sperm to be preserved for posterity; he lost his pride and his prestige at the same time as he began to find his fellow men more interesting and acceptable than his women.

The combination of these three factors – contraception, man's greed to profit from new inventions and his ever-decreasing masculinity – have all occurred, in effect, within the last fifty years. Man's failures of the body and mind managed to achieve for woman in less than a century a reversal of her social role established over thousands of years. In fact, as far as England is concerned, the last bastion of male dominance was stormed in 1989 when a Bill was first proposed in Parliament to reverse the old rule that a husband could not be found guilty of rape on his wife.

This is not by way of complaining about the situation, for which there may well have existed a certain historical inevitability. What needs to be underlined for the purposes of this discussion, however, is that although the practical and social role of woman has changed dramatically, it is somewhat more difficult if not highly speculative to determine whether concomitant and necessary changes have taken place in her psychological make-up. It is not good enough to say that boys and girls should be treated as though they were alike; femininity is not merely a matter of dress.

QUALITY OF SPOUSES

The difference in the instrinsic merit, as individuals, of the spouses, is a factor that needs to be considered, even though it must be readily admitted that it is, to a great extent, subjective and highly controversial. Nevertheless, that there is an imbalance in the present-day qualities of man and woman cannot be denied. It is a fact that this imbalance is now very marked and, if we ignore physical differences and handicaps, woman is in the ascendant.

Whether because of the losses suffered in two World Wars or whether as a result of the war of attrition which has been waged ceaselessly by women since the middle of the nineteenth century, but more violently since the 1940s, man at present is not performing so well as woman. Wherever one turns, woman is advancing and man is under pressure, if not following a downward slope. If we ignore the apparent inability of woman to compete with man on the artistic level, and if we take it for granted that, because of the way in which she has been brought up, but more particularly because of her need to assert her personality in the task of motherhood, woman does have a tendency to lack vision, there is no doubt that there is at present very little that women cannot do. Furthermore, they show marked dissatisfaction with their married partners, as evidenced by the statistics quoted.

There are, increasingly, more men who father children and then disclaim them, or fail to maintain them and/or their mothers, men who beat women, who abuse children. If the statistics show anything, they show that men are not living up to women's expectations. Apart from being tragic from the standpoint of man, his manhood and his masculinity, this development is highly damaging for society because of its effect on the children. What opinion can the young children, especially the daughters, of a marriage that has ended in divorce, hold of their father in circumstances where on the one hand the mother is awarded custody and on the other, in all likelihood, the father has performed badly by whatever standards one wishes to judge him (financial, sexual, moral and so on). What opinion can modern women hold of fathers who commit incest, who molest young girls, who go drinking with the lads instead of caring for their wives, who are homosexuals and, worst of all – if Kinsey is to be believed – who cannot maintain an erection for longer than one/two minutes. The quality of man is definitely declining whereas that of woman appears to be constantly improving.

One need not carry out too many investigations into the social or sexual habits of woman to ascertain that she knows what she wants and how to get it and, above all, she knows where she is going. Her stride is lengthening and its pride increasing proportionately: present-day woman consistently shows better qualities than her male counterpart.

This imbalance, which is becoming more marked with the passage of time, is not conducive to happy marital relations. Indeed, it is one of the most significant causes of the exceptional increase in the rate of divorce. Women cannot help comparing their spouses' performance either with their own contribution to the marriage and to the family, or with that of other men. By this standard, man is judged, and most critically, and is found deficient.

It cannot really be accepted that a woman who goes to the trouble of getting married, of establishing a relationship, of going out to work not necessarily to please herself but above all, to maintain herself and her family, wakes up one morning determined to break up the marriage. If she decides to do so, it must be because, in one way or another, her husband does not satisfy. D. H. Lawrence put it quite clearly when he said that the woman of today was the captain of the hymeneal barque. In relation to her, man has the choice of (a) being the lord and master who is honoured and obeyed, (b) the perfect lover, (c) the true friend and companion. I would suggest that (a) is out of date, (b) is unattainable. We are left with (c). A counsel of despair.

There is also a further consideration, namely that, ultimately, what woman appreciates most of all in a man are those manifestations which project power. It may be physical, moral or intellectual power, depending on the type of woman and man involved: but in all cases where a woman looks up to a man it is because of the power that that man is capable of exerting as far as she is concerned, it may be the power of his prowess as a lover, his high moral stance or his great intellectual ability. Woman wants, and indeed needs to look up to a man and when she does, what she appreciates most in him is power, whatever ardent feminists may say.

As Havelock Ellis put it,[23] the hymen is the anatomical expression of that admiration of force which marks the female in her choice of mate, since it is an obstacle to the impregnation of the young female by immature, aged or feeble males. This has been so since the dawn of history. The moment man first dragged woman by her hair into a cave he asserted his dominance over her; millennia of psychological heritage of this kind cannot be thrown overboard in one or two generations.

The dissatisfaction which woman finds with her married

partner nowadays is also due to the absence of the asserting of power by the male. Feminism has taught woman openly to restate her own femininity, power and sexuality; and in so doing, it has resulted in a psychological imbalance for the woman which has become one of the factors that are conducive to marital disharmony. It must also be acknowledged that in certain situations the more typically feminine requirements are transmuted into a different type of activity; but whilst this diversion of energies and finalities is a manifestation of our increasing technical expertise, they betoken a change of approach which is highly damaging for the woman's psyche.

It is difficult to see how this change of direction and emphasis can be redressed, save possibly within the framework of a totally different and new social system and, above all, morality for married partners which will dictate that woman should, of her own choice, prefer to be submissive rather than assertive. As far as woman is concerned, her psychological heritage, varied though it may be just like man's, proceeds like his from the behaviour of all her ancestors. On this basis, it could be said, with little fear of contradiction, that the psychological heritage of the female of the species has centred upon the essential function of being a mother whether she wants to or not, since her body was developed, or was created, with that function in mind and her whole being, so to say, rotates, both in the physical and in the psychological sense, around her potential motherly destination. Within this framework, the sexual act is the ultimate and most prominent manifestation of such essential finality.

Consider then, for a moment, how the woman is forced to react to modern pressures. First of all, she no longer has to be a mother if she does not wish to. Second of all, she is allowed by contraception to thwart the preordained aim of sexual activity: in other words, she comes together with the male on an even footing and society recognizes – indeed, nowadays demands – this equality. But her psyche is not yet ready for this; the little pieces of the jigsaw cannot be slotted in quite so easily. Tension is thus created in woman's mind, which is aggravated by her struggle for parity in the home and in the work place. Hence her dissatisfaction with herself, her mate and her role. Hence, too, her lack of fulfilment in sexual intercourse. We are told by psychologists who have dedicated a lifetime to this kind of investigation that the frequency of women's orgasms is constantly diminishing or they are becoming more and more difficult to attain. This is evidenced by her numerous sexual partners, her divorces, her unhappiness and her neuroses.

It has been stated by F. Lundberg and M. Farnham in *Modern Woman (The Lost Sex)*[24] that large numbers of modern women are psychologically disordered. According to such authors, the high rate of sexual dissatisfaction and of divorce cannot be an accident and is the result of a fundamental imbalance in the woman's psyche brought about by the pressures that we have mentioned above. They state:

> Male creativity is fundamentally a psychological freakishness and possessed by only a few men. Female creativity is a profound natural fact, like the movements of stellar bodies. The new age, with its values spouted out of panic and self-doubt, was tampering with this profound biological fact as it set about worshipping the male psychological freakishness.
>
> Some women attempted to make a virtue of the loss, reminding one of the fox and the grapes of the fable. Now, they said, women were no longer 'forced' to bear children. At this, they were overjoyed (they thought). This was much as though Beethoven or Michaelangelo, upon being informed that they had received a legacy, had been told that they no longer need bring forth great art. For now, they were free to spend all their time loafing or at lesser tasks.

Lundberg and Farnham (a scientist and a woman psychologist) go further along this road:[25]

> The less a woman's desire to have children and the greater her desire to emulate the male in seeking a sense of personal value by objective exploit, the less will be her enjoyment of the sex act and the greater her general neuroticism. A woman who does not want children, who resigns herself to the indirect social prohibition imposed on her, who accepts it as an advantage or who does not emotionally fully accept her children, invariably obtains reduced enjoyment from her

sexuality. Reduced enjoyment is part of the entire complex.

It should make it clear at this stage that I am not suggesting that all childless women are neurotic, any more than that no woman with children is. There obviously exist women who cannot have children either through no fault of their own or because of their mates' impotence or infertility; and not all of them are neurotic. Similarly, there may be well-adjusted women who have decided not to be mothers, without too much psychological aggravation. I am nevertheless stating a fairly general principle, the exceptions to which are less frequent than the present climate of opinion would have us believe.

SMOKING

A 1998 survey of 3,000 adults analysed by Chicago University shows that adults who smoke are 52% more likely to divorce than those who do not. The experts blame this not so much on the anti-social habit, but rather on the fact that people who smoke are said to have more psychological problems, including depression and anxiety; more particularly, that younger smokers enter adulthood with more psychological and family problems than non-smokers.

All this may well be true and topical. I would like to suggest a further reason, namely that the personality of the smoker is that of an individual who by definition will not necessarily care about the effect of what he/she does on others, or about the manner in which the environment is thus polluted.

SEXUAL INADEQUACY

The Russian writer, Leo Tolstoy, who died at a very old age, is on record as saying:

> Man survives earthquakes, epidemics, the horrors of disease and all agonies of the soul but, for all, the most tormenting tragedy has been, and is, and will be, the tragedy of the bedroom.

One might be forgiven for taking the view that one should not pay too much attention to what a Russian old man wrote in the nineteenth century. The trouble, however, is that despite all the sexual indoctrination provided by schools, the Press and, above all, television, if the figures that have been recorded earlier on are to have any meaning, it is a fact that the relationships between spouses at the beginning of the twenty-first century are more unsatisfactory that they ever were.

One may think of all the extra-marital activities, the need for titillation, the pornographic leanings of the printed, the spoken and the televised word, the inadequacy of the common man, evidenced both by the dissatisfaction of woman with his performance and the desperate search for remedies, such as Viagra, to correct erectile dysfunctions or malfunctions, and one will see there a clear record of the failures of modern man.

The term 'modern man' is used advisedly here, because in this context, it is somewhat difficult to pin the primary responsibility on woman. As a rule, a woman who is loved and well treated in the sexual sense will not even dream of committing adultery. There is an inherent stability in the sexual reactions of the average, normal and mentally stable woman which man can never hope to achieve, which is dictated by her reproductive ability.

This is not to say that there are no nymphomaniacs to be found, or no lesbians: but it is a fact of life that man is more likely to be stimulated into committing adultery by the sight of a mini-skirt than woman by the flexing of pectoral muscles.

It has to be said that this writer is not too impressed and, to some extent, discounts almost entirely the modern tendency of women to attend shows where men purport to strip in the same way as women have been doing since before Salome. These abhorrent manifestations of woman's sexuality are inflated by the Press and by film-makers and in the general sense are less frequent than a lot of people would like to believe. On the other hand, the husband's straying from the path of marital virtue is quite a frequent occurrence, and the wife's is now very common indeed. When a woman commits adultery, she is in the first place motivated by dissatisfaction by the performance of her husband in the general sense, and more particularly, at the sexual level.

It is the utter inability of modern man to deal with woman that is one of the principal causes of divorce. Maybe if Viagra were freely available to all men, there might be some improvement in the divorce rate . . . . .; but maybe not. The decay of man has gone so far that in the view of this writer, even if he could remedy his sexual failings by a daily intake of tablets, he would nowadays find it very difficult to manifest those qualities of intellectual masculinity and strength, of responsibility, concern and sensitivity, of tolerance and understanding, and above all, of patience, which are pre-requisites of a lasting marriage.

VARIOUS OTHER REASONS

Obviously, each separation or annulment has to be looked upon within its particular set of circumstances or, as lawyers put it, has to be judged on its own facts. There is a multitude of other reasons which affect the decision by the spouses to part and I list some of them for the sake of completeness, though the list is not exhaustive.

1) The higher standard of living. It is easier these days for people to afford divorce.
2) The decline in religious belief and, above all, in religious authority.
3) Life in cities which has made the insistence on a unified standard of behaviour and morality less important.
4) The fact that divorce has become easier to obtain.
5) The fact that people live longer. One must suppose that the longer one lives, the more one wants to change, although this is by no means axiomatic.
6) The greater frequency in marriages between parties of different nationalities and cultures and, above all, of different ethnic origins. Marriage is difficult enough without the added strain of totally diverse psychological and cultural heritages.

BECAUSE DIVORCE IS THERE

It may sound almost trite but, if divorce were prohibited,

people could not divorce. If people were not allowed to divorce, they would in some way or other find a *modus vivendi*, they would come to terms with each other's foibles, at least for the sake of the children. This aspect of the problem is a fundamental part of the present discussion and will be considered later.

NOTES

1. Southern Illinois University Press, 1930.
2. FM2 No 14 page 89 cited above.
3. 'Sexual Behaviour in Society' – Duckworth 1950, page 97.
4. *Sexual Behaviour in the Human Male*, 1948, Table 15.4.
5. McGraw-Hill Book Company.
6. *The New Women and the Old Men*, Secker & Warburg, London 1989, pp 108, 251-252.
7. Smith, Elder & Co, London, 1873
8. W.B. Saunders Company, Philadelphia 1953.
9. Saunders, *Sexual Behaviour in the Human Male*, Philadelphia, 1948
10. Rich & Cowan London 1943 page 53.
11. *op cit.* page 54.
12. Havelock Ellis, *Man and Woman*, London: Walter Scott Publishing, 1914, page 522.
13. See, for instance, Jesie Shirley Bernard in *The Future of Motherhood*, infra.
14. *The Future of Motherhood*, New York: Dial Press, 1974.
15. Henrik Ibsen, 'Et dukkehjem' (A doll's house), 1879
16. *The Future of Motherhood*, page 180.
17. *The Suicide of the Sexes*, *Harper's* magazine.
18. *op cit* p. 251.
19. pages 410-412.
20. *op.cit.*, pp 251-252.
21. Havelock Ellis – 'The Objects of Marriage' in Ruth Brandon, *The New Women and the Old Men*, London: Secker & Warburg, 1989.
22. *Marriage & Morals*, Unwin Paperbacks, 1929, page 23.
23. *Studies in the Psychology of Sex*, Volume 3, page 140.
24. Harper New York 1947, page 122.
25. *op. cit.* page 265.

4

Remarriage

There are those of us who have always found it somewhat repugnant to consider how the marriage vows, having been broken by a divorce, are repeated upon remarriage. No doubt, it could be said that the statements to love, cherish, etc., were honestly believed when they were made, whether on the first, the second or even the third and fourth occasion. The honesty of the belief in those statements, however, does not detract on the one hand from their absurdity, if they are repeated on remarriage/s and, on the other, proves nothing at all. A thief may honestly believe that, in breaking into somebody else's house, he is earning a living and has the right to do so this way: his belief, no matter how honestly held, does not justify his conduct.

If it could be put a different way, any honest belief in a particular kind of conduct cannot be judged subjectively: it must be judged objectively not by those who hold the particular belief, but by others who may either be around or have to sit in judgement upon the effects of the particular belief. By this token, there is more than an element of hypocrisy in taking a spouse for better or for worse today, divorcing that spouse and re-marrying, and repeating the same promises to take the second spouse for better or for worse.

The view that one adopts of remarriage obviously must be dependent on the view that one has of life generally. Those who tend to favour Freudian psychology or who are born pessimists, know, or believe they know, that remarriage is doomed to failure; those who are born optimists and believe that love, a many-splendoured thing, springs eternal, will no doubt wish to try their luck a second or a third, or more, times around. If society allows them to behave in that manner, it is an inescapable fact that they will not fight as they should to preserve their marriage.

The fact that the State from time to time is heard to pronounce in favour of the maintenance of a marriage, will certainly not dissuade those whom we have referred to as optimists: remarry they will. Furthermore, the pseudo efforts on the part of the State apparently to give support to the institution of marriage, which are not backed up by financial and tax inducements for those who marry, have children and establish a family, I personally find disgusting – just as the ancient Romans were disgusted by women who had several husbands whom they kept divorcing.

It is often said that the institution of marriage has not been damaged by divorce, but is merely evolving; in support of this notion politicians, sociologists and psychologists point to the very many situations where divorced people remarry. It is claimed that remarriage is proof of the inherent morality and responsibility of the individual and an inevitable consequence of the very many factors that are causative of divorce.[1]

Of course, some remarriages are a great success. This cannot be denied, even though it is debatable – because no statistical studies have been carried out – exactly what percentage of remarriages have such a felicitous outcome. The instances of happy remarriages are pointed out repeatedly as examples of the concept that divorce is a good thing where parties have failed in their relationship because they have gone on to a more loving and lasting and, above all, stable association. But to convert these obvious exceptions, for exceptions they are, into a rule of life seems a little unimaginative.

It has long been established[2] that the proportion of divorcing couples in which one or both partners had already been divorced, has been increasing steadily over the years, and that remarriages are at greater risk of dissolution than are first marriages. This is hardly surprising because the latter study confirms what the general public already knew, namely that men are more likely than women to remarry after divorce and, indeed, to remarry more quickly than women, in the same manner as men are more likely to cohabit than are divorced women.

This study also found that '... couples in which only one of the parties has previously been married, and where there are no stepchildren' have the lowest risk (of breaking up) whilst those marriages where both husband and wife are remarrying and both have children from previous marriages, have the highest risk'. Is not this concept self-evident because of the differing loyalties to one's own natural children, that would come into play?

In any event, all that these studies do is to confirm that remarriage is not very efficient. Furthermore, one must not forget that in those second marriages which emerge as happy and successful, it is clear that the spouses have learnt something from the mistakes they made first time round. But, surely, in the majority of cases where a second marriage lasts, as the religious vow provides, until death, the greater likelihood is that the reasons for its permanence are to be found firstly in the fact that the parties are unwilling to acknowledge that they have made a further mistake and secondly in the consideration that for that very fact, they will have tried their hardest to make the relationship work. Put differently, they bring to their second marriage the very qualities of industriousness, tolerance, understanding and, above all, perseverance in trying to get the relationship to work which, had they been present in the first marriage, would have made the union a success.

This is another reason why the concept of divorce is a wholly fallacious one because its very existence deprives the spouses of the opportunity of persevering in the relationship and of trying to make it work, come what may. It is that determination, as has already been remarked so many times over the centuries by writers of greater ability and understanding than the present one, which ensures that an uncertain or shaky marriage is converted into something more solid, rather than into the kind of shambles which inevitably will lead to a divorce.

It must be acknowledged that there is something incredibly romantic about the notion of a second marriage. There is a great sense of novelty and excitement in the new relationship, which starts off as a permanent second honeymoon. The spouses genuinely believe that at long last they are understood by their partner and are determined that they will not repeat the mistakes that were made first time round. They are both eager to please. They are as keen and as attentive to each other's needs as the waiters and owners in a newly-opened restaurant. They enjoy dressing up well, they are determined permanently to look their best, clean, scented, well shaven, open to new ideas, to different interests. The man who hated the theatre now becomes a lover of Shakespeare; the woman who only enjoyed Shepherd's Pie now is eager to experiment with diced Chinese vegetables.

The first marriage is considered as utter boredom and the new experience as wholly uplifting. Both spouses – as Alice Reed has observed – are on their best behaviour to try and prove a point. Nevertheless, exactly the same tendencies, attitudes and wishes preceded the first marriage and continued in the first honeymoon: accordingly, one is entitled to ask where the difference lies on the occasion of the remarriage. When the second honeymoon is over, the relationship will settle down in exactly the same way as the first one. It is conceivable, as we have just observed, that second time round there may be a reluctance to admit a second failure so that some couples may remain married possibly for as long as fifty years, even though they are not quite certain that they have done the right thing.

But can it truly be maintained that the spouses who made certain vows on the occasion of the first marriage ceremony, and repeated them on the occasion of the second or even third, have changed? Statistics seem to be against this. As Edmund Bergler has proved,[3] people who get married, divorce and remarry are in fact tendentially neurotic. Whilst it is obvious that their neuroses will not have helped the initial marriage, it follows, as night follows day, that when they remarry they are likely to repeat their previous experiences and therefore the remarriage does not stand any better a chance of success than the previous relationship did.

But before we look at any kind of statistical investigation into the chances of success of a second marriage, or indeed of any remarriage, we should consider briefly the reasons why people remarry in the first place. The primary one, it is believed, is that loneliness is something that most people do not enjoy. Human beings seek companionship and once they have been accustomed to a stable relationship with a person of the opposite sex, they have become more used to the needs of that sex and may believe that they will find it easier to satisfy them. Furthermore, by the time they reach the stage of remarriage, human beings ought to know how they are oriented sexually; a single person, on the other hand, may be uncertain whether he or she is homosexual or heterosexual.

In the case of men, it has been shown that divorced men are more likely to remarry than divorced women. American statistics show that three-quarters of divorced women remarry but four-fifths of divorced men do. Here again, the explanations are obvious:

a) Where there are no children, men may consider either that they are not terribly useful about the home on their own or that they would be more efficient with a woman around, or that there may be a social prestige to or need for being married.
b) Where there are children, it is clear that men need wives to care for the home and the children although where women already have children, some men may be reluctant to assume their burden.

In this context, it should be noted that men are more likely to pick up younger women whereas older women have a handicap when compared to physically attractive younger ones: this reduces the number of eligible remarriageable men.

Another noteworthy fact is that the traditional difference in remarriage rates appears to be lessening. There is also the deterrent effect of children upon the remarriage of women. However, as a result of greater moves towards sexual equality, and the greater accessibility of divorce, divorced women are much more acceptable socially than they were in the past.

People may remarry because they believe that society expects them to although, again, as noted earlier, this consideration is less important than it was. They may remarry to satisfy their sexual needs or in competition, so to say, with their former spouse. The remarriage says to that spouse: I shall show you that it was not my fault that we divorced, but yours.

There is a further motive which those who remarry are somewhat reluctant to admit, or perhaps have not been asked to admit; certainly the advocates of women's rights are a little hesitant about saying so openly: it is this. When people remarry, especially if the remarriage takes place soon after the divorce, it probably is because the divorce itself was brought about by some kind of extramarital relationship that has overtaken the marital status and has prompted one of the spouses to opt for a different partner. If one asked the man on the Clapham omnibus why people would want to remarry within one year of divorce, he would immediately say: 'Well, of course, they are marrying the party for whom or because of whom they broke off the first marriage.' This is a fairly commonsense notion but it is one that most authors are reluctant to acknowledge: the reluctance stems from the fact that divorce is fashionable as well as from the principle that people are unwilling to highlight what is 'wrong' – in the sense of having unacceptable consequences – about divorce.

The ease of divorce is in itself a cause of remarriage but it is difficult to find scientific evidence to support this concept. In the same way, not much evidence is forthcoming to explain whether a second or subsequent remarriage is more successful than a first marriage and, if not, why not. We have here a great problem to overcome and it is that no amount of Kinsey-type research can possibly be reliable in this context. Very few human beings find it easy to admit that they have made one mistake, let alone that they may have made two or more; so that whereas numerous reasons why a marriage may fail are provided (and there are innumerable case histories that show *ad nauseam* what went wrong with a particular marriage), there is very little information as to whether remarriages fail for the same reasons as the first marriage, or for different reasons.

There is quoted in *The Family in Social Context*[4] an early study by the American author, Monahan, for the years 1953 to 1955, which shows that divorce rates from second marriages are twice as high as those from first marriages; where one of the partners has been divorced twice before, the rate of divorce for the third marriage was higher still. The same study shows that divorce rates amongst the previously widowed are lower than those from first marriages. The reason here, however, is quite simple: widowers may well have been reasonably well adjusted people whose prior experience with marriage was not that bad. They may accordingly approach their second marriage with a different view.

Monahan's findings were unpopular with feminists and were challenged on more than one occasion; but the experience of the 1970s was summarized by Carter & Glick to show that as many as 44% of any remarriages occurring in the United States of America in the 1980s ended in divorce.

There seems to be no conclusive evidence as to whether men or women are more successful in their remarriages. What is undoubtedly true, however, is that in the same manner as divorce breeds divorce, remarriage breeds remarriage: this for two reasons. Firstly, a person who has already been divorced once, knows how easy or how difficult it is to obtain a divorce and to survive it. The process at least is well known and the traumas may be easier to tolerate second time round.

The second reason is that people who remarry obviously will want to make a better go of their second marriage than they managed to do of their first one: they will accordingly set themselves higher standards which will be proportionately more difficult to attain. And this is the reason why if a remarriage does survive it is relatively much more successful than any first marriage.

There are, of course, other considerations. Just as some people are accident-prone, others are divorce-prone. Put differently, one requires a basic personality to survive a marriage and if that is lacking, the marriage will end in divorce. It should be noted that this of itself has been considered one of the factors why remarriages ought to be more successful; the experience that one learns in the first marriage is said to be capable of being utilized in the second one because one can understand what went wrong the first time. Even taken at its lowest level, this means that a woman who did not know how to cook during her first marriage may nevertheless, with the passage of time, have learnt something about cooking and may be capable of applying that knowledge more successfully in the course of her second marriage. Equally, a young girl who married at 18 would not normally have a clue about how to use money, but the experience of divorce, the fact that she had to pay lawyers and negotiate a settlement from her husband, etc., very quickly teaches her to become proficient with money. She may thus be a very competent housekeeper in her second marriage.

A youngster may have lost a job and yet be married; five years later he may be in a better position to keep a job. Probably a failed first marriage, but a better chance of success second time round.

It is said, too, that as we mature we become wiser and more tolerant. Certainly, the fact that we have failed in our first marriage produces a major change of direction: we are determined to make a go of the second one.

There may also be mixed motivations such as the desire to make a success of one's social life, if not of one's family life, as well as the consideration that with the passage of time the parties themselves become less belligerent. One statistical datum, however, seems indisputed, namely that 60% of both men and women who remarried following divorce had children by their first marriage (averaging between them one and two, which is the world average for so-called 'civilized' nations). There seem to be no studies as to what happens to those children. There is statistical information[5] to show that one out of every four children in the USA is a stepchild. In the UK (1998) it is believed to be just under one out of every five.[6]

Here, it must be noted that it has been said time and time again that most of the remarried mothers were satisfied with their children's adjustment. Psychologists support this by saying that remarriage tends to make children more settled (whatever the trauma was that is associated with the divorce) in the sense that a new family is reconstituted. As is demonstrated in Chapter 5, there is no evidence whatsoever that this is really what the children feel: and the truth may be otherwise, since the children may well be tied to the past. It may be a form of wishful thinking on the part of those psychologists who lean towards divorce, since exactly the opposite conclusions are stated to be true by those psychologists who are against divorce (although there are not many of them).

Endeavouring to take a balanced view of these extreme positions, it would seem, first of all, that something is forgotten. The first marriage partners of spouses who remarry are, no matter what others think, themselves parties to the remarriage. The potentially disrupting factor here is great. It is often said correctly that when one marries a spouse, one marries that spouse's family: that is perfectly true, of course. What is forgotten is that when one *remarries*, one also marries the spouse's former partner and this does give rise to problems. Whether the former spouses are physically present or not, they are in the background; the children may have to be taken to see to the divorced parent; the maintenance cheque may be part of the expenditure of the second family. Especially where there are children who are not self-supporting, the previous spouse cannot be shut out in the same way that water is turned off at the tap: the occurrences in the memories of the children are not shut out either and it is clear that a potential for conflict is there all the time.

Finally, it should be recorded that most scientific studies that are available have concentrated on the difference between the reconstituted family and the original one.

At this stage one has to consider a moral question, namely: is the promise to love and cherish for life, once made, a vow that should be broken, or not? For this answer most people, even those who have remarried, would say that they would have preferred to stay married to their first partner and that if their failing marriage had been capable of being made to work, then they would certainly have not got divorced, especially where there were children. This sounds right and fair; but in reality it is not, for the simple reason that the statement is made by the very same people who did, in fact, get divorced and remarried. One must, therefore, pause and consider why, despite their belief as to their preference in staying married – which is stated to exist even after divorce – and despite also their conviction as to the genuine theoretical stability and indissolubility of their first marriage, they in fact took it upon themselves to break their marital promise. Whatever reason, valid or not, they might have had at the time that caused them to divorce, it was obviously their own individual convenience, their decision to search for happiness at all costs, the thinking 'You only live once and I can't continue to live like this', the desperate need for the assertion of one's ego, that prompted them at last to divorce and remarry. This of itself should not be criticized, for human beings are weak creatures and, depending on one's outlook, religious or moral, the same kind of conduct may be capable of criticism or of being applauded.

If it were a question of good intentions alone, remarriage should be successful or at least a woman/man should have an even chance of making it a success, whereas the statistics quoted show that this is not so. The need for personal fulfilment and to make a success of the 'new life' are no guarantee of success. One is not blind to the fact that, as a counsel of despair, some people may stay married second time round to avoid admitting a second failure. But when people remarry, they do not consider the possibility of a second failure. The woman is starting a new life after a period of unhappiness; she thinks she understands herself better, she has had to discover why her first marriage failed and therefore in so doing had no choice but to take stock of her own faults. In all likelihood, she understands men better and knows her own limitations in her relationships with them and knows, too, the limitations of the marital bond. She is inevitably older and that in itself is extremely important, because nowadays people marry far too young, whereas we can assume that they ought to be wiser with the passage of time. In theory, therefore, the woman stands a much better chance of happiness than before if, for no other reason, than because she has picked up more experience, so to say, in transit. The man himself is more mature, experienced, tolerant, readier to accept the restrictions of married life, looking forward to making a success of it second time round.

That is the theory and if the facts corresponded to it, it would truly be a wonderful thing! In practice, the gaining of experience of itself provides no guarantee that one will be able to put it to good use. It is a fact that a number of unmarried people live together nowadays and then get married; but if they subsequently divorce, just as easily if they had not lived together, they merely prove that experience does not count for much in personal relations. Apart from this consideration, statistics show that, generally, people who are divorced tend to marry amongst those who have themselves been divorced, possibly on the basis that because one has shared the traumatic experience of a separation, one is likely to be more understanding. Again, that may be theoretically true but one drawback is that it narrows the field of choice considerably; that may not necessarily be a good thing. The theory that by learning from one's mistakes, one avoids repetition of those mistakes is the result of a sort of reflex action of the Pavlow type. No matter how successful he was with his dogs, it seems a little more difficult to apply his principles to human relations.

In *The Challenge of Second Marriage*[7] Angela Reed of the then National Marriage Guidance Council provides very useful practical considerations and material. In justification of second marriages, she claims that whereas in the first one people come together carrying principally their own background, folklore, expectations, ideas, hopes and fears, in the second they not only bring all these things but also the history of their first marriage, the reasons for its conclusion and the feelings that they had about it: accordingly, she claims that this is a very good thing which makes for better relationships.

She does, however, concede that where there are children the situation is not quite so easy, particularly where there are children from both marriages of the parents in the second marriage.

Amongst the reasons she gives for people remarrying, there are not only most of the more common ones, already addressed, but also an additional psychological one, namely the desire to show personally and socially that it was not their fault that the first marriage failed. This is self-defeating and she admits that there are greater chances of people who have already been divorced, divorcing again after they remarry because they have already considered breaking off one relationship and therefore they could easily break the other. A simile that occurs to this writer is that the first divorce is like the first parachute jump: one may well go on jumping.

Angela Reed's sympathetic view of human weakness, though usually quite clear and perceptive, does result at times in a certain amount of wishful thinking. At page 15, for example, she says: 'One can look at the divorce rate from another point of view. Far from being proof of dissatisfaction with marriage, it can be taken as proof of the importance of having a good marriage and show that those marrying and remarrying are looking for higher standards, have greater expectations and demand more from their partners than ever before.' If this argument were carried to its logical conclusion, there would be no point at all in being married because the constant attainment of perfection would be such as to ensure that one would marry, divorce and remarry in order to reach peaks of perfection. Perhaps the same energy and the same time could be better spent at making the first marriage work.

Her objectivity, however, is commendable. For example, at page 29 she remarks: 'How is anyone to know how children really react – even the parent with whom they live?' As noted earlier, that it is too trite to say that children are too young to understand. As Susan Isaac has so sympathetically remarked in *Childhood and After*[8]: 'Too young to understand does not mean too young to feel.'

In a study carried out in New York in the 1960s, it was found that 'divorce, separation and desertion by the parent more than double the probability that the children would also become divorced or separated'.

On page 54 Angela Reed states: 'Changes in the law are very often a reflection of the way in which society feels and the change of emphasis of the divorce law might be taken to reflect the public admission of the fact that bad marriage is no marriage and that the partners involved should be released from it.' Whilst one understands the motivation behind this remark, it seems that she fails completely to see that there is no such thing as either a good or a bad marriage: any marriage is both good and bad and its result and survival depend solely on the personality of the spouses and on their determination to stay married.

She also observes that many neurotic people would choose divorce as a means of opting out of marital difficulties rather than staying in the marriage and trying to overcome them and that whenever this happens, the situation will recur in the remarriage. This is true but essentially it is a highly damaging admission, from one who endorses divorces, if carefully analysed, for it crystallizes the view that some marriages could be made to work if divorce were not permitted.

On page 60 she quotes Doctor Benjamin Spock as recommending that very young children should see their fathers often enough to keep the relationship alive and at least every week; at one or two years of age, the visits should increase in duration and at three or four, the young one should spend Friday or Saturday night at the father's residence. There are, however, practical difficulties in ensuring this where the parents remarry. Self-evidently, remarriage does not help this kind of situation at all and very few writers have considered the feelings of the father who merely has visiting rights and no custody. These range from distress for the loss of control over the child to the fact that he cannot provide the same accommodation or facilities as previously for his children, as well as his possible financial difficulties and the likely problems with his new wife, particularly where he contributes high maintenance to his former wife.

In her thoroughness, Angela Reed considers also the remarriage of the same spouses. As the reader will know, this writer takes the view that when parties who have divorced, remarry, they show how immature and selfish they were when they originally divorced. Angela Reed does not put it quite in that way but there surely is no other conclusion to be drawn. The problems of remarriage, however, do not stop there, for the greatest ones are of a psychological kind. Consider, for example, the situation of a wife who divorces her husband and marries her former lover: will it never cross that woman's mind that in the same way as he committed adultery with her, he might do so again with another woman? One of the drawbacks of feminism is that it has given woman the kind of freedom that can, in situations of this nature, be counter-productive for her. What is to stop a free-thinking woman from enticing the wife's former lover and present husband away from her?

The same considerations apply, *mutatis mutandis*, to the man. Furthermore, how often do men who have remarried, stop and consider that perhaps their former wife was not quite so bad after all? Their present second wife may be a brighter talker, and a better hostess, but the homemade bread baked by his first wife was better. One can multiply these examples. Ultimately, human beings, men and women, are all very much alike; there is not such a great difference between one woman and the other. True, a second wife may have nicer legs, a better smile, more intelligent conversation: but what about the other virtues of the first one that she may be lacking?

A further consideration is that there seems to be a certain absence of spontaneity in remarriage which is very often the result of pressure: pressure by the children, the relatives, the friends, the practical problems of everyday life. After divorce, a woman may think that it is going to be difficult for her to perform the two roles of father and mother and that she ought to give the children a father. A stepfather, of course, because the original father will gradually disappear from the picture. She may be unwilling to go through a lengthy courtship again and thus will be more inclined to remarry, if at all, someone who is already divorced. She may be incapable of coping either in the psychological or the economic sense. She is under pressure.

Equally, the relatives or the friends will put forward ideas or candidates: we all feel sorry for those who have been 'abandoned'. So, she remarries, either because she is convinced that she is doing the right thing, or because she yields to pressure. But even having got to the door of the church or the Registry Office the second time, the problems begin to loom all over again. Where there are children, there are problems of favouritism, too strict or too lax discipline, dealing with old habits, the previous parents; we have to consider whether we should pamper them or punish them, we have to think of their real parents, their real grandparents and so on.

In these remarriage situations where there are children, one of the most important roles of all is that of the stepfather. In passing, one is tempted to remark that the greater the number of stepfathers, the greater the weakening of man's authority generally. But let us look at the position of the stepfather. Leaving aside for a moment his own children, if any, he now has his own stepchildren, for whom he must accept some responsibility; but he is not their father, he cannot possibly feel for them the same way as he might if they were his own flesh and blood and, most important of all, he cannot assert the same kind of parental authority. If he carries the weight one associates with a father and which a man worthy of the label should have, he finds that his authority is seriously challenged by the children. This challenge may or may not be supported by their mother but is magnified throughout society by the ever-increasing number of stepfathers and, in this way, the standing of the male in society is reduced. Meanwhile, however, all the time he has to contend with the fact that there exists the real father. Some people suggest that, after divorce, there should be a clean break and the real father should be replaced by the stepfather to all intents and purposes. A suggestion of this kind is perfectly consistent with this writer's view that man has ceased to be important, for in our society we think nothing of swapping a real father with a stepfather.

Social workers have a tendency to ignore the problems that occur throughout in this kind of set-up: jealousy, inadequacy, irritation. There is no doubt that second marriages are going to develop them if there are children. The presence of children from the former marriage obviously makes relationship with the second one more difficult but even where there are no children, remarriages are just as likely to break down.

Here are some other more specific reasons why the failure rate in remarriages is high:

1) When, as is likely, they take place quickly, there will be the same lack of knowledge by one spouse of the other. Courtship is usually lacking since, particularly where the parties have already been married, they tend to get to the point rather quickly.

2) The man who marries a divorcee who has not been given custody of her children is likely to be disillusioned if he stops and considers that the woman he has now married has been known to the Court not to be fit enough for custody to be awarded to her. If he intends to have children, he ought to wonder whether she will make a good mother.

3) There may be difficult economic circumstances, particularly if maintenance is still payable to the former spouse, in which case the man is paying through the nose for the privilege of having got married a second time. There is no doubt that, normally speaking, divorce for the woman results in a lower economic status and that only through remarriage, in most situations, she goes back to the financial status she had before divorce, at least if she chooses well.

4) The question of pressure from relatives and/or friends and of the possible comparisons in all spheres with the previous spouse, man or woman, we have already mentioned.

5) There may also be what is known in America as a 'role failure'. Americans believe that people carry within themselves 'a repertoire of relationships which they are capable of sustaining, that they look for people with whom they can carry out these relationships' and that even if they do not find such people 'they attempt to impose their own repertoire on those whom they do

meet'. This is in a sense like walking on a treadmill. A woman who has a particular image of the man she is seeking, for example, the husband who can properly play the role of father, may be disappointed in her findings; she then tries to remedy the situation by moving from one marriage to another in search of the right partner but she never finds him, essentially because he is a figment of her own imagination.

We are now told that in the United States there has come about a kind of relationship which is of long-standing but free of ties. This is a relationship where man and woman are emotionally committed to one another but maintain different households: it differs from marriage because in this kind of 'boyfriend' relationship, the man is no longer the head of the household. There is no shared responsibility for maintaining home and family and, by definition, there will be no broken home when the relationship comes to an end. As part of this type of set-up, the man never takes up full residence in the house where his 'wife' lives but he is merely a casual visitor who helps the woman, if required, and her children in activities such as play, holidays, shopping and so on, thus performing all the functions that would normally be the true father's: but he is not the father and is not treated as such. In fact, he is a nothing: the woman is the queen bee.

This is a very good picture of what might be the future in a society dominated by women. Children will be born from injections of semen and men will be around merely to help. Ultimately, men will all be eunuchs because there will be no need for them to perform any real physical or psychological function, save occasionally to give the woman some kind of satisfaction, at her request. With the spread of what is now known as non-penetrative sexual activity, man will no longer even require his male attributes.

The relationship we have just described is the result of some insistence on the principle that since nowadays we all live longer, it is inconceivable that we could stay married for sixty years to the same person. A further development is that it is now accepted in America that we may have 'serial marriage':

this expression means that many people will divorce and remarry three or four times during their lifetime, on each occasion selecting the type of spouse who is more appropriate to a particular phase and moment in life.

The disruption that this system of mating will cause to individuals in emotional terms, coupled with the destruction of the family unit and the cost of the various divorces to the State, is so great as to be frightening. The argument runs that there comes a point in life when the spouses grow apart because of personality, career, outside interest changes. In such a scenario the departure of the children appears to remove the last reason for their staying together and at this stage they want to start a new life, have a clean break with the past and 'be themselves' again. It is even said that the second, third or fourth marriage may, in fact, present the most exciting opportunities for the future because the parties will be adults, will not be concerned with looking after children, will be mature, more understanding and so on.

All this ties in quite well with the 'emancipation' of woman. Angela Reed reminds us that in 1953 Kinsey showed that those who had had pre-marital affairs were most likely to indulge in extra-marital sex; the habit of seeking sexual variety having thus been established, it can only be reinforced by the fact that wives are working and participating in activities which were previously the preserve of males, in circumstances where travel is easy and they may be away from home because of their work; inevitably, affairs are more common.

Women, it is said by her, thus become more aware of '... the infinite variety of sexual experience which can be achieved with different partners and they may find it all the more difficult to settle into a stable relationship with a second marriage partner'. It is interesting that it is justified by 'the infinite variety of sexual experience': words of this kind display on the one hand contempt for concepts such as love, companionship, loyalty and affection; and on the other – and this is much more serious – a great ignorance of matters sexual, firstly because the variety of sexual experience, as any experienced philanderer could show, is fairly limited, and on the other because when it comes to matters of sexuality there never was, there still is not, and there never will be, anything new under the sun. It is pie in the sky to believe in the 'infinite variety of sexual experience': the ignorance that prompts these observations is too crass for comment.

The reader who rejects this view is referred to *The Comfort of Sin.*[9]

NOTES

1. See for example, *Break-up* by Dr Masud Hoghughi (McDonald Optima, London, 1989).
2. See *Marriage and Divorce Statistics* 1988, (HMSO, series FM2, number 15) and *Family Change and Future Policy* 1990).
3. *Divorce won't help* (Harper & Brothers, 1948).
4. Page 594.
5. Based on estimates. There are no recent USA figures on the percentage of children residing in step-families (per Stepfamily Association of America, Inc., 650 'I' Street, Suite 205, Lincoln, Nebraska 68508).
6. This is but an estimate. There will be no reliable UK data on step-children until the 2001 General Census. (Office of National Statistics)
7. Plume Press & Ward Lock, 1973.
8. Routledge & Kegan Paul, London, 1948.
9. *op. cit.*

5

Effects of divorce on the children

In all those situations where the parents divorce, one thing is reasonably clear, namely that it is the children who ought to be the principal concern of lawyers, the courts, the State and, indeed, of their parents. One cannot really feel too deeply for the parties themselves because, in the majority of cases, what befalls them is the result of their own character, temperament, behaviour and approach to life. In every divorce, at least one of the parties, if not both, has brought the situation to a head through mistakes, stupidity, carelessness, self-centredness or excessive enthusiasm. The spouses only have themselves to blame if they divorce; in a different sense from the Biblical one, they reap what they have sown.

This ought to be axiomatic, but the reverse reflects the approach of Western society. People appear concerned only about themselves. Whether motivated by religion (the so-called 'institutionalists') or humanistic feelings (the propounders of absolute freedom for all), they thought and still think about nothing but their own well-being and seldom about that of their children.

The neglect of the views of the children is normally explained away on the basis that, well, it cannot be done, they cannot really tell us what they feel. But it is not true that the children cannot be consulted; it is not true that the State is in no position to educate human beings to adopt different views about various aspects of life. The success of the campaigns against smoking and against driving under the influence of drink clearly shows what the State can do once it determines that it wishes to create an aura which makes certain forms of behaviour less socially acceptable, or more likely to be prosecuted by the criminal law. Indeed, the State actually goes so far as to eliminate particular kinds of so-called anti-social behaviour, as the enforcement of no smoking throughout the underground system and elsewhere quite clearly demonstrates.

However, in matters of divorce the State is reluctant to intervene, on the basis that individual freedoms must be safeguarded. This argument lies most uncomfortably in the mouths of those who have governed our country in modern times since the State has interfered with individual freedoms at every level of society and in every sphere of our activity. Encouragement is constantly given to surveys and studies whereby the State wishes to ascertain the views of its subjects; or so it is claimed. Many such interventions are futile.

For example, a survey of married couples was published in October 1989. It proved, assuming anybody needed to know, that wives are more likely to take lovers before their husbands take mistresses. This is not such an illuminating item of information as might appear at first blush. On the other hand, one would have like to see the results of a survey to deal with the question, for example, of whether children of divorced parents are more likely to commit crime than those from a stable home.

Such surveys are not carried out on the same scale, if at all. It seems that modern society proceeds from the premise that there is no great merit in instilling into children a basic morality when they are young. We seem to have ignored the practice of the Jesuits who maintained that once they had had a child in their care for the school years up to the age of seven, his soul was theirs forever.

We poll all and sundry about all aspects of their activities, we spend millions on finding out which washing powder fits which machine better: the opinion of everybody is sought, men and women are consulted about divorce. We still do not consult the children about the effects of divorce, any more than we wish to enquire whether juvenile delinquency and unhappiness can be prevented more successfully than AIDS. In short, we prefer not to know about the effect of a broken home on our children.

The reason is not far to seek. If we knew, we would have to adjust our conduct and our decision-making accordingly, and we would feel less free indiscriminately to pursue our self-interest and our dreams of happiness. It is insufficient to say, as Parliament has done, that the welfare of the children shall be the paramount consideration in matters of family law. We should try and carry this otherwise wholly commendable principle a step further.

The first point to be made in this connection is that, because it is born, the child has no choice but to be implicated in the relationship, good or bad, between his parents. In a happy marriage, whatever that expression means, the relationship between the parents causes on the whole no real problem for the child and is probably beneficial. In an unhappy marriage, on the other hand, the relationship intrudes into the child's day-to-day life and into its psyche. The spouses, when they quarrel, are incapable of considering the welfare of the child first and theirs second. In a perfect world, they should. But in a perfect world, if they put the children first, they would neither quarrel nor divorce.

There are arguments as to whether it is better for the child to be without parents, or to have parents who are divorced, or to live with either one or the other of his natural parents, or to live with the parent who has remarried, in a different family, than in the natural family where the spouses are unhappy. The trouble is that the situation after divorce is no different for the child from what it was before divorce. The relationship between the parents continues to intrude into the child's psyche and no one has been able to prove that the child is better off after divorce than it was before the parents separated.

It is at this point that one ought to consider whether, given that the child will suffer both before and after divorce, if his parents cannot get on (and let us face it, if they could not get on before divorce, they are very unlikely to get on after), the State ought to say that of the two evils, namely the suffering of the child before or after divorce, it prefers the former, for the simple reason that the maintenance of a union, no matter how unstable, is of greater importance for the structure of our society – as it is constituted at the moment – than its destruction; and that for children, stability is much more significant than any other consideration.

It is not, surely, correct to say that it is healthier for a child to grow up with a step-parent who does not quarrel with his wife than with his original father and mother in the first marriage of which the child was the offspring. The reverse must be true: it is better for the child to grow up in a home within a family, no matter how unsatisfactory the relationship of husband and wife. The reason for this is not far to seek.

Young children are like young animals: they have a very marked instinct for, what one might call, their own den. They are born within the bosom of a family unit in a particular home and they grow accustomed to their parents' behaviour, in the same way as they grow accustomed to the house. They partake of the nature of both cats and dogs in the sense that they are very fond of their own home, in the same way as they are fond of their parents.

Their home may leak when it rains, and some of its rooms may be cold in winter; their parents may quarrel or the father may beat the mother when he comes home from the pub on payday. But these patterns of circumstance and of behaviour are known to the child and they are constant: it is the constancy that provides the reassurance and this reassuring constancy is brought to an abrupt end, disappears entirely, when there is a divorce. This is something that the parents themselves are reluctant to acknowledge. If there were greater education before marriage, a health warning should be shown to all intending spouses to the effect that 'marriage seriously injures your children's health' because of the frequency with which marriages are now ending in divorce.

Later on in this chapter the concept of divorce as a bereavement is given some consideration. It is the death of the marriage and in some cases it is also the moral death of the individual and that is why it is said that, after a divorce, the parties go through a period of mourning in psychological terms because they both have to work out their feelings of disappointment, anger, bitterness, grief, regret and guilt (depending on which applies). It is almost as though, having been unwell, they have to go through a period of convalescence; they may recover, of course, but the scars remain. No equivalent literary or poetic description of what happens to the children after divorce comes to mind. What about their health and possible consequential illness? It is asking too much of them to keep up with the changes brought about by the mechanics and implications of divorce. Furthermore, in our society we have to recognize the fact that some children, even before the age of 16, will have to suffer the traumas of more than one divorce, occasionally even three.

In her book *The Challenge of Second Marriage*,[1] Angela Reed states: 'In an ideal world, when couples marry and have children, they should bind themselves to remain united and at least without physical violence until the children are old enough to manage independent relationships with each of them.' This particular feminist writer does not believe in the sanctity of marriage and accepts that divorce is right in certain circumstances. But even she is forced to make the point. One wonders why the need occurred to her to make a statement of this nature unless it be that she realized that children do suffer when their parents divorce.

The truth is that every single word in the extract quoted above is open to criticism. For example, the world is not an ideal place; indeed, anything but. People actually bind themselves for life when they get married, according to the words of the marriage ceremonies which we looked at earlier. It is impossible for a spouse to know today whether or not he or she will tomorrow commit physical violence. At what age are the children old enough to manage independent relationships? 16? 18? And what are independent relationships? Is not any psychological relationship dependent upon someone else or something else? In the true sense of the word, psychological independence can never be obtained.

This particular author is quoted here because she highlights the inconsistency of maintaining both that divorce exists and of refusing to acknowledge the damage that is caused to the children. She cannot have it both ways: either divorce causes no damage to the children, in which case there is no reason why the parties should behave in any particular manner, and should divorce at will; or it does cause damage to the children, in which case we ought to ask ourselves why we allow divorce to occur in the first place.

The principal study (published in the USA) which considers in some detail and on the basis of statistical evidence how children cope with divorce and what children think about it is contained in *Surviving the Break-up: How Children and Parents Cope with Divorce!* by Judith Wallerstein and Joan Berlin Kelly.[2] This is reviewed at some length later on.

There is no doubt, however, that it cannot be good for a child when parents split up. Few are the marriages which end up in the divorce courts without a history of anger, misery, tension, aggravation, or even violence. In this situation a child must suffer, essentially because he/she does not understand. And even where the child may be old enough to understand (and this is rather a farfetched hypothesis because very often grown-ups themselves do not necessarily understand why a marriage ends in divorce), the suffering is not reduced: indeed, it may be worse, since the better the understanding, the greater the suffering. If the break-up is brought about by specific conduct of either spouse, that conduct sticks in the child's mind as an example of either indifference or cruelty or whatever else may be applicable to the relationship that is coming to an end. It is a psychological tattoo which is ineradicable.

If pressed, most people accept that the immediate effect of divorce on children is traumatic. But on the whole, as we have seen, adults have been reluctant to come to grips with the reality of the situation, namely with the fact that, in most cases, the damage caused to children by divorce lasts well into adulthood.

Judith Wallerstein is the joint author of *Surviving the Break Up*.[3] She is also the founder of the Centre for the Family in Transition, in California, and is one of the very few people involved in counselling, both for parents and children, who has made a long-term study of the effects of divorce on children inasmuch as she has chronicled the development of 131 children in 60 families in the United States. The examination is by no means short-term, as most other such studies are. In the UK, for instance, we have nothing similar: those who have looked at the effect of divorce on children, and they are not that many, have considered these effects over, say, a maximum term of two or three years after divorce. In the Wallerstein study, however, children were interviewed throughout the subsequent period and even as long as ten and fifteen years after the divorce. Her findings are that the psychological damage caused to the children by divorce is substantial, not only in terms of their concern about forming relationships with members of the opposite sex, but also about having children once those relationships were formed.

In *Second Chances*, which she wrote later with Sandra Blakeslee,[4] Judith Wallerstein states:

> Children of divorce regard their childhood and adolescence as having taken place in the shadow of divorce. Three in five felt rejected by at least one of the parents, sensing that they were a piece of psychological baggage left over from a regretted journey. Almost half the children entered adulthood as worried, under-achieving, self-deprecating and sometimes, angry, young men and women.

Although she found as a fact that girls at first appeared to have adapted better than boys, she reached the conclusion that later in life they were unable to commit themselves to a man without anxiety and guilt and, in turn, they entered into multiple relationships or impulsive marriages which were at risk and which in most cases tended to end in divorce.

Another writer, Jack Dominian,[5] finds a close relationship between the broken home, psychiatric illnesses and personality disorders. He claims that significant correlations have been found between suicidal behaviour later in life, and parental loss in childhood. This may be otherwise explicable. He also finds that a significantly greater proportion of those attempting suicide came from broken homes and had experienced recent disruption of a close relationship in the previous six months. He also claims that '. . . there is good evidence to suggest that people from broken homes have an above average risk that their own marriage will suffer with the likelihood of disturbed personal relationships'. He underlines the concept of the disorganization in the life of the child who comes from a broken home. He quotes a Swedish study of delinquent boys, their parents and grandparents made in 1967. The author studied 305 delinquent boys and compared them with 500 attending child guidance clinics and 222 non-delinquent, normal children. He found that 42% of the delinquent boys were sons of divorced parents as against only 13% for the non-delinquent boys.

The difficulty, as far as children are concerned, is that they are torn between having to face reality – and that reality in most cases results, as we shall see, in their having little contact with their fathers, for example – and the constant hope that their parents might one day get back together again. This hope is in most instances dashed at a very early stage because about 45% of fathers lose contact with their children within two years of divorce. Whichever way modernists wish to look at the marital relationship, it is a fact that the image of the parents will remain with a child throughout his life: we may have terminated the marriage, but we cannot terminate the psychological tie, the blood tie, between parent and child. Nevertheless, divorce continues to rise and one child in four will see his parents divorce before reaching his sixteenth birthday. Nowadays, one child in eight lives with only one parent. As already mentioned, for 1998 the number of one-parent units is put at 1.8 million. In a letter published in the London *Evening Standard* of 26 March 1999, a teacher recorded that 'last year, more than 50% of my class no longer lived with their natural parents'.

□

So much for generalizations. Coming to more specific difficulties, let us consider some of the principal effects that divorce has on children.

There is ample evidence that, at most within three years of divorce, children, especially the younger ones, lose touch with the parent who does not have custody. Since by definition it is usually the father who finds himself deprived of custody, this means that, at a very tender age, children end up effectively by being part of a single parent 'family', inasmuch as they do not 'know their father'. It is not technically correct to call them fatherless children but, effectively, that is what they are.

The visiting or access system is unreal because in most cases it does not work. Even where both parents are keen to ensure its success and the one who has custody cooperates to the best of her/his ability, a most unlikely eventuality, it is a fact that children need their parents for twenty-four hours and not for two or three hours a day. They need the stability which comes from the knowledge that the parents are there.

There is still ignorance in our society about the consequences to children of fatherlessness, whether occurring naturally through death, or as a result of divorce. Very little research has been carried out into this point despite its obvious significance; there is no doubt that it is destined to become even more important with the increasing incidence of single mothers.

Throughout this chapter we must remind ourselves that the more emancipated the woman, the more inclined she is to be independent in her approach to children and, indeed, to having children, even when either she does not want to marry the father, or does not want to marry at all, or the father is no longer around, has abandoned her, or whatever. The consequences to children of being brought up in a home where there is no father have not yet been fully analysed and understood and although there is, for example, some evidence that childhood bereavement by loss of a father can be a factor in adult depressive illness, or that the absence of a father, no matter how occurring, whilst the child is under the age of two, may be a factor in other mental illnesses, there is no real conclusive view that can be formulated with any degree of confidence.

In her book *Social Science and Social Pathology*[6] Barbara Wootton makes the following point:

> . . . the majority of our twenty-one investigations are thus in agreement in showing high rates of broken homes against delinquents; various British studies place anything from 22% to 57% of their delinquents in this category, whereas control figures, when available, range only from 11% to 18%. It is clear, therefore, that the loss of a father increases the risk that a child, particularly if he is a boy, will become a delinquent by a factor of approximately two. Lack or inadequacy of parental support is a very determining consideration. There is a connection between emotional disturbance in childhood and delinquent behaviour.

This does not mean that every boy who does not have a father becomes a delinquent; but it must be common sense – and this view is reinforced by statistical data – that a child who lacks the guidance of a father runs a greater risk, indeed, a far greater risk of becoming a delinquent than a boy who is brought up in what is generally regarded as a normally constituted family. Boys who are brought up solely by a mother tend to become either effeminate, or surly and resentful.

The absence of a father has further consequences as far as a child is concerned. In the first place, the child becomes unsettled. Consequently, as already stated, he may turn to delinquency. He may become effeminate and turn to homosexuality. He may either become too close to his mother or end up by disliking women.

A further consideration is the increase in the number of runaway children. Sometimes, it is true, children leave home at an early age because they seek adventure; nowadays, however, more and more children leave home because they are unhappy there. In 1989 there were 25,000 runaway children recorded in London alone. All these are problems of some magnitude. As to the child being unsettled, it seems axiomatic that this is so: children are creatures of habit.

Terman and his colleagues[7] concluded that children who are strongly attached to their parents and have little conflict with them are more likely than others to be happy in marriage when they become men and women. 'Marital happiness appears to be a condition that tends to run in families.' This finding endorses in scientific form the commonly-held belief that children of divorced parents are more likely to divorce in their turn than those who come from stable families. Put more simply, you could say that divorce breeds divorce.

Indeed, divorce creates a vicious circle long before we dedicated any attention to the studies of Terman and his colleagues. It is surely common sense to recognize that if my parents lacked the adaptability, reasonableness and instinct for a sound choice of spouse and a stable marriage, I am unlikely to develop those same qualities when I grow up and marry. The proponents of divorce underplay this theme, since they are forced to argue that happiness can be found in a second home. It is, of course, true that if a second marriage is happy, it *may* be a better situation for a child to find himself in than a very unhappy first home. But there is no proof even of this.

On the other hand, it is a well-established fact that where there has been a divorce, even at times where there has been a remarriage, the parents remain lonely and this loneliness communicates itself to the children. The children themselves are manipulated by the parents and in turn learn how to manipulate both the parents and the step-parents. Examples are legion: the parents' views as to what should happen to the children inevitably will differ and each will want to keep the other one out; there will be problems with the new 'parents'. Overall, there always are complicated relationships and arrangements. Indeed, the practical difficulties are often so great that there is little doubt, as noted earlier, that most children would prefer the two parents to stay together, even though they might quarrel whilst cohabiting.

The psychological effect of the complications and the bickering may remain dormant for years and only long-term observation could determine which of the alternatives, namely an unhappy home with two parents, or a relatively happy home with one, or with a step-parent, is truly better for the child. Whichever way the decision might go, the burden is carried on by the child into whatever new relationship is established.

Misconceptions in this field abound. It is said quite cheerfully, and with conviction, that happy parents result in happy children. This, though often maintained as gospel truth, is proved to be inaccurate.[8] According to Wallerstein and Kelly the overwhelming majority of children interviewed preferred an unhappy marriage to a situation where divorce had occurred, no matter how happy the spouses might be in the second marriages.

It is against this background that one has to consider another of the major consequences of the parents' divorce, particularly where the child remains effectively fatherless; and that is, the development by the child of homosexual traits. It is this author's belief that one of the major consequences of marital breakdown, to which insufficient attention has been dedicated, is that it contributes to the spread of homosexual tendencies.

This is not an aspect that has been seriously considered either by those who have made a study of homosexuality or by those who have considered divorce and its effects. The reasons are not far to seek: on the whole, the former do not wish to consider that homosexuality is something that can be acquired because they feel that it is a perfectly normal sexual manifestation; as such, it is by definition uninfluenced in its determination, though not in its manifestations, by original behaviour on the part of others. Those who have considered the effects of divorce would not wish to add to the number of drawbacks which are acknowledged even by the believers in divorce as inevitable consequences of the breakdown of a marital relationship. But there can be little doubt as to the effect of divorce on the development of sexual tendencies.

As noted earlier, whenever parents with young children (let us say, of anything up to the age of sixteen or eighteen) divorce, it is both logical and sensible in any legal system that, as a general rule, the youngsters be entrusted to the care and control and/or the custody of the mother. This is amply proved by statistical data and needs no restatement. Despite the fact that the father in most cases is likely to be given certain rights of access, it is clear, as studies have shown, that, over the years, the degree of access by the father whilst a child is a minor, reduces, and his impact as a parent becomes less and less. The belief is becoming widespread that a father is only needed, if at all, to support the child financially and the psychological, let alone blood, bond between the two is discounted.

Where a male child is brought up solely by the mother, he finds it difficult to identify with a masculine role. Indeed, one can go so far as to say that it is almost impossible for the male child who is brought up by a mother who does not have a strong man by her side, to identify with the male role unless the *mores* of the society in which he grows up are strongly marked towards a heterosexual trend. One has to consider at this stage the objection to this suggestion that could be raised as concerns widows. In other words, does it follow from what has just been stated that the child brought up by a widow stands a good chance of becoming homosexual? The answer is in the negative and the reason is this: where the father dies, the child knows full well that he was removed from the scene, so to say, by accident and not by the will of the spouses themselves. In all likelihood, the marriage was a reasonably happy one. It is conceivable that the mother keeps photos of the father around the home, she has memories of him, she may mention him from time to time, she may compare features of her young son with those of her dead partner. The memories, if the marriage was a happy one, are usually loving ones and the picture that the child builds for himself of his father is almost an idealized one. Where there has been a divorce, however, if the father is mentioned at all, it is usually in the context of his having been useless, or violent, or a failure, a spendthrift, a bad provider, an adulterer, or someone who fails to pay the maintenance on the due date. There is no comparison between the two situations from the psychological point of view.

From the mother the male child derives warmth, affection, sensitivity and a tenderness which will enable him ultimately to make a successful partner; from the father the sense of discipline, the masculinity and those 'manly' qualities which, though badly devalued and debased in present-day society, are representative of the very features which woman naturally looks for in a man.

The male child even more than the female certainly needs both. Where the masculine traits are lacking, he becomes either too closely associated with the mother or finds himself in a position of conflict with her; in either event, his familiarity with, and understanding of, persons of the opposite sex – other than his mother – is badly affected.

And this is the reason why so many men are nowadays terrified by the women they see around them. The ever-increasing assertion by woman of her rights, her sexuality and her 'feminism' are anathema to certain males. They run for miles: they cannot understand it and inevitably they do not know how to cope with it. It is so much easier to find refuge in the bosom of one's sporting friends, or drinking or club pals.

One need hardly mention the fact that the divorced mother herself has problems. She feels a victim anyhow because she has been a failure and she may lack support. If the children are females, they may complain about the home; if they are males, the likelihood is that they complain because they have not got a father. One of the results of all this is a marked devaluing of marriage as an institution in the eyes of the children. It does not suffice for people to counter this by saying that marriage remains solid and popular because everyone wants to marry and, indeed, the mere fact that divorced people remarry so soon shows what a good thing marriage is. This is totally untrue. All that the hasty remarriage shows is that there is a fashion: it certainly does not prove that marriage is becoming stronger and the family more solid than it was.

But whatever may be the problems of the mother, the fact that she is working has serious consequences for the child because he loses his home comforts. When he gets home from school, there is no welcome. Although it is true that lights can be put on a timer, as a rule the house will look dark in winter, there may be no fire on, or if there is one on in the house, it may still be less welcoming. There is clearly a feeling of emptiness and the children do not feel quite so much at ease as they ought to. If they do not feel at ease, they have no incentive to get back home early. They go and meet their friends, they get into bad company, they turn to crime, they may even turn to drugs. The neglect of the house itself is apparent. Where both spouses are at work and there are children, there is usually an element of disorganization in the house. This is a common experience and hardly needs labouring. Running a home is a full-time job: the laundering is not up to date, the house is untidy, it may be unclean, certainly it is not dusted, there may be little in the fridge, nothing in the freezer, dirty dishes in the sink, washing piling up, shirts not ironed. There is general disorganization and chaos, compounded from time to time if the mother is ill.

This kind of scenario is hotly contested by most career women but they normally operate on a different social level. Usually, where a husband and wife are professionals, their income is sufficient to provide for adequate home help. But we are not concerned here so much with people who have money and who can compensate, on the practical though not on the psychological level, for some of the evils and disadvantages that have been mentioned. What about the social classes where the wife must go out to work as well and cannot afford domestic help? In those situations, the home is no longer what it ought to be by definition, namely a haven of safety. It becomes merely a port of call; children and parents go through it like ships meeting at sea in the night, but the sense of permanence, which provides so much for stable development of the child, has gone.

What the proponents of greater freedom to divorce tend to ignore, is the effect of the example of parents on children generally. It is common knowledge that children pay close attention to what their parents do; they are affected either positively or negatively by the way their parents behave to each other and to the world at large, by their habits of cleanliness, of drinking, of smoking and so on. Clearly, the children will be equally affected whether their parents maintain a marital relationship or divorce. If the latter, they in turn may wish to divorce where they do not agree with their future spouses: it is a self-perpetuating circle and unfortunately, although there exists in the USA a 'National Federation of Clubs for the divorced and the separated', with branches in many parts of the country, there seems to be no equivalent organization in the UK to take care of the children of divorced parents.

A further consideration is that the child must inevitably develop some rancour at the fact that a divorce resulted in stress upon him, and that this process was initiated by one or even both parents. Apart from being angry with his parents, he feels neglected and under attack mainly because he does not understand how it all came about. The child says to himself: 'If my mother or father loved me, how could they do this to me?' The mere fact that he asks such a question has far-reaching implications for his psyche. As part of this refusal, parents as a rule are unwilling to discuss the divorce with their children. It is as though they were either afraid of hearing what the children had to say or felt guilty about what they had done or are about to do.

It is often said that we should educate parents so that they are better able to cope with divorce. This seems a counsel of despair: it might be wiser to educate them so that they are better at helping each other and at caring for their children. The difficulty is that whereas we are in a hurry to educate people as to the facts of life, we spend no time trying to educate them as to the meaning of marriage, how to make it work, how to survive it, how to fight for it and how to stay married.

This is not the voice of somebody crying in the wilderness. There are plenty of people who would support the sanctity of marriage and some restraint over sexual freedom, there are many who abhor the violence upon and the raping of old women, who resent pornography, homosexuality and lesbianism being flaunted as perfectly normal occurrences or forms of behaviour; who have contempt for the profit motive and the institutionalization of economic dogma; who believe in their responsibility to their children and to society, who resent alcoholism and drug addiction and who feel that our society is depriving them of a wonderful opportunity to be happy and organized. These people, however, say nothing about the protection to be afforded to the children of divorced parents and, provided the child comes out of a divorce situation with one parent, they think it has not done quite so badly.

But it simply is not true that children can survive just as well with one parent as they would have done with two, because they then lack the experience of sharing. They cannot know what it means to share the love of each parent for each other and for the child. The reverse side of the coin is that whoever has the child, mother or father, will try to overcompensate for the absence of the other parent and will be either prepossessive or not at all possessive: relationships thus become confused and reactions unnatural. There may be some balancing of each parent's faults when there are two of them, but when there is only one, if there are faults, as inevitably there will be, these will strike the child with great force. If the woman remarries, there is the problem of the stepfather; if she does not remarry, she will have to harden herself up to the reality of life and in the process will inevitably become less feminine. That will certainly rub off on the children and, in the case of boys, as we have seen, will have a particularly damaging effect. The increased rate of juvenile violence, especially among soccer fans (or so they call themselves) has coincided with the very high rates of divorce and family breakdown.

In order to compensate for this and for the divorce rate it is now suggested that, when parents wish to divorce, the whole family should get together, bringing in an experienced mental health adviser who could thrash out the problems in the presence of the children. A family 'parliament' to avoid juvenile delinquency? How naïve can our society get?

Religious beliefs do not seem to be prevailing either. A Protestant ethic is clearly reflected in the attitude of UK legislature which, however, seems to have adopted a double standard, as it is only concerned with the personal well-being of the spouses and not really about the consequences of divorce as far as it affects the children. The most recent example of this lack of interest is the report of the Morton Commission. It will be recalled that the Morton Commission was appointed in 1951; its report was published in 1957. It listened to social workers, politicians, doctors, do-gooders, barristers, solicitors, priests, nuns and practically everybody under the sun: but the views of children were hardly represented. Put differently, it heard 'evidence' about and from all the people who for one reason or another had an axe to grind (whether it be for professional, economic or psychological reasons) but it did not take any steps whatsoever to ascertain what children themselves might think. It is of course, only too easy to say that this cannot be done. That is not true. Julia Wallerstein managed to do it.

One example might be that of a sensitive young girl who sees her unhappy mother forced to divorce her father. The natural reaction may well be along the lines: 'My father has made my mother unhappy: therefore, I cannot bear him/I don't love him/I hate him. My father is a man. Therefore, I cannot bear/love/I hate all men.' This is not so far-fetched a hypothesis in psychological terms. And the reverse situation would apply in the case of a young boy. The youngster cannot understand what goes on in his psyche but the effects are felt throughout his life and when he reaches a more mature age, it is easier to appreciate certain traits in character and general development.

On numerous occasions I have heard people in the age group 45-55 remark with bitterness that they deeply resented their parents' divorce which had a very marked effect on their own lives. In all the cases where this observation has been made, the speakers themselves had been forced into divorce. They could not help it. Their psychological make-up was such that they did not have the ability to make a go of marriage and just as their parents failed, so they felt deep down that they, too, were doomed to fail.

A further matter of concern, for the children themselves, is related to the actions by a disappointed parent who either feels that the legal system in the UK does not provide him/her with sufficient protection, or has been denied custody of the children, namely that of child-snatching. This is a much more common occurrence than people are led to believe. The highly publicized situations where a child, subject to the English jurisdiction, is taken abroad, especially to countries with different religious or political traditions (one thinks of countries like Iran, Egypt, and so on), are merely the tip of the iceberg. In practice, as every lawyer who is involved in family matters well knows, quite often a divorced parent, who has been denied custody, deprives the former spouse of the children. This, of itself, is a contradiction in terms. It has often been said that the best thing that a parent can do for his children is to love the other parent. The natural flow of affection between the parents communicates itself to the children. To the tragedy of divorce where the flow is interrupted, sometimes quite abruptly, and always detrimentally for the child, one superimposes a situation where the child becomes more of a pawn in the war between his parents than it was even in divorce.

The concept of a parent re-possessing, so to say, his children is very sad indeed. It must be heart-rending for the spouse, who is deprived of the children and who had believed that the court order made in his/her favour was the end of the matter; but, above all, it exacerbates the feeling of anger which children experience in any divorce situation. The anger is obviously related to the parent who brought the divorce about: as a result, the children are forced to take sides. Indeed, they may have been quite upset by the parents' inability to cope with them whilst the divorce was going through. But when it comes to their being 'snatched', the trauma is all the greater because the snatching crystallizes the need (in psychological terms) for the child to take sides if it is to preserve its sanity.

All too often (regrettably because of lack of money more commonly, but otherwise, because of lack of willpower or determination), the deprived parent acquiesces in the new state of affairs. Again, as with divorce itself, the situation is essentially of benefit to no one except lawyers and enquiry agents.

There is one further aspect of the damaging effect of divorce on children which is, in a sense, the most worrying and this is the reason why I have left it until last. We all know that, during the last decade of the twentieth century, there was substantially increased publicity surrounding the sexual abuse that children have been subjected to. It would appear that the UK is now in the grip of an epidemic of child sex abuse. (Included in this term, is incest and any other form of 'perversion' as far as children are concerned, both within and outside the family.)

The increase is often explained away by saying that it is not the number of occurrences that has increased but the likelihood, if not the probability, that more of them are being reported as time goes by. It is said that all that is happening is not that there are more incidents but rather that the very frequent attacks and other forms of abuse, which were part of the Victorian society and, generally what is termed the 'old order', are now considered much less trivial and acceptable than in the past and, accordingly, because we have a different perspective of the relationship between men and women, and more likely to be reported than formerly.

There is, of course, some truth in this and there is no doubt that in incestuous relationships, male predominance within the family in particular was a most relevant factor both in its inception and in its secretiveness. But the argument is only part of the story, since some of the worst episodes occurred whilst the children were under the care of social workers and not within the bosom of the family. Here, one could quote, for example, Jasmine Beckford and Kimberley Carlisle.[9] All we have done is to replace the family and the authority of the father with the social services department and the authority of the social worker.

The reality is that child abuse is a concomitant of divorce because where there is occurring, as is frequent nowadays, a total breakdown in the authority of the family as an institution, and of the father as head of the family, it is most likely that difficult sexual situations will develop.

It is clear, as far as the child is concerned, that where the parents are unmarried, there is less security within the family because of lesser commitment between the spouses. It has been recorded[10] that where people co-habit and have children, they are three times more likely to have a breakdown in their relationship, than where they are married. It is quite easy for a person who is unrelated to the child and is co-habiting with the child's mother, to have no feeling whatsoever towards the child itself and, therefore, to abuse that child. According to the report 'Who Cares?' by the Centre for Policy Studies:[11] '... almost half of all reported incidents of the three main categories of abuse, are committed by the new partner of divorced or separated mothers'.

In turn, parents who were victims of child abuse are more likely to commit it than parents who came from relatively stable and healthy homes. Indeed, Valerie Riches, the Secretary of the organization 'Family and Youth Concern'[12], has recorded that a number of research studies have found that a disproportionate frequency of abuse in parents arises out of broken homes and that one study, in particular, found that 59% of sexually abusive fathers, within its sample, had had divorced parents. If, as she points out, we bear in mind that these men would, in all likelihood, have grown up at a time when divorce rates were far lower than they are at the moment, then we can see how the problem is likely to increase rather than diminish.

According to the National Society for the Prevention of Cruelty to Children, the number of reported cases of sexual abuse of children increased twelve times between 1983 and 1988. Again, according to the NSPCC, 58% of the victims of sexual abuse live either in single-parent households, or in households where the man is not the father of the particular child.

In England in 1999 there were 31,900 registrations to child protection registers and 30,100 children and young people actually on such registers. As of March 1998 the number of children in care or looked after by local authorities was 53,300.[13]

It is beyond the scope of this discussion to consider the arguments which are put forward for and against the theory that because the traditional family was of a patriarchal type, there would inevitably be sexual abuse, on the one hand, and those which proceed from the premise that a broken home is more likely to be conducive to sexual patterns that are abnormal or perverted. The climate in which we live is not a happy one, as far as fathers are concerned. A number of them have actually developed almost a phobia about displaying perfectly natural and affectionate tendencies towards their children.

There is no doubt, therefore, that broken homes contribute to broken relationships. These relationships will inevitably include sexual exploitation. Thus, sexual abuse of children is more likely to occur outside than within the traditional family.

If this premise is right, then the increase in the incidence of child abuse is the gravest and most damaging indictment of the views that our society has adopted regarding divorce. Whether these views stem from feminism, consumerism or whatever other cause, it seems inescapable that there is more than a *prima facie* argument that, as far as the well-being of the children is concerned, divorce is a most negative, damaging and dangerous way of tackling the dissatisfaction of the parents.

Clearly, any argument which is founded upon the feminist theory that what we are witnessing is not an increase in the number of incidents of abuse, but greater sensitivity, alertness and willingness to report is not persuasive. As a matter of common sense, a stepfather or any male co-habiting with a woman who has young children, is more likely, if he is so minded, to abuse those children than the natural father. Whilst it is a fact that the natural father may and sometimes does abuse his own daughter, he is less likely to do so than a step-parent.

In fact, the particular consequences of step-parenthood as far as the children are concerned, would appear to this writer not to have been studied in sufficient detail. The authors who have dealt, either incidentally, or specifically, with the role of the step-parent have, as far as I can see, completely ignored the possibility that a step-father may be more inclined than a natural father to sexually abuse his children.

□

I thought it might be profitable to conclude this section by looking in somewhat greater depth at the Wallerstein and Kelly study. It is a careful review of sixty families in California and their children, after divorce, and for a follow-up period of five years.[14] This is a fundamental study of the effects of divorce upon children and it is worthy of much attention: until recently, it has been ignored. The authors themselves are conscious of the fact, as they put it, that as far as the consequences of divorce upon children are concerned the 'number of investigations ... is perilously low'. Or, as they also put it, this is a problem to which 'astonishingly little professional attention (has been) paid'.

The authors make a number of interesting findings of facts which they preface by stating that their work points '. . . to the strong possibility that the psychological effects of divorce could lie dormant for years and become visible at a much later stage of development, thereby underscoring the importance of long-term observations'. As far as this writer is aware, these long-term observations are non-existent for the reasons already given, but essentially because adults have made unwarranted assumptions about their children. The old school of thought was that the unhappily married couple should remain married for the good of the children. As Wallerstein and Berlin Kelly put it: 'Today's conventional wisdom holds with equal vigour that a marriage which is unhappy for the adults is unhappy for the children and, furthermore, that a divorce that promotes the happiness of the adults will inevitably benefit the children as well.' On the other hand, they find that this presumed community of interests between adults and children is not borne out by the facts that they studied.

I am greatly indebted to their work which could be summarized as follows:

1) Whilst only a few of the children interviewed thought that their parents were happily married, yet the overwhelming majority preferred the unhappy marriage to the divorce.

2) One can be a good parent and a 'bad' (in the sense of unhappy) spouse.

3) Despite the unhappiness of the marriage, the children felt that their parents were behaving quite well to them as parents.

4) Although an analysis of divorce as such did not form part of their investigation, the authors do recognize divorce as being either a stress-related response, or an impulsive decision, or a decision brought about by the attitude of others, with a resultant notable decline in the standard of

living of three-fifths of divorced men and three-quarters of divorced women. The decrease in the standard of living was particularly evident as far as mothers who have custody of the children were concerned.

5) Half the women interviewed in the study had worked part- or full-time prior to the separation. The authors do not say whether that circumstance of itself brought about stress within the marriage.

6) Another of the consequences of divorce is related to the attitude of the spouses. This ranges from feelings of anger, depression and inadequacy, to extremes of elation as a result of the hope that one was starting along a new road.

The findings, however, become much more significant and damaging to the cause of divorce when one starts looking at the great detail amassed by the authors. A total of a hundred and thirty-one children were interviewed ranging from the age of two to eighteen, over a five-year period. The authors are in no doubt that, both for children and adolescents, the separation and its aftermath were the most stressful periods of their lives, the children being intensely affected by the disruption of the family and worried about the future.

This worry appears to have been compounded by the fact that since the parents are so concerned with their own troubles, they find they have less time to dedicate to the children. Less than 10% of the children and adolescents either expressed relief or welcomed the decision to divorce. Over three-quarters of the children opposed divorce very strongly.

At a delicate age in their development, it is difficult to see to whom the children could turn for support when notified that the marriage was breaking up. Their sense of vulnerability and fear is very great. The authors found as a fact that one-third of the children worried that their mother would abandon them. All children felt sad and worried, lonely, rejected, angry, torn between conflicting loyalties and some of them even felt guilty, perhaps believing that it was their fault that the parents were splitting up.

One of the findings that is particularly relevant for the

purposes of this discussion occurs on page 53:

> The intensity of the fighting between the parents and the amount of violence within the marriage that the child witnessed were not by themselves associated with the child's feelings of relief at the time of divorce. Furthermore, we had expected that the quality of the parent/child relationships prior to the separation might influence the amount of distress the children experienced. Such was not the case. The children's preoccupation with the divorce and the intensity of their response were not linked to the quality of their relationship with the departed parent.

This finding is wholly consistent with the views put forward in this book. The child is concerned with having a family, and a home; and, above all, with certainty. Divorce brings about fear, regression, bewilderment, aggression, guilt and essentially overstimulates the imagination of the youngster at a time in his development where excitement should be reduced. Interestingly enough, as noted earlier, most children continued to hope that the parents would be reconciled. In some cases, psychosomatic illnesses developed such as headaches and stomach aches, cramps and asthma. In the case of the older children, they in turn became preoccupied about matters of sex and of marriage and I would suggest that it is at that particular point that the neurosis develops in the children of divorce.

The truth is that the discipline inherent in a clear-cut family structure is a very valuable asset for the child and as soon as the family breaks apart, the parent/child relationship, as Wallerstein and Kelly put it, 'swings free'. 'The chain of reaction so abruptly set off may reverberate for several years and lead to new relationships greatly at variance with those obtained when the family was together; relationships, indeed, that have no real counterpart in the intact family'.[15] I wholeheartedly endorse this comment, for it explains much that is wrong within our society, where relationships are already so confused. For example, just imagine what view a child can form when the parent after divorce, as is common, enters into an extended period of intense sexual activity. Lovers may appear in rapid succession, visit for shorter or longer periods, indeed, stay overnight: what kind of psychological grounding in relationships is such a scenario for a sensitive child? Couple this with the increased dependence that the child must develop with the parent who has custody and you will see what a kaleidoscope of feelings the situation develops, even if we discount entirely the fact that, if the mother is working, she cannot dedicate all her attentions to the child at a time when she is more than ever needed. As the authors put it:

> Although the sexual life of parents within an intact family is by no means as invisible to children as many adults believe it to be, the family system nevertheless provides guidelines for sexual behaviour. As we have already noted, one-third of the custodial mothers became involved in an active sexual life immediately after the separation. Only a few had stable relationships at this time; more had a succession of lovers.

This is almost rubbing salt into the wound inflicted upon the child.

The authors also found that visiting arrangements gave rise to great difficulties, as is common experience for those who practise in the divorce courts. There are a number of inherent difficulties but one of the principal ones is undoubtedly psychological. Fathers get depressed, they feel guilty, they become provocative, they quarrel with the step-father, they end up by not visiting.

The arrangements of visits is problematical, it needs to be planned, one has to see whether other children can come along, whether the visit can be shared with others. The atmosphere is not necessarily friendly and in certain situations it is openly hostile. A sensitive father may decide that he is better off staying away. In the same way that wives recover more quickly from divorce than husbands, the authors find that the girls they interviewed took the divorce situation more in their stride.

With the passage of time, the attitude of the children towards divorce did improve. This is ascribed by the authors to their maturity. I would prefer to suggest that it is the result of the inherent enormous adaptability of human beings. What cannot be cured must be endured, runs the old saying and presumably this is exactly what the children of divorce do. They adapt, of course: but what is the psychological price that they have to pay, particularly when they grow up?

Improvement there must be from the immediately post-divorce period to, say, five years later. However, all is not well. According to the authors:

> We were most surprised to find that five years after the separation, 56% of the children and adolescents continued to find little or no improvement over the pre-divorce family; 22% were highly gratified with the post-divorce family and the remaining 22% expressed a cautious view that the divorce family offered a modest or moderate improvement.[16]

If we were running the divorce system on democratic principles and if we accepted these findings of fact by Wallerstein and Kelly, then we ought to reach the conclusion that the children were no better off after the divorce of their parents: I suggest this bears out the point that divorce achieves nothing as far as the children are concerned. Nor is this surprising. As they themselves put it:

> It seems reasonable to propose that divorce is not likely to be beneficial to children unless the parent-child relationship separately or jointly can be maintained at the level of gratification and guidance which existed earlier within the pre-divorce family or unless these are improved.[17]

One is bound to wonder, therefore, what is the point of divorce? After all, the authors claim that they were startled when they discovered that 30% of the children interviewed were fully aware of the intense bitterness between their parents five years after the divorce, with consequent distress and poor psychological adjustment for the children. In other words, those particular spouses could get on with each other neither before not after divorce.

Remarriage made matters worse. The authors found that relationships between fathers and children often declined either after the father's remarriage to a woman with children or when children were born within the new marriage. This is perfectly understandable. Stepfathers quite often complicated matters in the long term, although initially children welcomed the arrival of a stepfather because of the grater security that his presence provided. This is an interesting finding of fact because it shows beyond a shadow of a doubt that children require two parents.

The authors' conclusions are as follows:

1) Contrary to expectations, many marriages that have been unhappy for the adults have been reasonably comfortable, even gratifying, for the children and very few of the children concurred with their parents' decision to divorce or indeed experienced relief at the time of the separation.

2) Unlike the adults, children did not as a group show an improvement in their psychological health during the years following the separation save in those situations where the father with whom they were cohabiting prior to the divorce might have been psychiatrically disturbed.

3) After five years, only one third of the youngsters were lively, well-adjusted and content with their lives.

4) Whilst divorce was found to be highly beneficial for many of the adults, the authors found no comparable evidence regarding the experience of the children. 'There is, in fact, no supporting evidence in this five-year study for the commonly made argument that divorce is overall better for children than an unhappy marriage or for its opposite argument, that living with an unhappy marriage is by and large more beneficial or less detrimental than living in the divorce family' (page 306).

5) Children of divorced parents became acutely conscious of the relationship between parents and step-parents and sometimes hyper-active in monitoring their behaviour.

6) The divorced family in which the burden falls mainly on one parent is more vulnerable to stress than that where there are two.

7) The incidence of depression at five years after divorce was higher than that observed at eighteen months.

8) Children in the nine-to-twelve-year-old group were

particularly vulnerable and liable to stress.

9) At the time of the family break-up, the parents themselves were less capable of being good parents, or put another way, the major hazard that divorce poses to the psychological health and development of the children lies exactly in this diminished ability of the parents to perform their duties to their children.

In conclusion, it is self-evidently the case that the effect of divorce, or lack of both parents, no matter how or why occurring, is dramatic for the children: it makes them divorce-prone themselves, is highly damaging to their psychological development, may make them more inclined to be homosexuals, will stay for them as an unhappy memory for the rest of their lives, affects their scholastic and academic attainments, may turn them into criminals and is a contributory factor of considerable and mostly under-rated importance in the increase of mindless and sexual violence, child-abuse, perversion, soccer hooliganism and disrespect for authority. In short, where children are concerned, divorce is a dramatic, traumatic and selfish disgrace, and should be avoided at all costs.

NOTES

1. p.214.
2. Grant McIntyre, 1980.
3. Grant McIntyre, 1980.
4. *Second Chances* – Corgi, 1990.
5. Dominian, Jack – *Marital Breakdown* – Longman & Todd, 1968
6. Allen & Unwin, 1959.
7. 'Psychological Factors in Marital Happiness' op.cit., p.34.
8. *Surviving the Break-up* by Judith Wallerstein and Joan Berlin Kelly, Grant McIntyre, London, 1980, especially at page 10.
9. They made the headlines in 1985. Classic situation of cruelty, neglect and murder of step-child, with failures of social workers involved. The outcry results in a public enquiry, much press debate and parliamentary questions.
10. Social Trends – 28, 29, 74, 87, 88, 89 – ONS – the Stationery Office
11. Published 1989 – London – ISBN 1870265734
12. 322 Woodstock Road, Oxford OX2 7NS
13. NSPCC Library, January 1999.

14. *Surviving the Break-up; How Children and Parents Cope with Divorce*, Grant Mackintyre Limited, London, 1980, and Basic Books (USA), 1980.
15. *Ibid*, p.99.
16. *Ibid*, p.116
Ibid, p.198.
17. *Ibid*, p.199
Ibid, p.215.

6

Effects of divorce on the spouses

It is often said that a separation between the spouses constitutes the death of the marriage, and divorce is its burial. But to look upon divorce as either the death of the marriage or, as people do more commonly, its burial, is to play with words; they may well be convenient to summarize what happens in fact, but it is wishful thinking to assume that, once the parties have divorced, their marriage ends up six feet below ground. The previous marital relationship keeps rising from the dead like a phoenix; all too often, the ghost of Banquo comes back to haunt the former spouses in all shapes and forms.

The ease with which some people embark upon divorce should not blind us to its consequences. It is true that nowadays people are more than ever determined to live for the moment and to grab what they can today, probably because they are afraid of tomorrow. Our personal fulfilment is our new religion. Nevertheless, one has to wonder why such people get married. Nowadays, they can achieve all the comforts, sexual and otherwise, that marriage provides without troubling to tie the knot.

It is a very romantic notion that inspires those who get married. The partners start out wishing to share their common tendencies and feelings but are not entirely aware that, with the ever-increasing tendency to marry outside one's social class and into different backgrounds, both educational and religious, that task becomes more difficult. The spouses blind themselves to this fact and still enter marriage with enormous expectations of success and happiness, to a standard which is quite unrealistic and which is totally divorced from a more natural approach to relationships, for they fail completely to realize that expectations inevitably carry with them conflict. At a time when woman is trying to redress the balance of power, and emerging from centuries of official subjugation, she finds it increasingly more difficult to even out her expectations. She becomes less controlled, less submissive, more determined and more assertive.

Her demands increase proportionately with her expectations and the fine balance in the relationship which is needed to make marriage a success is upset by a reluctance to adopt the principle of give-and-take. Each party wants to live, first of all, for himself or herself, and secondly for the spouse; 'let live' is lost sight of. At the same time, psychologists and sociologists encourage spouses to be honest with each other in an endeavour to redress the lack of communication to which attention has already been drawn. But nobody wants to hear the truth, and extreme candour can be positively dangerous, especially when spouses who have not communicated for a long period of time suddenly spurt out all that they have bottled up over the years.

What very often seems to be missing in the relationship is any sign whatsoever of any notion, no matter how remote, that the survival of the marriage is based on some form of self-denial and self-sacrifice. Once the parties are divorced, however, they are hit by the reality with which they had failed to come to terms previously. In the first place, it is common knowledge that the health of divorced parties, as indeed that of anyone who is experiencing problems with or within the marriage, starts to suffer. In the initial phase after divorce, a phase that can last several years, the divorced person may sleep too much or too little, may lose appetite or tend to over-eat by way of compensation, may go through stages in which no interest can be found in anything under the sun, may be either easily provoked and hypersensitive about the divorced state, or totally insensitive to it, can be either very angry or very ashamed about what has gone on : the psychological reactions vary from individual to individual. Habits are abandoned or acquired; people may start smoking or become addicted to pills, to alcohol or, more commonly nowadays, to anti-depressant or tranquillizing drugs. Very many divorced people have to seek psychiatric treatment.

It has been recorded time and time again that the suicide rate amongst divorced women is considerably higher than amongst the non-divorced: it is three times as high as that amongst divorced men, and four times as high as that amongst married women and men respectively. The psychosomatic illnesses that highlight the trauma of any kind of separation are particularly prominent and noticeable in the case of divorce. They show in stark form how the break-up of a marriage is something major. In a strange sense, the more casually the relationship was entered into at the beginning, the more dramatic the divorce becomes, even though it may not have been ruled out entirely when the marital vows were expressed.

Divorced people are apt to become very lonely indeed. No analysis has been made nor, indeed, would it be easy to make one, of the cost of the telephone bills of divorced parties. The telephone seems to be the most obvious way in which to keep open channels of communication with the outside world and to compensate for the ever-increasing sense of loneliness. Some divorced people dive headlong into new relationships whilst others avoid them altogether. It is worth repeating here (as is widely known) that it is not easy to find new partners. Men and women get set in their ways, they have developed their personal experiences, tastes, ideas about life and it is even more difficult (second time round) to find someone who slots in. Of course, they may find it easy to have casual sexual experiences but these are in turn problematical because they result in a disassociation between physical activity and feeling which must be upsetting, particularly when the divorcee is already labouring under some kind of spiritual misapprehension. All in all, the divorced person of either sex is on an emotional see-saw and finds it difficult to adapt for quite a while. In the case of the woman, however, there is the additional problem that she may well be financially dependent on the husband. She may be paid alimony for the children; but those women who can make a go of it or have a career upon which they can rely are probably very much in the minority; the mere fact that the ex-wife is receiving money from her former husband keeps her practically, and often emotionally, bound to him.

In a very strange sense, this dependence, burdensome though it may appear at first sight, can be a good thing because the woman will try and avoid quarrelling with her former husband in order not to prejudice payments and with a view to avoiding having to go to Court to recover arrears. She may even have an interest in keeping him happy without causing him to spend too much so that he may treat the children as he would have expected them to be treated whilst he was married to her. Whereas this in turn means that she never really gets totally separated from him, it does have a beneficial effect as far as the children are concerned.

If she has custody of them, it is debatable to what extent she will find it an easy task to be a single parent and, when she remarries, there is the problem of the step-father. There is a further difficulty which complicates the whole picture and it is that most divorcees were people who, at heart, wished to be married: they were not loners, they had not decided to spend their life on their own. They did make a major mistake and that was the wrong choice of partner. For this reason, it is likely that they will go about choosing another partner and at that point they will make the same mistake again. The question of remarriage is considered separately. However, suffice it to say at this stage that there is a self-perpetuating factor in the divorce situation. Whereas it is true that some divorcees vow never to remarry, the position is not quite so simple. If that particular person felt the need to marry in the first place as distinct from cohabiting, the psychic make-up must have been such as to dictate marriage. The human psyche does suffer in divorce but it does not change overnight from black to white.

A further point to be considered is the usefulness of the divorcee to himself, his immediate or not-so-immediate family, his employers and society as a whole. We hear of the studies that have been made of the days lost to work in factories or in the office through alcoholism, back-ache, or absenteeism for other reasons. Few have taken notice, let alone any count, of the performance of the divorcee in the work-place or in the professions.

There is a further aspect of the matter requiring consideration. We are so brainwashed at present by feminist politics that scant attention is given to the consequences of divorce as far as men are concerned. It is true that usually one is more interested in what the woman has to say, because she is closer to the children and more directly affected by a marriage going wrong; or at least, so it appears. On the other hand, the reader will recall the point already made to the effect that the initiative for divorce, in nearly three-quarters of the cases, comes from the woman.

As far as man is concerned, he is just as likely to suffer from divorce and, in fact, as we have seen, more so. Those who have studied this condition have been able to prove conclusively that not only, in most situations, man is the reluctant partner in the divorce proceedings, but also that he is the one who is more likely to regret the divorce and to suffer from it. The suffering is not only of a practical nature in the sense that he has lost the convenience of a home, with all the comforts that are normally associated with it; nor is it related to the fact that it is well established that, within three years at the most after divorce, most fathers have lost touch with their children, if they did not have custody of them; nor do I have in mind the situations where wives behave improperly or unfairly to their former spouses, especially if they remarry; nor am I interested in the view that all divorced men for whom I acted professionally, or dealt with in any form, complain that they are the losers, not only from the psychological but, above all, from the financial standpoint. These are really incidentals for present purposes because they are the necessary consequences of having adopted divorce as a principle to deal with marital unhappiness.

The work of Judith Wallerstein and her *Second Chance* written with Sandra Blakeslee, as to the effect that divorce has on children, has already been discussed. It is worth underlining at this stage, however, the compounded effect of divorce, whereby the children of divorced parents, in their turn, marry and are divorced. In the case of the man, his already anxious, insecure and unsettled psyche receives a blow from which he is unlikely to recover.

Proof that man is more emotionally affected by divorce than woman, is to be found in the fact that more men remarry, and faster than women: this shows how they are in urgent need of another close relationship with a woman. Cynics have stated that the reason why divorced men remarry faster than women is that they seek those domestic and sexual comforts which are denied to them whilst they are single: for example, they do not wish to go the launderette when it can be so convenient to find the shirt beautifully ironed, hanging in the cupboard. But is this really a representative picture? Indeed, I personally find it difficult to believe that present-day woman is such a good housekeeper and that present-day man is so spoilt. The truth is that the sense of despair and helplessness, which comes to both men and women with divorce, is greater in the case of the man. Whether it is because he suffers in silence and prefers not to confide his problems to his pub mates – whereas the woman will, quite freely, chat to her friends about her difficulties, after she has recovered from the initial shock – or whether it is because man is fundamentally weaker, where feelings are concerned, than woman, is a matter upon which this writer would formulate no view. Suffice it to say that the problems of men have not been dealt with in the literature in the same depth, and so voluminously, as those of women.

Essentially, there appears to be only a handful of English studies that deal primarily if not exclusively with the problems of men after divorce. Of these, one might single out *Surviving Divorce – Men Beyond Marriage*[1], and *Divorce and After; Fathers' Tales* by Mary Macormack.[2]

Most men are said to develop some form of mental illness of

varying intensity after divorce. It may last for up to three years and often for longer periods. And what about the usefulness of those men to society – in terms of ability to cope with their employment or their professional activity – which must be substantially reduced during the period that they are so affected?

Some attempts have been made to cater for 'the victims' of divorce. For example, there are a number of bodies and organizations that carry out thoroughly commendable work in an endeavour to 're-settle the victims of divorce'. They are usefully listed in the sympathetic paperback *Divorce and After: Fathers' Tales* by Mary Macormack,[3] and nothing that I have either said or shall say detracts in any shape or form from my admiration for the dedicated people who staff these support organizations. But if one considers carefully what they do, one is entitled to reach the conclusion that they, also, are concerned with the symptoms or the consequences of divorce and never with its causes. They cannot be, it is not their function: the legislature has arrogated to itself the task of telling us that divorce is probably good for us and that is why it is so freely available and is something quite acceptable to society.

The 'Campaign for Justice in Divorce'[4] is concerned with financial injustice, and the 'Advisory Conciliation and Arbitration Service'[5] tries to reconcile couples. 'Families need Fathers'[6] tries to redress the balance consequential from the facts that only about one man in ten gets sole care of his children and that 50%, or thereabouts, of non-custodial parents, lose contact with their children after a couple of years (and by definition this means that the fathers lost contact with their children within a very short period of time after divorce), 'Gingerbread' offers support to single parents.[7]

The 'National Council for the Divorced and the Separated',[8] the 'National Council for One-parent Families',[9] the 'National Family Conciliation Council'[10] and their equivalent Scottish and religious bodies, all try and shut the stable door after the horse has bolted. The 'National Marriage Guidance Council',[11] of which we have all been aware for a very long time, has now changed its name to 'Relate'; it is as though it acknowledged that there is no point in trying to give guidance about marriage because marriage has ceased to have any meaning and what we ought to try and do is to get people to communicate. It is the reverse situation, really, because marriages normally break down for the very reason that people have failed to communicate and there seems little point in people communicating after they have divorced.

We also have now in England a 'National Step-Family Association'.[12] The neologism 'step-family' began to make its triumphal appearance in the 1990s; but how far do we take it? Shall we have the first step-family, the second step-family or even the third and fourth? How many families can one have? Surely, there were only ever two families, namely, the family into which one was born and the family which one created when one married. Obviously, this view was wrong and we shall have to learn to acknowledge that parents can quite easily and conveniently, and just as effectively, be replaced by step-parents. This is certainly the theory: those who have to live with day-to-day problems, know how untrue this concept is and what difficulties arise because step-parents come into the picture.

There appearss to be only one organization catering for the children themselves, namely the 'Divorced Child Research Group'[13] which is not one of the major organizations and seems to be focused more on the needs of unmarried fathers rather than on children. Nor should this be surprising, given the fact that the parents themselves do not appear to think about the children too much when deciding to divorce. Very often, too, the parents are under pressure from society as a whole since there are times when we seem to regard divorce as a moral duty where the spouses cannot agree.

□

Having had to speak professionally time and time again to divorced women (with children), who are now in the 45-55 age group and who divorced in their late twenties or early thirties, I can confirm that they all claim that they thought hard and long, as the expression goes, before taking such a serious step; that they were saddened once they decided that their marriages should terminate; that they were concerned for their children. Nevertheless, the decision had to be taken. The justification put forward always was along the lines that 'it was my life that I had to think about', 'you only live once and I could not continue living like that', and similar expressions which highlight the personal drama, which was genuinely felt, of the individual caught in the web of an unhappy marital relationship.

No criticism of such women is intended here. But the point needs to be restated that none of them put the wellbeing of their children first: in some form or other, for one reason or the other, each of them put their happiness first. How can we expect the State, therefore, to give priority to children? We do realize, very fully indeed, that to put our personal happiness before that of others is a fairly normal event and a failing of most of us, and I include myself. The fact remains, however, that once parents have procreated, they have taken a conscious decision to undertake responsibilities for their children within the framework of which selfish considerations, no matter how human and understandable, ought to be discounted and, at any rate, ought not to be countenanced and endorsed by the law.

The State ought to take a lead here, if the individual is incapable of controlling his selfish instincts. For reasons which may be either hygienic, political or economic, or a combination of the three, the State, as we have seen, does purport to take a lead in other spheres to dissuade the individual from embarking upon conduct which, by being detrimental to him, is also, in some form or other, expensive to the State. Suffice it to mention smoking and drinking, human weakness which the State is trying very hard to control by creating a financial, physical, psychological and legal environment where the individual is effectively discouraged. The State could, if it wished, do exactly the same with divorce. After all, the glorification of the feminist principle that woman is mistress of her body and, accordingly, of her future, is beginning to prove as costly to the State, and to society, as the uncontrolled intake of alcohol or of smoking, whether primary or secondary. It is also worth recording at this stage that it is not a coincidence that the period which has seen the greatest rise in the divorce rate in the UK also coincides with increases in the abortion rate.

In the last three-and-a-half decades, since David Steel, the proponent of the abortion legislation, managed to provide some appeal for women, but not enough to get his party elected, the rate of abortion has escalated. Indeed, at the beginning of the new millennium, we might be forgiven for maintaining that instead of being the solution to some unfortunate woman's physical or mental difficulty, abortion has now become a form of contraception. A look at some of the figures will easily endorse this point. In 1968 there were a total of 23,641 abortions in England and Wales. In 1971 there were officially recorded 94,600 abortions in the United Kingdom. Given that it is unlikely that the inclusion of Wales and Scotland can account for such a substantial difference in the two figures just quoted, it is obvious that the increase has been dramatic. The equivalent figure for 1997 was 179,746. One should note at this point that it is very often said that a number of women from other parts of the world come to England to have abortions. It is a matter of record that of these 179,746 recorded abortions, only 5% (9,601) relate to non-resident women. Of these 179,746 abortions, a very noticeable 116,425 were to single women.[14]

Adopting a method of calculation popularized in the United States, the rate of abortion per 1,000 women in 1997 in the United Kingdom (women in the age group 14 to 49) rose from 8.4 in 1971 to 13.4 in 1997, and in September 1999 it stood at just under 14 per 1,000. This means effectively that on average 14 women out of 1,000 in the United Kingdom have at least one abortion. It is interesting to note that our neighbours across the Channel in Holland have an abortion rate of 6%. Indeed, figures published even more recently[15] confirm that abortions are running at the highest ever level, since in the third quarter of 1998, 46,000 women in England and Wales had an abortion. This figure represents an increase of 3% over the same three months in 1997.

The Office for National Statistics had indicated that for the whole of 1998 the total abortion figure is expected, when officially recorded, to top 180,000 for the first time in England

and Wales. This is said to be happening also because the safeguards imposed by the Abortion Act 1967 are no longer observed. In 1968 there were officially recorded 23,641 abortions in England and Wales. This figure rose steadily over the years and for the latest recorded year, 1998, stands at 187,402.[16]

We all know how figures can be interpreted differently but the reader will surely agree with me that there is a very close, indeed, there is an ineluctable relation, between the divorce rate and the abortion rate. They both stem from the feminist and modern creed that gives priority to woman over everything else, they both show that something is wrong either with the person involved or, with a society which postpones, as a matter of avowed policy and intention, the interests of the child to that of the mother. What they do also show in my submission is that the motherly or motherhood instinct is gradually being bred out of woman, for the greatest claim that any mother could make, apart from that of procreation, was and still is, that she loved and cared for her children. This claim ceases to have any real significance at the moment when, in divorce, the interests of the children are postponed to that of the mother and, in abortion, – which is almost an analogous situation, – the interests of the unborn and yet viable, if not living, child, similarly are forced to take second place.

□

The clamour of women for divorce, which has grown even louder in the last thirty years, has manifested itself in a rather unusual recent situation concerning the Jewish faith. On 1 December 1999 the Chief Rabbi of the United Synagogue in the UK sat in the religious court (*Beth Din*) together with Rabbis from the Sephardi community. The purpose was to resolve what was stated to be a rather controversial divorce case by the Jewish system of mediation/negotiation.

The Jews have a problem. Under Jewish religious law an orthodox woman who has obtained a civil divorce cannot remarry until she receives her husband's blessing, which is manifested by the 'Get', that is to say the religious divorce. It often happens that husbands cannot or will not resist a civil suit for divorce but are reluctant to grant consent to the latter step because of their religious beliefs. This creates a situation where women of the orthodox Jewish faith are considered almost as slaves. But at least, as has already been remarked above, no allegation of hypocrisy can be levelled against the Jews as far as divorce is concerned because in their wedding ceremony the parties do not vow to live together until death.

NOTES

1. Wheatsheaf Books, 1983 – a study by Ambrose C Harper and Pemberton
2. MacDonald Optima, 1990
3. *Ibid*, pp. 158-162
4. 177 Green Lane, Shepperton, Middx TW17 8DY
5. Brandon House, 180 Borough High Street, London SE1
6. 134 Curtain Road, London EC2R 3AR
7. 16/17 Clerkenwell Close, London EC2R 0AN
8. 74 Biddulph Park, Chase Terrace, Burntwood, West Midlands WSY 8JQ
9. 255 Kentish Town Road, London NW5 2LQ
10. 9 Tavistock Place, London WC14 9SN
11. Herbert Gray College, Little Church Street, Rugby, Warwickshire, BV21 3AP
12. 18 Holton Place, London EC1N 8RU
13. Now no longer active
14. General and Demographic Series AB, number 24, pages 1 and 3
15. *The Times*, 17 February 1999
16. General and Demographic Series AB, No. 26. Of these, only 9531 abortions were to non-residents of England and Wales

7

Effects of divorce on society

When we look around at the ever-increasing rate of personal and social violence, the spread of drug-taking, the ongoing contempt for life, disregard of old age, disinterest in those worse off than ourselves, lust for money and power, the glorification of the profit motive and of sexual abuse and deviation (one need only consider the numbers of cases of incest and child abuse), we must ask ourselves whether these features are, as some claim, an inevitable consequence of the fast-moving, technological age we live in (not least the profound impact of television); or whether it is not a coincidence that all the damaging, unhappy and soul-destroying features that we have listed above are related in some form or other to a breakdown in morals which is either caused or aggravated by the constant diminution in the value of the family as a social unit.

It is not within the scope of this book to consider this particular problem save to ask rhetorically the question: why is it that all these features have become more prominent, in this country at least, at the same time as the rate of divorce has increased beyond any reasonable bound? I accept, of course, that this may be a chicken-and-egg situation and, having posed the rhetorical question, let us move on to more fundamental issues.

It needs to be said that the grave difficulties we all have to face nowadays lie in the obvious lack of an anchoring point for the energies and the values of the members of society. As I see it, there are three essential groupings upon which the individual relies for support and reassurance. They are, historically, the family, the Church and the State – convenient nouns to identify a certain type of relationship. In the family, the individual finds the reflection and manifestation of his love and his need to procreate; in the Church, he finds a representation of the afterlife or the Superior Being; in the State, he finds a practical level of protection against other individuals. The family provides an outlet for love, the Church for hope and prayer and the State for patriotism; each of them serves a different purpose at varying times in individual lives.

Nowadays, however, these concepts seem to have lost their meaning. We have already seen how the importance of the family is being whittled away by the modern developments of feminism, firstly, and divorce, secondly and mainly. As regards the Almighty, considerable doubts are being expressed, much more frequently and vociferously than in the past, as to His existence; and where has patriotism gone? The expression 'my country, right or wrong' seems to have lost all its meaning.

Against this background it is hardly surprising that the individual develops neuroses, for he has nothing solid on which to rely, he has no place or idea into which he may seek refuge or solace. He is left to consider that he is surrounded by lack of discipline, absence of values, inordinate and gratuitous displays of violence and greed, and a desperate search for sexual satisfaction.

In the view of this writer, divorce does not help; quite the contrary, it compounds the damage. Indeed, the effect of divorce upon society is at least as great as that on the individual spouses. After all, society is no more than the aggregation of the individuals that live in a particular location at a particular moment in history.

In May 1990, the police disclosed that during the previous year, crimes of sexual violence against women in the London area increased by 28% over 1988. The incidence of rape was 14% greater than in the previous year. The police went on to make two observations, the first factual, the second speculative. The factual statement related to the knowledge by the rapist of the woman he had attacked; friend, distant relative, neighbour, social acquaintance. The police then recommended that women should do more in order not to provoke rapists. Whilst it can be readily accepted that a sick man may be precipitated into committing crimes of violence by scantily clad girls or women in provocative postures, it is surely a nonsense to accept that women's behaviour can do more than tempt the healthy male. If I am not violent, I do not convert myself into a rapist by being either provoked or teased by an attractive woman.

The factual statement that the rapist in most cases already knew his victim is, however, much more significant. It shows two things; firstly, that men, even sick men, who commit crimes of violence are growing lazy in their pursuit of females; and gutless. Lazy, because they prefer to go for the prey that is readily available rather than having to stalk her. And gutless, because I should have thought it requires more courage to stalk a woman and then assault her than entice an unsuspecting acquaintance or friend into a car or flat and then molest her.

The significance of the statistics quoted above, however, is different. They show the ever-increasing lack of respect in which woman is held nowadays. Her dignity has gone. It is the view of this writer, at least, that a marked contributory factor to this loss of dignity which results in increased crimes of violence against her is her behaviour within the bosom of the family. Woman is no longer seen as the mistress of the household, the mother of the children, the queen of the family sharing the throne with king man. Woman is rather seen as the creature who is increasingly assertive, finds men wholly unsatisfactory most of the time, takes the initiative in divorce regardless of the well-being of her children, is a single mother because she wishes to remain one, takes on one lover after the other when she separates from her husband, adopts a step-father for her children in place of the natural, blood parent, proclaims mastery over her body instead of considering herself an instrument of nature; in short, is less worthy of respect than she was even two generations ago. These considerations are not the result of any kind of logical analysis, for men who sexually molest women are hardly capable of using logic: they follow their blind, perverted instinct. But they are part of the overall subconscious of even the healthy male, let alone the sick one.

Statistics are not available to show how many men who sexually molest or rape women come from broken homes. The sophistication of our computer techniques that would easily allow this item of information to be determined has not been applied to collating data that might show the causal connection between divorce and sexual crime in such stark form. Perhaps those who govern us are not interested in the information or at least in ascertaining whether there is anything in the point. Moralists tend to put their case too dogmatically and often in a manner which is verbally violent and extreme and as such receives less attention than it probably deserves.

But, as already noted, I am not too concerned about the existence of statistics to prove the point, for I rely on the probability principle. The probability is that insofar as divorce causes broken homes and affects the psychological make-up of the children, it may cause them to turn to crime because they have become unbalanced. There is no reason why they should not also turn to sexual crime.

Finally, I would like to say, just as unequivocally, that I do not share the view of those – see, for example, Dr Masud Hoghughi in *Break-up*,[1] – who maintain that people who divorce are likely to be of greater benefit to society than those who do not, essentially on the principle that they are displaying an ability to conduct themselves according to their own wishes rather than with the more or less spurious moral tenets of the society in which they live. I challenge this view, not because I am concerned about the fact that their self-assertiveness is contrary to society's need to have individuals who conform. Quite the reverse, in fact, for I am strongly in favour of the individual who is prepared to pit himself against society out of belief in the wisdom of whatever cause he may be supporting at the particular moment in time.

I do so on exactly opposite grounds to those of Dr Hoghughi, namely that I do not recognize that the marital relationship is, as he puts it, 'for enjoyment', anymore than it is acceptable to argue that it is '. . . a catalyst or precursor to wider self-assertive tendencies in society'. We must surely look upon marriage as something much more fundamental which is, at least the moment when children appear on the scene, quite removed from the enjoyment aims of the parents and is in fact the performance of a duty to the children, to society and, ultimately, to oneself. It is hard not to come to the conclusion, naturally ordered, that when people marry and have children, the spouses are robbed of their freedom and made instruments of the life urge.

This concept that the parties are really abandoning their freedom when they marry, and particularly when children arrive, has a long history. It was set out quite clearly by the fathers of the Roman Catholic Church, but they might be said to have had a vested interest. On the other hand, nobody could accuse Montaigne of having any particular vested interest. As he said in his *Essays*:[2] 'A man ought wisely to husband his liberty but after he hath once submitted into bondage, he is to stick unto it by the laws of common duty or at least enforce himself to keep them.' Nor can we accuse H. G. Wells, a libertine essentially, of having any vested interest either. In *An Englishman Looks at the World*,[3] in the chapter headed 'Divorce', he makes the following points:

Divorce is a change in the marriage law. Divorce is not one of those things that stand alone and neither divorce law nor the general principles of divorce are to be discussed without a reference to antecedent arrangements. On page 208 he states:

> There is certainly a very strong and logical case to be made out for a marriage bond that is indissoluble even by death. It banishes step-parents from the world. It confers a dignity of

> tragic inevitability upon the association of husband and wife and makes a love approach the gravest, most momentous thing in life. It banishes for ever any dream of escape from the presence and service of either party or of any separation from the children of the union. It affords no alternative to 'making the best of it' for either husband or wife; they have taken a step as irrevocable as suicide.

He then goes on to argue that the maintenance of a marriage that is indissoluble and that precludes the survivor from remarriage and that gives neither party any external refuge from the misbehaviour of the other, whilst making the children the absolute property of their parents until they grow up, would cause no very general unhappiness. Indeed, according to him, the very rigidity, the entire absence of any way out, would oblige innumerable people to accommodate themselves to its condition and make a working success of unions that, under laxer conditions, would be almost certain to be dissolved.

As he puts it, 'a few more crimes of desperation perhaps might occur' which, however, would have to be balanced out against an almost universal effort to achieve contentment and reconciliation. There might be more murders by jealous husbands or by jealous wives and maybe traffic in poison would go up; but the impossibility of any remarriage would operate to restrain the impatient.

From this he goes on to argue that if marriage is not to be indissoluble, then it should be dissoluble at will and mentions in support Bernard Shaw, though considering that Shaw's view of marriage, namely that marriage should be terminable at the instance of either party, would be no marriage at all but merely an encounter.

As Wells says on page 212: 'I believe in the family as the justification of marriage. Marriage to me is no mystical and eternal union but a practical affair to be judged as all practical things are judged – by its returns in happiness and human welfare. And directly we pass from the mists and glamours of amorous passion to the warm realities of the nursery, we pass into a new system of considerations altogether.' He then goes on to review what happens when the children come along:

they have the strongest claim against both their parents for love, shelter and upbringing and this both the legislator and the State should acknowledge because they have the strongest reasons for seeing that these things exist, even at the price of considerable vexation, boredom or indignity to the spouses.

He claims that, deep down, most parents have great stores of pride, interest, natural sympathy and passionate love and devotion for their children and this should be harnessed in marriage rather than be scattered on divorce. On page 215 he makes a fundamental point: 'Divorce as it exists at present is not a readjustment but a revenge: it is the nasty exposure of a private wrong.'

Even in the case of insanity, he adopts the same strict position on the basis that '. . . so far as insanity goes, I perceive that the cruelty of the law would but endorse the cruelty of nature. But I do not like men to endorse the cruelty of nature'.

He goes on to criticize the concept of taking divorce through the courts on the basis that the emotional breach of the marriage bond is as private an affair as its consummation and that it is unjust to have personal feelings thrashed out in a court room. It is true that George Bernard Shaw was of the opinion that '. . . divorce in fact is not the destruction of marriage but the first condition of its maintenance', but he was to all intents and purposes an eccentric and at the end of the day one is bound to be suspicious of how great his knowledge of women was.

There are, of course, others who have looked upon divorce as a policy of insurance and, on the basis that marriage is an experiment, have adopted divorce as the insurance that will cater for the situation where the marriage fails. Even Nancy Mitford is on record as saying that '. . . women as well as men ought to have a great many love affairs before they marry as the most critical moment in a marriage is a falling off of physical love which is bound to occur sooner or later and only an experienced woman can know how to cope with this. If not properly dealt with, the marriage is bound to go on the rocks.'

These considerations show on the one hand the importance that everybody attaches to marriage and, on the other, the logical tenability of the indissoluble theory of marriage. At the same time, it should be recorded that H.G. Wells was quite pessimistic about this situation generally. In the book just quoted above, at page 3, he was already making the observation 'we have fallen behind in the quality of our manhood', a point which is very much part of the agenda in this discussion.

In fact, Wells' view as to the standing of this country and, to some extent, its moral fibre, is endorsed at page 68 where he makes the following statement:

> It is almost a national boast that we muddle through our troubles and I suppose it is true and to our credit that by virtue of a certain kindliness of temper, a humorous willingness to make the best of things and an entirely amiable forgetfulness, we do come out of pressures and extremities that would smash a harder, more brittle people, only a little chipped and damaged. And it is quite conceivable that our country will in a measure survive the enormous stresses of labour adjustment that are now upon us, even if it never rises to any heroic struggle against these difficulties. But it may survive as a lesser country, as an impoverished and second-rate country.

I cannot help sharing his pessimism. We have indeed become a second-rate country. It is possible that the reason is that we have abandoned our moral view of the family as a unit, just as it could be argued that it is the other way round, namely that because of the high rate of divorce we are no longer a first-rate country.

Both are over-simplifications; but the fact of our fall from prestige as a nation and the attainment of the second highest divorce rate in the Western world are not mere coincidences: there must be a causal nexus between the two. There is no doubt that remarriage is on the increase proportionately almost with the increase in the divorce rate. It has been calculated in the UK that during the age period between 20 and 24 years, the likelihood that a divorced woman may remarry is more than twice as great as the chance that a single woman would marry in the first place. This likelihood increases with the passage of time so that, at older ages, the differences are even more in favour of divorced women remarrying.

There is thus created a vicious circle. Except in those limited number of cases where remarriage does in fact work, what is established is a self-perpetuation of unhappiness and contempt by woman for man. Incidentally, we should mention that a comparison has been made with widows and this shows that in the age group 25 to 29, widows are more likely to remarry than single women are likely to marry originally, although widows are less likely to remarry than divorcees are. In the United States the figures are over one million divorces each year. The probability in the US that the first marriage will end in divorce is about 1 in 2, and somewhat higher in remarriages.

Studies show that separations are more frequent during the first year of marriage than any other. The length of marriage to divorce is longer in first marriages than in remarriages and that is obvious: once you remarry you know the ropes and you get out of it more quickly, as already observed. There appears to be an inherent attempt to attain perfection in the relationship relying on the expectation that one's performance will improve each time. As Doctor Johnson put it, remarriage is 'a triumph of hope over experience'. But it is difficult to know at which point to stop. Where does the process of acquisition of experience and perfection reach fulfilment? On the third remarriage? Can it be conclusively presumed that at the fifth remarriage one is experienced?

As regards mediation, it is hard to be impressed, save negatively, by the latest developments. Although it is true that the mediators have to ask whether there is any change of the differences between the parties being capable of reconciliation, it is the practice to ask the question solely for the sake of the record, and then to pass on to other things. The other things are the arrangements as to finance and children. Quite clearly, the purpose of the mediation process is to endeavour to eliminate some of the bitterness existing between the parties and trying to convince them to come to a conclusion on which they can both agree as concerns such matters. The principle is that if the parties agree a solution they are more likely to honour it than if it were imposed upon them by the court. To achieve this, they may now even get Legal Aid

(Family Law Act 1996, Part III).

This is all good stuff, but it has got nothing to do with the indissolubility of the marriage and that is why, having mentioned the matter for the sake of the record, we need make no further reference to it. Equally negatively, the Family Law Act 1996, is a piece of legislation described by at least one lawyer as aimless, useless and tattered; 'family law reform now having entered a directionless phase', especially since the Lord Chancellor stated recently (July 1999) that he would postpone indefinitely the Introduction of Part II of the Act, dealing with marital breakdown.

NOTES

1. London, McDonald & Co., 1989.
2. In the John Florio translation of 1580.
3. Cassell, London, 1914 pp. 207-217.

8

The one-parent family

The choice of words for this chapter is made for the sake of simplicity of understanding. The phrase is in very common use and, as the figures quoted already show, it reflects a factual situation, namely, that there were 1.8 million single parents in the UK in 1998. According to the Government's *General Household Survey*, published in March 2000, one in four families in Britain is now headed by a single parent, with nine out of every 100 families headed by a mother who has never married and who has no steady partner. This means that the proportion of one-parent families has increased from 8% in 1971 to 25% in 1999, and that the number of 'lone' families have more than tripled – from 7% in 1971 to 23% in 1999.

In response, as published in the *Daily Mail*, Hugh McKinney of the National Family Campaign was quoted as saying: 'This is what happens when you pursue policies designed to discriminate in favour of single parents. Until the Government starts recognizing marriage again through the tax and benefit systems, these figures will continue increasing, to the detriment of countless children and future generations.'

The expression 'one parent' originated in what is known as

The Finer Report (1974) published by HMSO, London, in two volumes; it stated that it was a Report of the Committee on One-parent Families.[1] The Report defined a one-parent family as:

'A mother or a father living without a spouse (and not cohabiting) with his or her never-married dependant child or children aged either 16 or from 16 to (under) 19 and undertaking full-time education.'

The expression has been used consistently by the Department of Social Security ever since and previously by its predecessor, the Department of Health and Social Security. There is in fact no statutory authority for it as such, and like many other things that happen in the United Kingdom, its use has been accepted, unchallenged, and allowed to go by default. In my view, the heading is a clear misnomer because there is no such thing as a one-parent family if, by that expression, we mean, as present-day British society does, that a woman who is unmarried has determined to have and keep a child. It seems that, theoretically at least, a family is the union of a man and a woman, with their children. The noun cannot be used to describe and, above all, dignify alternative situations. Allow me to be more specific.

As a matter both of theory and practice, bearing in mind that, in most situations, a young child will be almost inevitably in practice, if not in law, in the custody as well as in all likelihood, the care and control of its mother, there are only the following situations where a woman, who is unmarried, can consider that, with her child, she forms a family:

1) The woman gets pregnant by accident whilst unmarried, has the child and does not marry its father.

2) The woman gets pregnant by choice and decides not to get married.

3) The woman is divorced.

4) The woman was married, but the father died.

In all these situations society has adopted the use of the simple expression – one-parent or single-parent family. That is a convenient elliptical form to describe differing situations, as demonstrated above.

The likelihood of this kind of family having any beneficial effect upon the children is not very great because, in every situation except the last one, that is to say except for widows, the child is deprived, as from birth, of the second parent. It is interesting to note that it is almost a universal trait in human beings, that certain organs are duplicated, almost as though they were made to complement each other in the same way as man and woman are. For example, most of us at birth, in the normal course of events, have two eyes, arms, legs, gonads, Bartholin glands, Fallopian tubes, lungs, halves of brain, ears, nostrils, rows of teeth, kidneys. Medical scientists no doubt will be able to give us other examples. One should note, as well, that until recently, it was always assumed that a child was to have, and be brought up by, two parents.

It is a challenge to nature to consider that children can make do successfully with one parent. For this reason, I take the view that the expression one-parent or single-parent family is unfortunate. I cannot think of a better one to replace it, but I feel compelled to underline its inappropriateness. Going back to the four situations described above, however, in the first instance, where a woman becomes pregnant by accident and does not get married to the child's father, we have a perpetuation of something that has been with us since the dawn of history. We are quite accustomed to dealing with the situation, really: either the grandparents take over, or the woman marries someone else, or she copes as best she can. Whilst it may be unfortunate that the rate of illegitimacy continues to rise, almost in inverse proportion to the spread of reliable contraception, we must accept this as one of the sad facts of life.

Equally sad, is the situation where the mother is widowed, particularly if this happens at an early age. Again, society has learnt how to cope with this type of situation, the remedies not being too different from those applicable to the first situation.

Situations 2 and 3, however, are less amenable, namely where a woman decides to become a mother and makes a conscious decision not to marry either the father or anyone else, and where there is divorce and the woman has to bring up the child on her own. In the first case, we are back to the concept of moral consumerism. I want a child, I shall have a child, so runs the argument: I do not want a man, I do not need a man, so continues the argument. The woman does not stop to consider the needs of the child and fails completely to ask the question whether the child itself may need a father.

This divorcing of procreation from continued care for the rest of the child's life, or at least until its maturity is, in a very strange sense, almost a sadder feature of our British society than divorce itself. One may sympathize with the inability of a mother to continue to put up with a husband, who may be uncaring or violent, sexually deficient, a bad father and so on; but it says a lot more for the depths to which woman's appreciation of, and respect for, man has fallen that she can actually make a policy decision to be fertilized without the expectation of continued companionship. What this means, surely, as previously noted, is that the role of the father has now degraded so substantially that he will soon become redundant.

This is not such a far-fetched hypothesis as the reader might consider at first sight. After all, in his relationship with woman, man has, until recently, performed essentially three functions:

a) he has been the breadwinner
b) he has been the protector of the family
c) he has contributed to procreation

If we carefully consider these three roles, we find the following facts:

a) the role of the man as breadwinner has reduced substantially. Women very often earn as much bread for the family as men and, in some situations, the mother is the real bread-winner.

b) the protection that a man can afford his wife and family has also dwindled. He can no longer go about beating up those who may wish to cause him or his family injury, he cannot use offensive or even defensive weapons, he no longer stands in front of his family with a spear in his hand, a picture of pride and masculinity, in the same way as the gander stands in front of his flock hissing at the wolf that is endeavouring to attack it. The State has taken over or, perhaps more correctly, has purported to take over, man's function as protector of his family.

c) We all know of the spread of Aids and we are all, each in our own way, fully aware of the divorcing of the sexual from the procreative function brought about by reliable contraception. Within this context, one does not find at all surprising the changes, developments and refinements in female sexuality, the spread of pornography and the profitable business in the sale of sexual aids. Man appears to have fulfilled his historical function.

Leaving aside the more philosophical aspect of the consequences (or causes) in the rise of single-parent units, it is a fact which any teacher of experience can confirm that the scholastic attainments of children, especially under sixteen years of age, who come from such a unit, are very much lower than those of their schoolfriends from stable homes and two parents. This consequence, which is potentially serious for society as a whole and certainly damaging for the individual, is discounted by those women who believe, for whatever reason, that they are better off without a man. For all we know, they may be right about their own well-being; but what of their children's?

Here, too, there are major inconsistencies in woman's psyche, for at the very moment when civilization enables her to be freed from the servitude of procreating, some women nevertheless wish to give birth to fatherless offspring. At this point, let us note the fact that the sexual act is of no concern to the community until a child is born; but the birth of a child is, in fact, a social act. As Havelock Ellis put it, it is not what goes on in the womb that counts but what comes out of it, since the community is invited to receive a new citizen; accordingly, it is invited to demand that that particular citizen shall be worthy of a place in its midst and that he/she shall be properly introduced by a responsible father and a responsible mother. He quotes Ellen Key as saying that the whole of sexual morality revolved around the child.

It is a pity, for our own purposes, that Ellis does not take this point to its logical conclusion because he does not consider at all what the effect of divorce is on the children, save in an aside on page 468 where he says: 'It is possible – that is a question which society will have to consider – that a woman should be paid for being a mother on the ground that she is rearing new citizens for the State.'

It is hard to resist the temptation of quoting from Ellis once more, and hopefully for the last time. In this context he cites[2] *again* Ellen Key as stating that '. . . although there may be a few exceptional cases in which women may withdraw themselves from motherhood for the sake of the other demands of their personality', the fact nevertheless remains that 'as a general rule, the woman who refuses motherhood in order to serve humanity, is like a soldier who prepares himself on the eve of battle for the forthcoming struggle by opening his veins', which is very poetic, but hardly constructive.

NOTES

1. Commissioned on 6 November 1969 and presented to Parliament in July 1974 by the then Secretary of State for Social Services, Barbara Castle, a childless spinster.
2. *op cit*, p. 587.

9

Why no divorce?

Whilst one may have great personal sympathy for those whose marriages are shaky, and much more for those whose marriages collapse, from the standpoint of principle and of the protection of society as a whole, the well-being of the individual is almost totally irrelevant because the best interests of the majority of the members of society are paramount.

Judged by this yardstick, divorce is an open admission of failure. This is not to say that those who remain married, even though unhappy, may not themselves also be failures. But there is an element of hypocrisy in every kind of social order and, at least as far as they are concerned, by remaining together they refrain from acknowledging openly that they have not succeeded. The divorcee, however, has no qualms about admitting his mistakes. In an almost Catholic manner, he/she feels the cathartic effect of confessing to the whole world the truth about his/her private life. The more people so openly acknowledge their failures, the more there is a lemming-like tendency to throw oneself over the cliff of one's psychological sanity. It is as though there were some kind of force that impelled the divorcee to acknowledge failure, whilst at the same time proclaiming to the world that the next round would be a success. What is worse, in so many ways, is that this failure is endorsed by legal and social recognition.

In the experience of this writer, this combination of psychological self-destruction and naïve optimism characterizes most divorcees. It is as though by proclaiming to the world that the next time round they will make a better job of it, they will have compensated for their initial mistake. For mistake it undoubtedly was. As discussed earlier, the failure, for whatever reason, occurred; and must in most cases, particularly in the twenty-first century, be laid at the door of the individuals concerned. I say 'particularly in the twenty-first century' because I firmly believe that in an age of comparative or at least apparent sexual enlightenment, when the means of knowledge and the technology that should assist us in making a success of our personal relationships are greater than at any previous time in history, it is inconceivable that the individual can escape responsibility for errors of judgement. Because of his mistakes, the divorcee interferes with the family set-up. It is this interference that we must now examine in some detail.

Let us start from the premise that anything which derogates from the principle and, consequently, the strength of the family as a social and psychological unit, is objectionable and is to be avoided. I readily accept that some of my conclusions would have to be completely different if I proceeded from other premises such as, for instance, that the family no longer has a contribution to make to society and to the individual and that everything should be governed and inspired by the community and the State.

I reject these latter approaches and wish to maintain that at present there is still no unit, and no concept, which can replace the family. I readily concede that mine may be in part an emotional reaction, at least as far as the issue of the family is concerned; I am reassured, however, by two considerations.

The first one is that I am not alone in stressing the strength of and need for the family unit. Having argued for the family, I logically argue in favour of marriage, and indissoluble marriage, at that. As Westermarck put it, 'marriage is rooted in family rather than family in marriage'.

The second reassuring consideration is that it cannot be

mere coincidence that the breakdown of the family encouraged by a liberalization of sexual conduct and endorsed by divorce on demand, coincides with what I can only term a very unhappy period in our moral and social history.

As already observed, the breakdown of the family is the principal cause of most of the evils of contemporary society. To choose but one of them, namely the ever-increasing numbers of rape, committed on elderly or infirm women, one is right to ask rhetorically how likely it is that the youngster brought up by a loving mother, loved and respected by his father, with or without siblings, in a permanent, stable and happy home, would commit rape on an elderly, or indeed, on any other woman. The reader should consider the probability of this occurrence.

Psychiatrists will tell us that it is possible, no doubt. Of course, it is possible: as Euripides said, it is possible that what we consider death is really life and what we value as life, is no more than death. Anything is possible save to keep alive when your time has come. But it is highly improbable.

Family, like marriage, is most important. Because it normally gives rise to children it is part of the intimate structure of society and, whilst theoretically it is an institution concerned with sex, it is much more than that. It ensures that the child has the benefit of both parents. It shows him what love between man and woman is about. It provides a home, a refuge, stability, continuity, certainty and guidance. It is almost a pre-human institution, which ensures the perpetuation of the species, above all because, as Bertrand Russell has correctly observed,[1] it preserves the habit of having children.

The reader will by now be fully aware of this writer's fundamental concern about the children. It is they, in particular, who suffer when the family is broken up. It is they, in particular, who gain by the unity and affection of the parents which provides them with safety and gives them the right outlook on life. It is in the family that they can see how their parents cooperate, how affection and companionship prevail over boredom and individual leanings, how sexuality is reconciled with sociability and restored from boredom. That feminism is contributing to its break-up is surely a matter of considerable regret. What feminists fail to see is that it is only the family which protects individuality and provides variety: the moment it is broken up, we shall all be swallowed up in the uniformity of a state-governed society. It is odd to observe that feminists who campaign for the emancipation and the individuality of woman will, in fact, end up by making woman more of a slave to the State than she ever was to man.

Thus, anything which interferes with the family as a unit is not only morally wrong and practically dangerous, but is also contrary to reason.

Divorce, therefore, is a wholly unsatisfactory concept. It may be useful, at this stage, if I summarized the reasons for making such an assertion:

[1] There is no doubt that if marriage were indissoluble and if its indissolubility were suitably advertised and explained to youngsters at an early age, and glorified in the same manner as some brands of jeans, shampoos or cars are, the number of unhappy marriages would reduce. I am not blind to the fact that no system on earth could ever eliminate unhappiness in personal relationships, but, as has been consistently argued, this is not a field where the happiness of the spouses takes precedence. It is the well-being of the children which is fundamental and, as far as that well-being is concerned, an indissoluble marriage is more beneficial than a 'happy' divorce.

When we know that we enter into a relationship for ever, not only are we much more careful and thoughtful about its inception, but we make the best of situations which could be termed a bad job in order to force the relationship to work, simply because there is no choice. It is choice that creates dissatisfaction and tension. A person with poor vision cannot see that the grass is greener on the other side of the fence.

[2] The second reason is that the alternative to indissoluble marriage can only be, both practically and logically, divorce at will. If we have divorce at will, we have to consider as inevitable two consequences namely, (a) that the family disappears and (b) that there is really no point in getting married in the first place.

If society considers either that the family is needed or that marriage is, (I fail to see how the two can be separated but our

Western culture is trying very hard to achieve that result), then I would suggest, as a matter of common sense, that free divorce is no answer to anybody's problems. In this situation, the reverse of what I have said at (1) applies, namely that the moment people know that if their relationship is unsatisfactory they can divorce, they will not commit to ensuring its success, or give the same care and attention that they would if they thought that they were going to be joined for the rest of their lives.

[3] One might be forgiven for being overawed by the fact that so many people divorce. Personally, I think the physical possibility and frequency of human conduct does not provide its moral justification. It is, of course, true that the sexual revolution, so called, is based upon self-fulfilment and relies on the principle that eventually we shall have wealth without having to work for it, sexual freedom without marital problems, and self-absorption without loss to the community. But these promises are not borne out by the facts and there seems to be a general consensus of opinion that many who divorce regret the step they take within an average of two to three years after the decree absolute.

Whether this happens because they draw comparisons with their former spouses or whether because the second honeymoon, like the first, is soon over, is a little difficult to say. It may well be that a contributory factor is that deep down in their psyche they were not really convinced that they should get divorced in the first place. As A. Alvarez has so sensibly stated in *Life after Marriage*:[2]

> Neither a sexual revolution nor enlightened legislation can eliminate overnight more than a thousand years of divorce taboo. It lives on like a ghost, chilly and half perceived, generating a kind of moral shudder even in those to whom religion no longer means much and society does not accuse. Pride, or the super ego, takes over where the Church and community leave off and no amount of acceptance of understanding or social indifference lessens the sense of personal failure.

Nor should anyone be impressed, save negatively, by the

speed at which, as a society, we have changed our attitudes towards divorce. Indeed, the mere fact that things have changed so quickly is reassuring in a sense, for it shows how quickly things could be changed back. It is not only a question of psychology. One can be perfectly consistent and say that no marriage should ever come to an end, except in the case of death of either or both spouses. This concept of the indissolubility of marriage is not merely religious; it is essentially practical, is in accord with nature and has as much logical justification as divorce may have; especially when there are children, the indissoluble nature of the marriage becomes much more readily acceptable. This view has been expressed many times already and I shall refrain from re-stating its reasons and details.

According to Augustus Strindberg in his preface to *Getting Married* written in 1884, marriage 'so frail and so full of stumbling blocks' only holds together because the partners have one interest in common, the thing for which nature has always intended marriage, namely the children. Carl Jung himself made the same point in *Marriage as a Psychological Relationship*, published in 1925. According to him, '. . . normal sex life as a shared experience with apparently similar aims further strengthens the feeling of unity and identity . . . . The individual will for self-possession is broken: . . .'.

It seems to me that both George Bernard Shaw and the others who have looked upon marriage as an experimental phase, completely miss the point. You can experiment and, indeed, you should, before you get married, but not after. The state of marriage is not made for experimentation but for permanence. Admittedly, it is wishful thinking to believe that marriage is going to be a bed of roses. As Carl Jung put it, 'seldom or never does a marriage develop into an individual relationship smoothly and without crises. There is no birth of consciousness without pain'. What happens nowadays, is that as soon as a little pin-prick is felt, the parties are off to the divorce court.

4 But it is not merely a matter of suffering or of disappointed expectations. This is not a situation where the individual well-being or happiness or hopes have any true

significance. Marriage is a social and political fact and the freedom and happiness of the individuals must take second place to considerations of an entirely different nature. In *Sexual Behavior in Society*[3] Alex Comfort makes the point that '... the biological argument for monogamy is largely dependent upon the existence of children; .... It is clear that the stability or otherwise of the home in which childhood is passed, is probably the most important single factor in character structure. Changes of parent and breaches of parental harmony have far-reaching effects on the child. It is therefore true, without reference either to the Church or to the State, that from the point at which marriage is fertile, it is indissoluble to the extent that its dissolution may have harmful social effects'. The State has an interest, both in the maintenance of the marriage and in its success, particularly where there are children. This is the reason why a line needs to be drawn between marriages that are 'infertile', for whatever reason, and marriages where there are children. I am not alone in this view.

Writing in 1948, in *Divorce Won't Help*,[4] Edmund Bergler makes the following fundamental point:

> It is quite conceivable that couples of future generations will decide to have children only after a few years of marriage, when they are already reasonably sure that their marriage is a stable one. At some time in the future, it will be commonplace that having children involves a voluntarily accepted obligation on the part of two people to make their marriage a stable one and by this is meant first, that there will be no divorce and second, that the conflicts of the parents would not reach such proportion as to endanger the psychic health of the children.

Put differently, the parties would have to reconsider their attitude to each other, even where there is a psychological imbalance. In order to achieve this, we should have to educate woman, above all, to the importance of her role as mother because in almost every normal marriage, its fate is decided mainly by the wife and not by the husband. It is a myth that the husband is in control.

As Pascal put it, the he-man is not the glory and shame of

the universe. On the basis that men are no mystery to women and that there is not a psychology of marriage simply because a woman intuitively does not take man too seriously, I think it is right that women should be reminded of their task. In this context, it is worth recalling Kipling: 'The silliest woman can manage a clever man but it needs a very clever woman to manage a fool.' It is common knowledge that every woman manages her husband, who is often a fool.

5 Nor should the benefit of the continuity in parental control over children be forgotten. The rosy suggestions made by some as regards the advantages of children being reared, in our enlightened society, by the community and not by the parents, leave one quite cold. In fact, I personally find the notion abhorrent and consider it totally at variance with my understanding of child psychology in our pattern of culture, whilst I would not deny that it might be appropriate to some other system.

6 A further striking consideration is that it appears to be true that human beings seldom change during the course of their lifetime. We remain basically the same. If this is right, we learn nothing from our experiences also because, as Oscar Wilde put it, 'experience is the name everyone gives to his mistakes'. We keep making mistakes and it is the sum total of our mistakes that represents the sum total of our experience. Terman and colleagues[5] come down very heavily on the side of the theory that one of the greatest dangers to marriage is the persistent morose temperament of one or both of the spouses.

This finding was made in 1938. Perhaps it is fair to say that people appear to be less happy now than they used to be. We have all become more introverted, more selfish, less forgiving, and less inclined to smile at others and above all, at ourselves. We are surrounded by ugliness, violence, greed, sexual perversion and abuse: it is difficult to develop a happy temperament against this kind of background. On this basis, it is hardly surprising to find that many more people divorce than previously for, if Terman and colleagues are right, they must all be less happy than they were, actually and temperamentally. Quite clearly, divorce at will is not providing greater happiness, rather more misery. On this particular aspect, the reader is referred to Oliver James's *Britain on the Couch*,[6] a brilliant analysis of the consequences of divorce.

[7] But there is a more fundamental reason why I take the view that divorce is a fallacy. It is clear beyond any shadow of a doubt that there is no greater factor to ensure the success of a marriage than the determination and the will of the spouses. It is solely that determination to make the marriage work that ensures that we overlook, or at least forget, the foibles, patterns of behaviour, attitudes and other unacceptable features of our spouse. We are forced to exercise that will and that determination either by religious beliefs or by our own personal conviction as to the binding nature of the marital relationship. But there would be no need for either will or determination to remain married if there were no divorce. Married we would all remain, happily or unhappily. I take the view that if an unhappy couple were forced to remain united, they would endeavour to make the best of a bad job.

[8] One aspect of the consequences of divorce which receives practically no attention whatsoever in all the divorce literature concerns the problems that divorce causes for the natural family of the divorcee, man or woman. By this I mean their parents, brothers and sisters. No mention is found, except very rarely, of the suffering caused to the parents of a divorcee. It is true that, if my analyses are correct, these are more likely to have been divorced themselves. But it must be acknowledged that not all parents of a divorced spouse are divorcees themselves and in any event, there is always a first time. There are perfectly respectable married couples who have been joined in matrimony for twenty, thirty or even more years, who are suddenly confronted with the sad fact that one or more of their children has decided to divorce. The shock, particularly in the case of parents who have known no other marriage themselves, is very great.

Nor should the brothers and sisters of divorcees be ignored: they, too, are important not only because they will be emotionally affected by the decision to divorce but also because the decision itself may strike a discordant note in their psyche, at least as regards the success of their own marriage.

They must wonder whether, in fact, they may not themselves wish to divorce or whether there may be something wrong with their siblings that has resulted in their being unable to cope with the pressures of marriage. If they are married themselves they will surely be concerned; if they are unmarried, they may be put on their guard as regards getting married.

The position of the co-respondent in divorce proceedings is also a factor. The co-respondent, man or woman, is affected by the divorce in more ways than one. He or she may be the actual cause of the break-up of the marriage or purely an accidental one; may be forced to consider whether a marriage or remarriage would perhaps 'sanctify' the adulterous relationship; or may decide, as the expression goes, 'to run for miles'. Co-respondents, in turn, have families. They have their own family if they are married, and their natural family, if they are not. In their case, too, the same considerations as have been made above concerning the parents, the brothers and sisters of the divorcee, apply.

Divorce does not solely affect the parties. If it did, we would be much less concerned. It damages the children, of course, but it has repercussions as far as all the other members of the family go and its ripples spread through society to much greater effect than the spouses themselves believe. The web of relationships and interferences which a divorce creates is much wider and tighter than might be generally perceived.

9 A further detrimental consequence of divorce is the impact that it has on housing, particularly at a time when there is a shortage. As a result of divorce, a couple, with or without children, who were living in one home, end up living in two. It is conceivable that remarriage may not necessarily cause this result in certain circumstances; but, broadly speaking, the number of divorces that occur, apart from being a source of income to psychiatrists and lawyers, is also of great interest to estate agents and builders, since it exponentially swells the demand for housing.

At a time when housing is in short supply, when the availability of homes in the rented sector has reduced dramatically in the lower ranges and where the rental of the better class of property, particularly in the major cities, has increased out of all proportion to real values, it seems odd that the State should not discourage the splitting up of couples, with its consequent effect on the demand for housing.

10 Furthermore, it should not be forgotten too easily that there are a number of totally different respects in which divorce is a waste of human resources, nor is it a coincidence that it is spreading at the same rate as that at which we squander the physical resources of our planet. In the first place, there is the enormous cost in time, effort, money, traumas and personality loss/adjustment to the parties themselves. If only a third of the time, for example, that is spent quarrelling, planning a new life, instructing lawyers and attending at their offices, going to court and so on – the list is endless, as anyone who has been through the process of divorce knows only too well – had been utilized in an endeavour to make a go of the marriage in the first place, a divorce might not even have come about.

11 There is also the consideration that the personality of the parties has to undergo great adjustment. Whichever way one looks at the matter, from the standpoint of the spouses, divorce is a disturbance, not only in the domestic and practical arrangements of the spouses' lives but, above all, of their personality. The parties who were relying upon marriage as a stable arrangement find themselves suddenly unsettled. Of course, if we were to regard marriage as merely the union of two people in love, then the disturbance would be slight, because the moment it becomes intolerable to their dignity that they should continue to live together, they would be only too pleased to part company. But it is not so easy as that because marriage, except to those who view life through the rose-tinted glasses of romanticism, is a status which not only creates legal consequences but which, in turn, is almost always in its inception some form of economic disturbance for both man and woman. For instance, work may have to be given up, or re-arranged, resources have to be pooled, efforts made. We all know how the withdrawal from marriage, even of one partner, causes all sorts of questions of financial adjustments and the problems of compensation for the

physical, mental and moral damage that occur are much greater than those appertaining to the division of furniture, effects, and may be, even of children.

There is no doubt as to the change in personality of the parties affected because the whole basis of life is altered when a marriage goes and we all know how, as soon as conditions of life change, personality itself is affected. The further problem to be faced is that in the process of change which is initiated by divorce there does not seem to be an end product as far as the personality of the spouses is concerned. There certainly is as far as the legal system goes, but since personality is in a constant state of flux and is always being adjusted in any event, divorce, of itself, is negative.

The matter does not end there, however, since it may well be that whatever victory we score in getting rid of our partner, we dearly pay for. The maladjustments following divorce have already been reviewed in an earlier chapter. One hardly needs reminding of the periods of impotence, inability to cope, depression, neurosis, frigidity, over-reaction, hypersensitivity, promiscuity, etc., etc. What needs to happen is a total reconstruction of the ego of the divorcee, in order that he/she might recover some form of psychological sanity and ensure that the bad habits which brought about the divorce are turned into good ones, that economic problems are overcome, that social relationships are sensibly reorganized.

Put differently, divorce necessitates a personal readjustment which is exceptionally difficult and which in most cases is almost impossible to achieve because if the divorcee had the emotional intellectual and economic stability necessary to achieve this restructuring of his personality in the first place, it is unlikely that he would have married that particular spouse, or, having married, that he would have failed to find a solution to the marital difficulties which brought the divorce about. It is only very few people who overcome the disrupting effect of divorce and who emerge from it purified, strengthened and better able to cope with similar types of problems; there is no doubt whatsoever that most people come out of a broken marriage with personalities which are badly in need of repair and which they may well find it exceptionally difficult to put right. In other words, divorce benefits only a select few in the same way as only a very limited number of remarriages emerge as successful.

To establish a system which brings about the huge number of divorces documented earlier for the sake of a few people only who might benefit from it, is exactly the same as supporting the indiscriminate spread of pornography and violence simply because there are a few people who may indirectly benefit from them. The conflict between acceptance and rejection of the divorcee's past on the one hand, and the need to come to terms with the reality of the present situation on the other, is enormous.

Those who acknowledge divorce as 'a useful and necessary social remedy' are fully aware of the difficulties just mentioned but they react to them by saying that the spirit can actually emerge enriched and encouraged from the breakdown of a marital relationship. It is almost saying that if bad food does not actually kill you, it will at least fatten you. The same people, however, do not pause and enquire what happened to strength of mind and purpose in the first place.

The terminology used is interesting. 'Divorce' comes from the Latin verb *divertere* which means to turn aside, to go in different ways or, as the dictionary puts it, to have a 'complete or radical separation of things formerly connected'. I think that the terminology of our subject-matter is as inaccurate as the concept itself. In the first instance, as any divorced spouse knows, the separation is never complete and in the psychological sense it is far from radical. It is certainly complete as far as the law is concerned; but only in that sense can it be supported. It cannot be radical: the parties have been accustomed to each other for a more or less long periods of time, and for millennia prior to the parting, their psyche has been used to the idea of a relationship between man and woman.

According to the term used, the parties have desired to go different ways, to find new routes. But that premise, too, is false because there is no certainty that a new route will either be found or be a better one. The parties do not know what obstacles will be found on the new path they have chosen to follow: pot-holes, obstacles, brigands?

It is a form of wishful thinking which highlights the fact that divorce is a most imperfect implement, as can be shown by the consideration that virtually every writer on divorce accepts that it would be better if divorce did not exist. Even such a sympathetic sociologist as Willard Waller in *The Old Love and the New*,[7] who dedicates much effort to analysing what awaits the divorcee, is quite conscious of the fact that it would be better if there were no divorce. The following extract makes clear his thinking:

> If we would do away with divorce, and the problem of readjustment connected with it, we must do away with unhappy marriage. Marriage is strongest when people know what is expected of them in it, and happiest when it is strongest.
>
> Every detail of every arrangement, with the responsibilities involved in every privilege, must be written on the walls of every schoolroom. Love cannot conquer all and sex is not enough to keep people together, especially if they do not agree as to the manner of its expression. Let us work out new matrimonial institutions and begin preparation for marriage with birth, for one way of making everybody happy – surely a worthy object – is to let everybody know what to expect . . . . .

The schools have a fundamental function to perform in re-educating society to a new view of marriage, since at present the lack of preparation for marriage is tragically inadequate. Society does not demand, and indeed does not even expect that anybody who gets married should be prepared for it. Anyone may marry provided he/she appears to fulfil the exceptionally meagre requirements of the law.

He may be scatterbrained, immature and maladjusted and may know nothing whatsoever about the responsibilities that marriage brings with it, just as he may be incapable of carrying a normal economic load: yet society assumes that marriage can be entered into by even the most poorly prepared. Whether this assumption follows the fact that society assumes that success in marriage will come naturally or whether it is because society does not care, is a little difficult to determine. I suggest that it is the latter, but am not sure: so often in our society great damage is caused not by wilful default but merely by lack of forethought.

12 Children could be taught that our present Calvinistic ethic of harder work for greater profit is not conducive to a happy marriage. Of late, our politicians have attached great importance to the profit motive, practically discounting leisure. It is a work ethic in which man is so engrossed that he can no longer see the wood for the trees. If, as now appears to be the case, women have the upper hand, it is obviously because men are not fit enough to have it themselves. The rise of woman since the beginning of the twentieth century is by no means an accident: it has coincided with the failure of men to adjust to change, a failure to realize that their mission in life was altering, a total lack of historical sense and perspective, at the same time as all that they set out to achieve was monetary success.

This attainment of success and economic status has resulted in man dedicating too much time to his work and too little time to his wife and family. If Diogenes were around in his barrel nowadays and were consulted by a married business tycoon, I suppose he ought to tell him to go back home immediately to make love to his wife rather than rush to the city to make money.

The resultant neglect of woman is hardly compensated by the fact that man has made a success of his career. It is a fact, as noted earlier, that, psychologically, no matter what anyone says, woman likes a strong man. Different women are attracted by varying shades or types of power: it may be physical strength, mental ability or sexual prowess, political success or the power of any kind of public recognition, the successful stewardship of industry, or the pure power of money. Whatever it may be, woman likes to be led although she wishes to be heard. Where she is not led, her claim to be able to exercise rights that although allowed to her by law are denied to her in practice, becomes paramount and irresistible and rises proportionately with her contempt for man.

This contempt is compounded by the fact that in a marriage it is normally the woman who sees what is going wrong long before the man does. In fact, some psychologists and social workers maintain that men seldom see that the marriage is not going as it should be, and that it comes as a great shock to them to find that woman suddenly leaves without warning. Women clearly have different sensitivities and are alert to different dangers and, within the marriage, are always on the look-out for signs of danger. In those situations where woman is given the opportunity of being loved, the marriage may survive. Otherwise it fails. If man is spending all his day pursuing money, he will inevitably neglect his wife.

13 A much under-played aspect of the consequences of divorce is the economic one. It is interesting that in our present-day society where money is considered a priority, the test of success, the pre-requisite of private and public recognition, the *non plus ultra* of human performance and attainment, we have the absurd position that only in rare circumstances does divorce benefit the spouses and the children in financial terms.

We have addressed the question of the great cost, both in monetary, psychological and effort terms, to the parties themselves, and consequent loss of productivity. But the matter does not stop there. Save in the somewhat exceptional circumstances where a divorcee remarries either above his or her station, or a person who enjoys much greater wealth and income than the former spouse, the standard of living of the divorcee will usually fall. The spouses who divorce may well have to support each other even after divorce. There may be children who need to be maintained. Where there was one home, two are created; where there was one meal, two have to be prepared; in all likelihood, it will cost more.

Many readers will have experience of the effect of a husband and wife pooling resources, whether it be by both going out to work when they can or by the wife scrimping and scraping, as the expression goes, on the housekeeping money to balance the family budget. The joint effort on the spouses does result in the ability to maintain and improve the household, gradually but steadily, so that at a certain point in time, once the children are gone or are self-sufficient, the spouses may – health permitting – enjoy the benefits of the efforts made through the years, of their hard work, of their savings, of what they gave up, in effect, to achieve a certain standard of living and a certain position in society.

Most of this collapses when a divorce comes about. There are lawyers' fees, there are expenses incidental to the sale and purchase of new homes, possible relocation of the children, maybe even boarding school for them if the finances allow. Any divorcee, unless wealthy or fortunate, will be able to confirm the drop in the standard of living after divorce. The economic impact may be great or small, depending, of course on circumstances; but there is no doubt that in the majority of the cases, it happens. It is interesting to observe that our desperate search for happiness causes us to discount even such an important factor as the economic one.

14 Another detrimental aspect of divorce is that indulging in it is not going to help anybody simply because quite a lot of people who get married are, in fact, neurotic. The point is made by Edmund Bergler in his book *Divorce Won't Help.*[8] According to him, quite a lot of people who get married will not be successful simply because of their own personality and neuroses. He puts it on the basis that the neurosis itself becomes the third party to the marital relationship and causes the divorce.

When the parties then remarry, clinically they are repeating their previous experiences. If, in fact, they are neurotic, then we should bear in mind that psychologically because of the existence of four parties to every marriage, namely, the spouses and their psyches, problems are compounded. The parties think that they are making their own decisions but these are predetermined by their psychological make-up.

Bergler makes the further point that neurotic people do not fall in love: all they do is to search for one another with uncanny regularity. As a matter of interest, my professional experience endorses this particular observation in its entirety. As far as those people who are neurotic are concerned, they assume that by changing the external factors they will be able to resolve their inner conflicts. Of course, one cannot generalize these remarks to all divorcees. Not all those who divorce are neurotics; not all marriages end in failure simply because the psyche of the parties is deficient. But it is true to say that one does not learn from experience in marital conflict for the simple reason that our emotional life is not governed by rational considerations; rather by unconscious feelings upon which experience has either no or a very limited effect. Sometimes, though not often, women change type, that is true. If initially they looked for a dominant man, after their first divorce they will look for a weak one; and vice versa. But that will not help them because the problem lies within themselves.

As far as Bergler is concerned, neurotics who marry are unconscious gluttons for punishment: they seek defeat, humiliation and failure. They are what he terms psychic-masochists.

15 According to Bergler, divorce is based on a number of illusions. The first illusion is that the next marriage will be more successful than the former one. People fail to realize that in the great majority of cases they arrive at divorce not by chance, but because they have unconsciously provoked the situation. It is true that it may be the chance conduct of a partner that precipitates the divorce (like a one-night stand, as the expression goes). However, every person has in his unconscious an apparatus enabling him to understand the unconscious of another person. This is a point that he derives direct from Freud: in the result, there is no change in the choice of a marriage partner.

The next illusion is to the effect that the woman may say 'I don't need a husband anyway', 'I'm better off without a husband'. Bergler considers that this is the result of fear and it stems from a stubborn refusal to acknowledge the defeats sustained in the battle of marriage. A further illusion is the belief that children will adapt to the new situation. This is not borne out by the facts. The children of happy marriages find that the wall of their parents' love for each other is impenetrable. There's no opening, there is no chance of replacing a rival: accordingly, the child accepts the inevitable and projects his wishes elsewhere, or modifies them. In other words, the child grows up because he accepts reality.

On the other hand, in an unhappy marriage the conflict between the parents offers the child some hope that he may be able to displace and supplant his rival, namely, the parent of the same sex; and divorce especially becomes a danger point as far as the child is concerned, because it causes it to develop a fixation with the prospect of increased conflict. Since the majority of children remain with the mother, the situation is even worse because they will develop an even stronger Oedipal attachment (the position would be exactly the reverse in the case of a girl).

Where there was a balanced situation before the divorce, the divorce causes it to precipitate. For the girl, divorce is the danger point of unconscious homosexuality; for the boy, of either homosexuality or hysteric mother attachment. Another illusion is the fact that our society preaches that monogamy is the result of puritanical teaching from which we should be emancipated. Monogamy is acquired in the nursery because, in a typical family in Western culture, the child is confronted with one father and one mother. It is true that every child passes through the phase in which it identifies with the parent of the same sex and wants to take the place of the parent of the opposite sex; of course, in a healthy situation he grows out of it. However, by being instilled with the idea of monogamy at an early age, he can no longer reject it on any moral, logical or even ideological ground. Accordingly, the child is predestined to become monogamous whether he likes it or not, so that when he remarries he has a psychological 'chip on his shoulder'.

We must never forget that the divorced individual, especially the man, soon after the divorce usually finds himself in the position of a castaway and, more importantly, of a failure. A failed husband, possibly a failed father, someone who could not make a go of a relationship. The divorcee finds that he has to face diverse and ill-defined troubles and is '... highly motivated towards developing defence mechanisms and compensations in conflict with himself, always present, sufficiently well that he can go on living effectively. The divorced woman must in most cases face also the problem of economic rehabilitation: she must learn to pay her own way'.[9]

On the problem of reorganizing his life, Willard Waller mentions (a) an attempt to cheapen sex, (b) promiscuity, (c) the finding of a real substitute, (d) the dispensing with sex altogether and replacing it with alcoholism, gambling, card-playing, social diversions, work, athletics, religion and art. He then has to cater for his wounded pride. Either he justifies his divorce by repudiating his mate (and then he has only got himself to blame because he chose the wrong one), or he takes the blame himself for the divorce and then he considers himself an even greater failure. Even if he thinks that it was six of one and half a dozen of the other, his judgement is still at fault because he could have chosen more carefully.

There is, thirdly, the question of the habits that are disturbed because, when a marriage goes, many little habits disappear that were part of it and cannot be restored quite so quickly, whether it be the time of cooking or the missing of the material comforts to which marriage had accustomed the spouse, for the husband a clean shirt, nice and ready; for the wife, a car or whatever. The woman has to consider earning her living and that is not easy, particularly for the older woman. It should also be remembered that all parties have to deal with the rebellion within themselves because conflicts do occur, particularly where, as is often the case, it took a long time to reach the divorce decision. There are a number of readjustments to be made.

16 One of the least carefully considered aspects of divorce is the effect it has on what Willard Waller calls the 'margin of heterosexuality'. He states:

> To modify the famous *bon mot* of another generation, it is divorce which is the touchstone of heterosexuality. One who is but weak in his preference for the other sex on account of undue attachment for someone in his own family, which partially precludes a love object of the opposite sex but does not preclude one of his own sex, is likely to be easily discouraged and to find a little joust in the lists of heterosexual love all that he is interested in attempting. Such a person may be clinched in the homosexual role by an unhappy marital experience. Others whose homosexual drives are latent will yet experience pronounced personality problems; it is submitted that such cases are much more numerous among divorced persons than is commonly said.

The results are not proportionate. Fewer women may turn to other women, because they wish to remarry for one reason or the other (mainly for economic reasons, particularly the older woman). Waller also makes the point that, although proof on a statistical basis is not available, the first few months after divorce seem to produce more suicides and, in general, resentment towards society.

17 A most important point to consider is the impact of the group upon the family. Society has relaxed its efforts to preserve the home and it has also ensured that the group takes a hand in actively splitting a married pair apart. It would appear that the group succeeds where the old love fails. Certainly, old love can linger on. Frequently, one marries the first person with whom one has a serious love affair and the fact that the love affair has culminated in the marriage shows that there was complete emotional involvement. This is particularly true where the parties, especially the woman, had not had much previous sexual experience. For example, a man may go on loving his former wife because if she was the first, she was also the one who had the opportunity to form his taste. I maintain, in any event, that there must be a biological intimacy which binds together people who have mated. Waller describes this bond as 'something which holds a woman to her ravisher or brings a man back to the woman who has often given him sex satisfaction. If a marriage has been reasonably satisfactory, reasonably peaceful, reasonably close over a reasonably long time, the wonder then is not that people should go on loving after it has been broken but that it could ever be broken'. In other words, the first love, the real love, never gets a rival.

Because of the dissociation of this impulse towards the former spouse, sometimes that love seems to grow stronger, at least in the sense that the emotional involvement continues: whether it be memories of events, or whatever, common anxieties concerning the children, or the fact that time mellows our pictures of the past, or that we hanker after our youth. That is the reason why sometimes people remarry the spouses they have divorced.

The existence of unrecognized conflicts in the mind of the

divorced person renders him or her liable to the peculiarly unfortunate phenomenon of love at first sight which is always pathological, partaking of the character of a compulsion; and which rarely turns out well. The past is permanent and whilst we may forget certain of our experiences, we do not cease to carry them with us. Whether experience is assimilated depends on acceptance of the experience by the ego; dissipation of the emotion connected with the experience; a more or less stable rearrangement of one's fundamental impulses; rearrangement in such a way that all aspects of past experience are utilized positively.

The basis of life is altered when a marriage goes, either gradually or suddenly, but it cannot be avoided, and there are so many changes that have to be faced, habits that have to be reorganized, memories that have to be erased, that those divorcing think it is a very difficult task to adjust. The reader will recall that broadly the same point is made by Edmund Bergler.[10]

18 One of the principal reasons proffered in support of divorce is that it allows the spouses to make a new life for themselves, especially if they remarry and the second marriage is successful.The difficulty divorced people have to come to terms with is that we are the product of our parents, of how we were brought up, of how we have lived, of our experience as youngsters; we are the effect of a number of causes over which, very often, we had, and continue to have, no control.

If, therefore, we made a mess of our first marriage (whether because we were not ready or fit for it, or too young, or uncommunicative, uncaring, or perhaps expected too much from the relationship, or emotionally immature, and so on), we will inevitably find the same difficulties second time around, unless we are exceptionally lucky.

The eternal fallibility of human nature is completely discounted by our divorce laws. Divorce is assumed as not only an appro[illegible] option for all those who have failed in one relationship, [illegible] and above all, a social tool. Just as the Roman[illegible]heir citizens food and games in the circus, so [illegible]s divorce and remarriage. The unquestioning[illegible] concept of divorce highlights a logical hiatus in the modern mind. The over-reaction to the strictures imposed upon women in past centuries is excessive. In a sense, there is a form of conceit here, by woman at least. The conceit, I think, stems from woman's confidence in herself and her ability to hold a family together. Since she always was stronger than man and quicker to adapt, she feels that even if she discards her spouse, she will find it easy to make new friends, come across another mate, create for herself a new chance ahead, establish a new life. She forgets that she remains married to her first husband, regardless of what the legal position is. The psychological tie, as we have observed, cannot be torn off as easily as the wrapper of a condom.

No effort is made to consider whether it is rational to divorce. After all, we must start from the common premise that divorce is a response to a stressful situation. The divorce decision may itself be an impulsive one; indeed, the more impulsive the decision to marry, the more likely to be impulsive is the decision to divorce. But, as I see it, rationality does not come into it at all. What divorce shows, and this is why I see it to be wholly fallacious, is that exasperated feminism is prevailing over discredited 'masculinism'. It shows that the war between the sexes is being won by women.

We tend to forget nowadays that the war of the sexes has always existed. It is overdramatized at times, and on other occasions it is played in a minor key: but it is still very much there. The boys bundle off together to the pub, the girls to their gossip. The getting together with one's own sex is an escape from the aggravation of the other's insensitivity. Man is clumsy, selfish, puerile, incapable of understanding, insensitive and rough; woman is aggravating, pedantic, moody, etc. There is nothing unusual in these differences which balanced human beings take for granted and have learnt to cope with.

But no matter how progressive woman becomes, the lurking feeling that the man is or can be an enemy is always there. Her make-up is said to be her 'warpaint' which is aimed at appeasement, but it is also a mark of aggression since woman is constantly on the warpath of feeling, she is on the warpath of showing how attractive she can be. That is probably the reason why no woman wishes to be watched by man whilst she is putting her make-up on, because she would then be revealing one of her secret weapons to her enemies.

This war of the sexes is kept under wraps in a happy marriage. There are skirmishes and sometimes even battles; but peace is made as often as war is declared and marital life continues, on the whole, unaffected by the underlying tensions. It is in divorce that the war breaks out and the guns are blaring on all fronts. The enmity, the bitterness, spite, aggravation, pettiness, and selfishness, all surface together. The dirty linen that was kept hidden is now washed in the public eye of the lawyers, the courts and the press; and that itself is an obscenity. Conduct that was acceptable – if not encouraged or even tolerated – when the parties were more or less on the same wavelength, is now thrown at the other spouse as wholly objectionable and as a reason for terminating the relationship. There is no doubt that the emancipation of woman has contributed to the difficulty in maintaining marriage as the kind of institution our grandfathers knew. It is not only a question of adaptation, in the sense that present-day woman no longer accepts that it is up to her to adapt to the husband, rather she expects the husband to adapt to her; but also of the greater variety of choice of partners available in today's world. The more progressive we become, the more difficult it seems for us to find happiness through life with a single partner. In those societies where marriages are decided by the parents, it is said that they can be quite happy marriages and the parties are not often tempted to stray from the path of fidelity.

It really depends on one's outlook on life and, above all, on the availability of alternatives. The difficulty that the spouses face nowadays is that there are so many alternatives open to them that the temptations become much more difficult to resist. It is easy to be virtuous and faithful to your spouse on a desert island. However, women themselves fail to see that if we equate marriage with a state of health, then, as others have said elsewhere, we must equate divorce with illness. But just as we judge the state of health of individuals by the number of times that they frequent their doctors or hospitals, so we are entitled to question the state of health of our society. Healthy people do not need doctors and happily married people do not need divorce. The provision of divorce is equated by some to the provisions of hospitals: but the difference, it seems, lies in the fact that people do not go out of their way to make themselves sick, whereas people actually take the trouble of embarking upon divorce. Here we find the state is just as much to blame as the individual. In the same way as the state provides social security benefits for those who are in need of economic assistance, so it provides freely-available divorce for those in need of emotional help. It does not stop for a moment and consider either why the unemployed came about in the first place, or why the emotions are disturbed.

It is clear that the state, when it comes to divorce, is merely endorsing the ruthless approach of the individual. I have to agree with Edmund Bergler[11] when he claims 'we are witnessing today the rearguard actions of a beaten army of masculine diehards. The shouting and the tumult are loud but the battle of the masculine prerogative has already been decided'. Some day the children of the diehards will smile condescendingly at their fathers for the futile way they hit their heads against the wall of emancipation.

My complaint, however, is that there is no logic whatsoever in comparing woman's right to equality, and her emancipation, to both of which she is clearly entitled, with her need to divorce. This need is brought about by her own ruthlessness in personal relations. Man, of course, shares in this ruthlessness, as we have already seen, for example, in the reaction towards the consequences of divorce on the children. Divorced parents take the view that unless the child is obviously maladjusted, he has not suffered from the divorce and they try hard to fool themselves that this is so. They do this for the sake of their own conscience, but they also do this because they are concerned primarily with themselves and only secondarily with their children. Nothing must stand in the path of their presumed happiness, self-expression, independence and progressiveness.

19 Formerly, couples who quarrelled nevertheless refrained from divorcing, even though they might have. They did so for a number of reasons. (a) For the sake of their children. This used to be the case as regards most unhappy marriages and there is no doubt whatsoever that there are sound practical, emotional and psychological reasons for the inaction of some unhappy couples. (b) For property considerations. These may still apply nowadays but, with the effective redistribution of landed estates, they are becoming less important. (c) In order not to hurt each other unduly. Maybe this was so at one time but, with the increasing emancipation of woman, her feelings towards her male counterpart have become less tender. (d) In order to avoid social prejudice to each other, but especially to the husband. Again, we are becoming less concerned about what society thinks. Ruthlessness governs us more than hyper-sensitivity; and in any event our approach to life, nowadays, is of a different kind. None of these considerations seems to have any great significance and certainly none should nowadays be put before our own happiness.

The determined assertion of woman's personality and rights has, however, resulted in her becoming full of contradictions, for she has been so busy copying and developing male attributes that she has lost sight of her own tendencies and has been quite unable to develop a special style. She may have acquired outward freedom but her inner feminity has not kept up with that development. As Edmund Bergler puts it:[12]

> '... every new movement shoots beyond the mark. Ridiculous exaggerations will be eradicated by mutual consent, simply out of inner necessity. This will entail the removal of "emancipation chips" from the shoulders of both sexes. What we see today are dissatisfied men and dissatisfied women. One cannot say that women were unprepared for their great journey into freedom: the propelling energy with which they have undertaken it, proves the opposite. The unprepared person was the average man. He's still confused and dumbfounded and fights back with anger, irony and constant reminders that women are at bottom sexual things.'

20 One of the reasons for divorce is the belief that we can change our destiny. Hence the thought that a different, better or new spouse will give us different and greater enjoyment, as a change of motor vehicle might. How often we may all of us have thought: 'If only ...'. Two little words, but so full of meaning and, in effect, so dangerous. If only my wife/ husband were like this or like that, felt or behaved towards me in a particular manner, could respond as I should wish to my innermost thoughts and desires, strike in the right vein the vibrant chords of my psyche etc etc. 'If only . . .' my spouse were truly my twin soul, the person of whom I had always dreamt when I was young, the fixed idea, the inchoate expression, the unclear dream on which we all, from time to time, focus in certain unutterable moments of passion.

It seems, however, that in most cases the problem lies in ourselves rather than in our spouses. It is not wrong to dream of magic and perfection in personal relations but to assume that reality will, in fact, correspond to our dreams is infantile. One spouse is very much like any other and it is wrong to build a philosophy of life around dreams when we should be working harder at making our reality more pleasant and, if not wholly satisfactory, at least acceptable. Of course, love is a wonderful thing; but lasting marriage requires many additional traits and feelings which no amount of rosy expectations of a relationship can bring about. Divorce simply will not help when our own psychological make-up is deficient. It may sound trite to say it but, remarkably in many cases, dogged determination to make a relationship work can sometimes achieve results beyond all expectations.

21 The feminist ethic loudly proclaims that women must free themselves of all fetters imposed by men; but when it comes to divorce, feminism seems quite meaningless because it is not only women who suffer in an unhappy marriage. There are countless men who are not quite as bad as they are made out to be by their wives, who suffer because of the way they are treated by them and who in fact are just as unhappy as a woman might be in similar circumstances. When it comes to unhappiness, there is no distinction whatsoever between the sexes. When it comes to the consequences of unhappiness, as we have seen, it appears that, overall, women fare better than men, in any event.

The family unit, the interest of society in the preservation of some kind of psychological sanity, and the children, are all factors of great significance and have to be considered in priority to the wishes of the partners. In particular, as regards the children, their future stability and well-being is paramount and for their sake the spouses may well have to be content with less than they longed for because, compared to the education, advancement and happiness of the children, firstly, as potential parents themselves and secondly, as members of an increasingly unsettled and unbalanced society, the dreams of happiness of the spouses pale into insignificance.

Those of us who practise in the divorce courts or who perform social work in this particular field know only too well how mean, embittered, resentful and vengeful warring spouses can be to each other. In my experience, they do not deserve the facilities and attention that society and the legal system dedicates to their bickering. The money the State pays out for the purpose of destroying one marriage in order to replace it with another which is just as likely to fail could much more profitably be employed in educating our youngsters in the art of marital or social relationships, or at least, devolved to charitable purposes.

Divorce is self-perpetuating and creates both an aura of acceptability, if not respectability, around marital break-ups as well as whole generations of people who are divorce-prone. Its very frequency shows that it is the wrong remedy for the very old difficulty of incompatibility between husband and wife. Although not enamoured of the powers of the State, as I have said several times already, I think that this is a situation in which the State should intervene and make it known that the good of the many takes precedence over the expected greater happiness of the individual. This is by no means a new point. It was made nearly ninety years ago, although in different form, by Havelock Ellis.[13]

Ellis accepted that spouses ought to be allowed to renounce their vows. In fact, having defined divorce by mutual consent as a natural goal, he goes on to qualify his permissiveness by adding the following statement: 'Provided, of course, that no rights of the parties themselves or of the children are injured, for it would seem to be logical that the exit from marriage should not be made more difficult than the entrance.' He also makes the further point that it must be accepted that if impediments are placed in the way of divorce, it is essential that impediments should also be placed in the way of marriage so as to diminish the need for divorce.

The trouble is that the divorce movement has conventionalized the ideal of marriage by making happiness its primary aim so that, inevitably, when people are unhappy, they should separate permanently. The divorce movement has concentrated attention on the erotic element as though that were not only a highly important element but also the actual sole content of marriage, and therein lies the fallacy, since marriage is a personal bond rather than a sexual one, the marriage partners constituting a unit.

From the late twentieth century, to the present, we have been looking at marital relationships through lenses distorted by our desperate need to give vent to our ever-increasing dissatisfaction with ourselves which is part and parcel of what I would term the present day cosmic restlessness and dissatisfaction. It is true that within this framework some men are proving absolutely useless, but this is a dangerous generalization. Even where man is living up to woman's expectations of him, there still are problems because she is unclear as to her true role and her requirements of life. Present-day woman appears to be under considerable pressure from her psyche, feminism, and the avowed need to gain money in order to assert her independence. Against this background, there exists in the soul of every woman a tug-of-war of feelings. The sufferers are, of course, the children.

At the same time as the rate of divorce increases, society actually encourages woman, by continued pronouncements and financial inducements, to go out to work; at a time when a considerable number of men are unemployed, women are asked by society to leave the home and effectively to deprive some of the unemployed of the possibility of work, to the detriment of their personal integrity and their dignity. The moment woman goes out to work, she has to find help to look after the children. The State encourages employers to provide creches and facilities for the women who are at work. All this appears to make little sense. One is bound to wonder whether it might not be easier if woman stayed at home looking after her own children in the first place.

22 In divorce, officialdom's chrism or, perversely, 'State blessing' is placed upon the break-up of the marriage and the spouses then have to try and cope psychologically and economically with two families, whereas there was only one previously. Efforts must be made to retain jobs and friends, to overcome the difficulty of being the odd one out at dinner parties, if invited, in re-establishing relations with the opposite sex or clarifying, defining and maybe even legalizing those with an existing partner and, above all, explaining the situation generally to the children. In particular, of explaining to them the existence of that partner as well, assuming, which is unlikely, that they did not know already.

Those who have been through divorce will know exactly what the picture is. The result is an enormous drain on the physical, psychic and economic resources of any person. It is all good work for psychiatrists and lawyers, of course, but it is all a nonsense if one stops and considers how many people unnecessarily earn a living out of human misery. There is almost something truly obscene about profiting from the weakness of fellow human beings. We should not ignore either the drain on the National Health Service. The doctor gets to know of marital problems long before the solicitor; and the State pays for his time, the tablets, the tonic, etc.

23 Only those who have never had anything to do with the legal aspects of divorce and custody of children can possibly maintain that divorce is a necessary and sensible process. Whilst the law prescribed that proof had to be provided of a matrimonial offence in order to obtain a divorce, the spouses went through a process of throwing mud at each other in the witness box, washing their dirty linen in public, providing prurient details of sexual behaviour which they had at least tolerated, if not actively encouraged and enjoyed when relationships were bearable, and which suddenly became repulsive to them. All this, to the delight of process-servers and enquiry agents as well as media people seeking titillation for their readers/viewers where, in effect, there was only stupidity and misery. The adversarial system of

the proceedings benefited them and the spouses' lawyers; but no-one else.

It must be admitted that things have improved now that, effectively, we have divorce on demand, since, as discussed earlier, it is no longer difficult for two human beings to show a judge that their marriage has 'irretrievably broken down', without expanding too much on the nature of their marital relationship. But the mud-slinging still occurs where monetary aspects have to be determined and, above all, when dealing with the custody of minors. The sadness of any kind of wardship proceeding can only be understood if experienced. Walking through the corridors of the Courts of Justice, wherever they may be in the country, one can always recognize instantly the parties who are involved in divorce proceedings. They huddle together, three or sometimes four at a time, almost like conspirators, and there is a marked sadness about their appearance and posture.

There is invariably a pettiness in any kind of custody hearing. The time wasted in endeavouring to determine which is the better and more caring parent, what should be done about access (the days, times, frequency, conditions, bath-time, feeding time and so on) problems about money, and education of the children. All these require hours and hours and hours of tedious consideration, preparation, aggravation and discussions inside and outside Court. What a waste it all is of human ingenuity and effort which, if channelled towards preserving rather than destroying the marriage, might well have saved it. And all the time the poor child is treated as a shuttle-cock, bounced from one parent, social worker, welfare officer, *au pair*, nanny, or whatever, to the other; living in one house with one parent and spending time in another. It is hardly a surprise that children of divorcees should become unsettled, violent and neurotic. The underlying assumption, as discussed earlier, that one can determine that the child can make do with just one parent is not only mistaken but is totally fraudulent.

Of course, there are exceptions. Of course, there are single-parents – usually mothers, sometimes fathers – who work exceptionally hard and conscientiously to achieve the best for their children. I discount entirely the fact that to some extent their efforts after divorce are inspired by the realization of having failed their children in the first place by splitting up the marriage and state, unhesitatingly, that one should have nothing but admiration for those few – for a few they are – who come through it without having caused their children too many traumas.

As to the difference between a separation and a divorce, I would say that they are quite substantial. In the first place, a separation upholds the principle of the indissolubility of marriage and this is of fundamental importance to the psyche of the spouses and to the views that society comes to adopt about divorce. In the second place, the concept of the family is not only maintained, but safeguarded. And in the third, the separation may serve as a sabbatical, after which the parties might be inclined to adopt a different view of life and of each other, having had time to consider the implications of their conduct, vis-a-vis, the children. Furthermore, it is possible that as a result the love that must have existed before the parties got married is rekindled, almost as if the separation blew fresh air over the smouldering embers of a passion long forgotten.

Maybe the passage of time will enable one or other of the spouses, or indeed both, to see that the action which might have precipitated them into getting divorced was perhaps not so serious, or the faults that were causative of the break-up of the marriage could, with some patience, be tolerated.

How often, especially in the Anglo-American world, a woman rushes to see solicitors when her husband is caught with his pants down. She feels affronted, slighted, and perhaps polluted by that breach of faith. Maybe she ought to think twice before rushing to see solicitors. The same considerations apply, of course, to the man. I appreciate fully that I could be open to the criticism that because I am over 60 years of age, my view of marriage and of the trauma that divorce causes to children is not modern, that I am no longer 'with it'. I suggest, however, that those who are minded to level such criticism at this attempt to engender a debate on the fundamental issue of divorce should spend some time reading an article that appeared in Part 3 of *The Times* of Tuesday 20 July 1999 under the headline 'Parents Should Stay Together, Even If They Don't Love Each Other'. The person interviewed and responsible for this quoted headline was a 15-year-old girl, attending what was stated to be one of the country's premier schools, a horsewoman, who represents both her county and her country.

Her parents divorced when she was five, then ten years later she acknowledged the scars of that event, and argued that if her parents had really loved her, they would not have divorced. 'Parents can't say that divorce does not affect the children. It does, and everybody knows that. It hurts. It hurts knowing that you were not enough to keep a family together. Parents always say they are not leaving because of the children. Is that supposed to make the children feel better? Does that take all the guilt off the child's shoulder? No. It's all rubbish. Children feel that they weren't enough to keep their parents, that their parents didn't love them enough to keep them together.'

The interesting thing about the article is that there was a postscript to it by the young girl's mother. I quote only one sentence from it: 'What she says is true.'

NOTES

1. *Op. Cit.* page 122.
2. London, Macmillan, 1982
3. Duckworth, 1950, page 89; republished, Pelican, 1964, under the title *Sex in Society*.
4. Harper Bros., New York, 1948, page 62.
5. *op cit*, page xx.
6. Century, London, 1997, especially pages 150 to 157.
7. South Illinois University Press, 1930, pages 312, 313.
8. Harper Bros., New York, 1948.
9. *ibid.*
10. *Divorce Won't Help.*
11. *op. cit*, p. 212.
12. *op. cit*, p. 211.
13. *Man and Woman*, London, Walter Scott Publishing Company, 1914

10

Remedies – a personal view

The reader should not expect too much from the title, since I readily admit that it is always easier to identify problems than to provide cures for them and, whilst it is theoretically conceivable that society could put an end to the ever-increasing rate of divorce and its detrimental effects, I fully realize that this cannot be easily achieved in a democracy. So, for the sake of argument, and by way of providing this writer with some 'literary licence', let us assume that the powers of a dictator are at my disposal. I would, accordingly, decree the following:

FIRST DIKTAT

That amongst the subjects in the school 'curricula' there would be the teaching, not only about the physical aspects of sex, but above all about personal relationships and more especially about the significance, the purpose, the difficulties, the traumas and, perhaps, the joys of indissoluble marriage. Incidentally, many, including myself, consider sex education fairly irrelevant. It has been pointed out by K. B. Davis (*Factors of Sex Life for Twenty-Two Hundred Women*[1]) as well as by others, that it is conceivable that the positive results of sex instruction may, in individual instances, be offset by the wholly unintended effect of causing the mind of the child to become preoccupied with matters sexual. The undoubted truth is that young people, more than ever, need a course on marriage.

If one looks at the matter dispassionately, the survival of a marriage requires as much ability, if not more, on the part of the spouses as is displayed by doctors, lawyers, engineers, drivers and others. We have to find money to spend on teaching many subjects in our schools and to provide degrees at university. We even consider nowadays that it is important to teach youngsters 'the facts of life'. The time is not far removed when, in addition to the essential elements of sexual behaviour as understood in the physical sense, we may even wish to teach our children, at an early age, so called sexual techniques.

If you wish to become a doctor, you have to comply with many conditions and spend many years in preparation before you are allowed to practise; if you wish to take a car onto the public road, you have to pass the driving test. And so it goes on. But no tuition, and obviously no tests, are imposed upon those who wish to get married. That is a great pity because if youngsters were taught what marriage really entailed, what its difficulties were, how inevitably there would be disappointments and setbacks, dissatisfaction with the oddities of one's spouse, deficiencies of response, inability to understand, differences of approach; if young girls were made to appreciate some of the obvious reactions of men in all fields; if both the respective spouses were taught not to expect miracles, nor impossible orgasms of the kind described in cheap and nasty literature, not to anticipate performances that are out of this world and in reality are open, in all likelihood, only to a very small percentage indeed of the population of this world; if there were constant sermons on the fact that married life is not a bed or roses, that the grass is not greener on the other side of the fence, and constant reminders of the words of the marriage services of all established religions, at least in the United Kingdom, (namely, that one marries for better or for worse, for richer, for poorer, in sickness and in health and, certainly, until death us do part), it might – but it is true that one can only speculate – still, it might result in the spouses not rushing to see their solicitors at the first sign of misunderstanding, dissatisfaction, insensitivity, or whatever.

Sociologists and politicians would probably counter this respectively by saying that there is no need for what is being suggested because human beings know it already and the State has not got the money for this kind of exercise. As to the former answer, one would say that there is every need, judging by the divorce figures; and as to the latter, well, I make no comment, save to say that it is one of the oddities of our lives that money can always be found by any State to do what the State wants to do and never for what the citizens wish should be done.

A module on married life could become a very easy and inexpensive adjunct to a Social Sciences course, which could be made compulsory. It would cost the State a little more but it would, in all likelihood, save us all a lot of money ultimately.

In this context, it should be borne in mind that, leaving aside illnesses, the four major events in life are birth, the choice of a career, marriage and death. We have no control over birth and death: they will occur no matter what we desire, save in the situation where a person commits suicide, in which event that person controls at which point in time and under what circumstances death occurs. But, exception made for suicide, birth and death are occurrences about which we ourselves need to do very little. We are left with the other two, namely, the choice of a career and marriage.

The modern education system is particularly insistent on giving sixth-formers the widest possible range of advice as to the career they should choose. Indeed, there are established organizations, some of them quite efficient, whose principal business is to interview candidates and determine their suitability for a particular career. Parents spend a lot of time discussing with their children what their future in life is going to be. All in all, we wish them to make informed decisions and try and educate them accordingly. This is right and proper: it is knowledge that may assist us in making a sensible choice.

When it comes to marriage, however, there is nothing of the kind. The State has enshrined in the law the principle that there is a minimum age for marriage. It has ensured that there is a minimum qualifying residence period. Those are the only two meagre requirements which are stipulated by the State for what is probably an even more significant event in a person's life than choosing a career. There is no education, no pre-condition, no insistence of any kind on a trial period. Once a person has decided to get married, the marriage will take place: the formalities are minimal.

It is difficult to determine why this kind of lack of concern persists. It must be obvious to those who govern us that, at least in the United Kingdom, most people are making a conspicuous mess of their marriages: as we now know, more than half those who get married, divorce: it is obvious that they made the wrong choice. And they usually divorce rather quickly, which means that they realize early on that they have made the wrong choice. The quicker the realization, the more likely it is that a proper choice could have been made, given better preparation on the part of the parties to the marriage.

What is needed is greater interest by the State in marriage as an *institution*. Children should be educated as to the obligations and responsibilities engendered by marriage. In a strange sense, it is more important to teach them about marriage than about the facts of life because the facts of life are very often self-evident, whereas the commitment, loyalty, consideration, flexibility, forgiveness, sympathy, understanding, affection, tolerance and determination, all necessary to try and make a marriage work, are anything but self-evident, particularly in a society like ours which is actuated by selfishness, contempt for authority and greed.

We would not allow anyone to practise law, medicine, become a priest, a vet or drive a car, without considerable tuition in the essentials. Why should we blissfully embark upon marriage, theoretically for life at least as far as the marriage ceremony vows are concerned, without some kind of education?

SECOND DIKTAT

That no marriage be solemnized either by the State or by the Church unless the intending parties had firstly recorded their interest in being joined forever in a marital relationship and then had waited a minimum of two years before the ceremony could take place. Even at this point in time, I would wager that if such a rule were applied the number of people getting married would probably be halved within five years. I am not too concerned about what the intending spouses do with their lives and with their sexuality during this two-year period. I have already drawn attention to the fact that sexual experience before marriage is of itself no guide whatsoever to a successful marriage: indeed, quite the reverse.

A very perceptive writer on divorce is A. Alvarez, from whose work we have already quoted. In *Life After Marriage*[2] he claims that his first wedding night had not been a success. Hardly surprising, so he says, since he had met his wife only seven weeks before and had married 'in a dream'. One is bound to wonder whether this is sheer lunacy: it is absolutely essential that one ought not to be dreaming when one gets married!

From an experience of this kind, Alvarez runs a whole philosophy of life and I heartily congratulate him on the success of his second marriage. But as he himself says:[3] 'I was an absolutist of the orgasm before I had had enough experience to ensure even sexual competence.' And that is presumably why, quite aptly, he quotes Socrates: 'If you can get a good wife, you become happy; if you get a bad one, you become a philosopher', which is probably very unkind to Socrates' wife Xantippes.

Nevertheless, Alvarez is anything but blind to reality since, according to him, it is absurd to place too much reliance on sexual attachment. He knows as well as we all do that sexual attachments are notoriously unstable and if we think only of erotic gratification, as most couples seem to be doing nowadays, then the risks of dissolution must increase.

The two-year period has not been chosen at random. It is a compromise between this writer's personal and professional experiences and the finding of Terman's 'Psychological

Factors in Marital Happiness'[4] to the effect that their samplings showed that the highest scores of mean happiness – according to length of engagement for both men and women – were respectively 73.4 and 72.4 in the engagements that had lasted five years or longer. This could be a freak finding, but is confirmed by the consideration that the respective figures were 71.1 and 71.5 for those engagements that lasted between three and four years, dropping to 64.7 and 66.5 respectively for engagements of less than two months. Again, Terman has provided scientific evidence for old concepts like 'marry in haste, repent at leisure'.

THIRD DIKTAT

That no marriage be solemnized unless the parties had both submitted to a medical examination and had been apprised of the results thereof, which they had approved and accepted; and had acknowledged in writing their obligations to maintain each other and the children, if any, by the grant of immediate irrevocable instructions to any employer or bank or other financial institution, where any monies of theirs could at a later date be found, to set aside for the benefit of the spouse and any children, minimum sums determined on the occasion of each budget speech by the State.

FOURTH DIKTAT

I have always subscribed to the view that no man should get married unless he is at least thirty, and no woman unless she is at least in her mid-twenties. Statistically, it is clear that people are getting married at much younger ages than in the past, though the pattern may now be changing. Early marriages are doomed to fail, statistically. Some couples, who were sweethearts in their early teens do, of course, make a success of it: but in my experience, they are few and far between. The lower the age at which the spouses get married, the greater the likelihood of the marriage ending in divorce.

For this reason, if the powers of a dictator were available, I would decree that no man could get married below the age of twenty-five and no woman below the age of twenty.

FIFTH DIKTAT

That the State itself provide each married mother with minimum weekly, monthly or yearly payments, sufficient to maintain her and the child in any event, that is to say, well apart from the earning capacity of the husband, thus emancipating her from whatever psychological subservience she might feel – if she were not earning any money or did not possess any – towards her husband. Similar payments would be made to existing unmarried mothers during any transitional phase of, say, a generation.

Payments of this nature would acknowledge the importance of motherhood both generally, and particularly as far as the State is concerned. They would obviate any need on the part of the mother to go out to work, even discounting the consideration that they would represent a substantial psychological 'boost' for those mothers who, tied to the children and to the kitchen sink, must very often wonder whether their usefulness is, after all, quite so great as our forefathers used to think.

Whilst the primary purpose of the 'recommendations' under this diktat is in fact the recognition of the importance of motherhood, coupled with the practical benefits that in such manner the 'stay-at-home-wife' would obtain, they would achieve the very positive result of ensuring that the mother is in the house, as the pivot of the family, and is not just another worker in society. The payments themselves would continue to be available whilst the child is in full-time education. They would cease, obviously, if the mother went out to work.

You may say that the State cannot afford to finance motherhood. As to this, I would respond by saying that the State appears to be perfectly able always to find funds when it decides that they are needed for specific purposes; and in the second place, that motherhood will become so important that it will be a worthwhile idea to subsidize it.

SIXTH DIKTAT

That the State itself determined that there were two types of marriage, namely an accommodation or companionate marriage and a true one. The parties would be free to choose whether they wished to be joined in marriage for the purpose of keeping each other company or for the purpose of procreating children. The former type of relationship would be purely conditional and dissoluble at will; the latter, indissoluble by definition. The former would automatically transform itself into the latter as soon as a child was born. Put differently, there would be an imposition upon the spouses not to divorce once there were children.

Such a proposal, as indeed the others put forward above, are achievable if people wished to, without any loss to society and indeed with the possibility of substantial gains for it, both spiritual and economic.

There is, however, a great deal of unclear thinking about the situation. Lack of clarity of thought seems to be a common feature of present-day society, fuelled in part by the constant heavy bombardment of communications from the mass media, which tend to highlight the more titillating and less settled developments and ideas, causing utter confusion in the minds both of adults and, above all, of youngsters. As noted earlier, the more extravagant a notion, the more farfetched a hypothesis, the more extreme an expectation, and the more unorthodox the behaviour, especially if it has sexual overtones, the greater the indiscriminate publicity that is given to it. The noise of the bombardment is deafening; the mind can no longer cope.

If there were agreed parameters to judge the news, the latest theory or whatever that is being thrown at people, the position would not be so serious; but there no longer are any. Religious belief, integrity, patriotism, the family, the good, the beautiful, the true, are all values to which our society attaches little, if any, significance. Where they exist, they act as a filter; it is as though from the petrol tank of public news and information, the parameters acted as a carburettor. But the filter is unclean, and clogged; the engine of the mind splutters and grinds to a halt or, if it runs at all, it is a hesitant, uneven march, with the fear that it might pack up completely at any moment. Against such background of muddled and uninspired thinking, it is very difficult to believe that the recommendations set out here would achieve any success.

It is a bit like our attitude towards certain forms of modern art. There are people who, when they see a blob of paint on a canvas, find it difficult to understand what it means; and if they had to speak the truth, when asked, would be inclined to say that they did not like it or perhaps even that it was rubbish and a waste of space or public funds. Nevertheless, they are afraid to express such a belief, of turning round and calling the blob rubbish, lest they should be termed non-conformist or should be considered ignorant and not 'with it'. The bluff is thus perpetuated and nobody is willing to call it. No one wishes to go up to the painter of that particular blob and ask him to explain what it means, lest he should be taken to task as a Philistine.

The same consideration applies to many other situations in our society but, above all, it prevails where divorce is concerned. Divorce is now so entrenched a tendency that its eradication would require extremely hard and unpopular measures, which no government would dream of taking. Nobody wishes, or indeed, dares to ask those Members of Parliament or of society who think that divorce is a good idea, how they justify such a belief when viewed against the damage it causes to children, its unsettling effect on society, the cost to us all, and so on. Can you imagine the votes that would be cast for any candidate who was ever heard to suggest, no matter how faintly or indistinctly, that he was against divorce? Can you see any political party uttering any sound whatsoever (other than towards greater liberalization) about divorce, in their manifesto? And yet, it is not as if I am canvassing for anything that is objectionable *per se*. If it is proposed that children should be educated not merely to the facts of life as they are called, but to their responsibilities in marriage, there is nothing untoward about that. If it is proposed that people should think long and hard before getting married, are we not merely repeating the wisdom of our grandparents? If it is proposed that the children should be taken into account when parents decide to divorce and suffer as a result, are we not saying something with which most people would be inclined to agree?

An incredible number of restrictions upon individual freedom already exist in our society, which we accept more or less gladly in the interests of the well-being of the community as a whole. We now can hardly drink if we intend to drive; we are no longer free to drive along our roads because they are choked by traffic; we are not allowed to smoke in some public places; we are not permitted to burn a certain type of fossil fuel; we are subject to a plethora of laws which interfere with our freedom of action, if not of thought; our home is no longer our castle, since as has been calculated recently, there are at least seventeen classes of public or quasi-public officials, from the Customs man to the gas man, who have right of access to it whether we wish them to enter or not; it is now suggested that we should all be tested for AIDS. And so it goes on. Against this background, what price individual freedom?

If we accept – and we must, as law-abiding citizens – that these restrictions on our unfettered judgement to do as we wish are imposed for the welfare of society as a whole, why should we not accept that certain types of marriage should be indissoluble? This is a matter where the choice of the individuals and their happiness or success are totally irrelevant since it is the well-being of society as a whole which is paramount.

NOTES

1. Davis, Kathrine & Ayer, B., New York, 1977
2. *op. cit.*
3. *op. cit.*
4. New York, McGraw-Hill, 1938

11

What next?

The outlook is not rosy. The principal reason is that one can never put the clock back. In a different sense from the context in which the expression was first used[1], freedom once conferred cannot be revoked. We cannot nullify the emancipation of women, we cannot expunge from their way of thinking their newly-acquired freedom; and apart from any other consideration, such emancipation has become much too convenient for all of us and, above all, for the State. If women do decide on a new role for themselves, no amount of wishful thinking by men is going to frustrate their purpose.

It, therefore, makes a great deal more logical sense to focus on them rather than men, for it is women who will have to decide where they want to go and what they wish to become: theirs is the choice, but it is not going to be an easy one to make.

Torn between the myth of absolute equality, which rises phoenix-like from the ashes of two world wars, and her historical background of natural compliance and enforced subservience, it is easy for woman to over-react and discount entirely the higher function assigned to her by nature. A balanced view needs to be taken and this is not made any easier by the obvious inequality that exists at the moment between the sexes. The present-day superior features of woman, to which attention has already been drawn as a very real potential motive for divorce, are almost forcing woman to convince herself that it is she who should take the initiative in order to put right what men have obviously done wrong. In so doing, it is making us all forgetful of her primary role, which is being gradually depreciated.

As woman turns away from being a mother, so she brings about changes in the natural order of things which, because of their violent nature and unexpected consequences, both women and men find it difficult to cope with. It is a very awkward balance to be preserved and no amount of bickering between the sexes will prove at all useful in this context.

When confronted with the uncertainties that the emancipation of woman is creating for her, sociologists point out her strength and the fact that no-one knows what woman is capable of achieving. This observation has been made from time to time by ardent feminists and was given its logical formulation by John Stuart Mill when, in 1869, he wrote his essay 'The Subjection of Women'. He argued that men had gone out of their way to enslave the minds of women by inculcating into them obedience and fear and by educating them only to develop those qualities which men appreciated in women, namely submissiveness, dependence, attractiveness, and so on.

There is obviously an element of truth in the observation, but to go on from that, as he does, that '. . . the nature of women is an eminently artificial thing – the result of forced repression in some directions, unnatural stimulation in others', seems to ignore completely the fact that there are some women who are perfectly happy in the role with which they are more commonly associated and that is a role which our society may well have to care for in a particular fashion.

I have recently re-read John Stuart Mills' essay on the 'subjection' of women and whilst I am in broad agreement with its aims, I object to some of its rationalizations. Where, for example, he argues that no man can claim to understand any woman, no matter how many he may have known and of what kind, simply because such understanding is not open to man 'until women themselves have told all that they have to tell', I could not help feeling that this was a fairly negative, if not impotent, approach to judgement formulation.

On the other hand, no matter who is right – that is to say, whether it be true that we have not heard the full story of women and there are greater revelations in store for us – or whether it may not be proper to consider that all of us have different roles to perform in society – it is an undoubted fact that we shall all have to determine what we expect women to do.

Accordingly, it is said that we have to develop a 'new morality' on the principle that any society must improve because, if it does not, it ends up by going backwards. An existing new morality is said to stem from the principle of individual freedom, for it is only in freedom that one achieves happiness. This is, in fact, the theme of John Stuart Mill's essay, and it is one of its fundamental weaknesses because it proceeds from a premise that has been repeatedly challenged, particularly by Freud, namely that there is no difference between men and women.

It seems to me that we must question the validity of the statement, that it is only in freedom that one can find happiness. But surely that depends on the person involved, the circumstances, the moment in history. Clearly, the peasants under Louis XIV thought that they were most unhappy; and they probably were. They fought for freedom and they established those qualities of libertarianism upon which Western civilization of the twenty-first century is still based. But political freedom is one thing, personal freedom is a totally different concept.

To think of calling for a new morality is nonsense, not least because there is a fundamental stability in the concept of morality which is above all change. Whether it be enshrined in the Ten Commandments or whether it be part of the reasoning, thinking, logical man's view of life, there are certain tenets which remain unalterable and they form the core of any kind of morality. What is needed is not a new morality but a more careful application of the existing and long-standing moral concepts to the new situation that has arisen as a result of woman's independence.

Woman will simply have to make up her mind what she wishes to do and to be. If, as some scientists have suggested, her androgen levels are high, either because it is the way she is born or because, maybe she has been injected with drugs that may have raised them, then let her by all means compete with man, if competitiveness is what distinguishes her, and do anything that man can do. A lot of women are doing just that and are proving very successful at it.

Clearly, if all women decided not to procreate and be mothers but to compete with men by behaving like men, our race would disappear. It is obvious, therefore, that the perpetuation of the species, the continuation of the life of our society and of our planet is dependent not only on the survival of the fittest, as Darwin put it, but on the survival of woman's procreative ability and availability. It is that availability that the State will have to ensure and I have suggested that one of the principal ways of ensuring it is to pay women for being mothers and one of the most important ancillary ways of achieving that result is to decree that divorce is not available to spouses once they have children.

The State can no longer ignore the particular problem. Figures published by the government actuary's department in January 1999 confirm the long-held belief that marriage is ceasing to have any significance. Also because people can no longer see any financial benefit to getting married. Currently, 55% of those aged sixteen or over are married, compared to 66% about eighteen years ago. It is estimated that by 2021 only 44% of women will be married, and fewer than one in ten men. What will happen, according to these projections, is that over the same period the number of couples cohabiting will double from the present 1.56 million to over 3 million. Marriage will be a thing of the past.

It goes without saying that the State may not wish to perpetuate a situation where the family unit carries any weight, and decide to eliminate the father completely. This is a policy decision which this writer is unlikely to influence in any manner whatsoever, save to observe that if the present trend of divorce continues unabated, the patriarchal family will completely disappear. We will then be left either with a matriarchal type family (the noun 'family' is used here in a very loose sense because, as already pointed out, it cannot apply to the situation where a woman brings up a child without a man) or a set-up where both mother and father disappear from the picture and as soon as the child is born, he is brought up by strangers on behalf of the State. This is an idea put forward by Plato over two thousand years ago and it still has not caught on. Let's hope it never will.

It seems, however, that Bertrand Russell was absolutely right when in 1929[2] he made the point that '... cooperation in the serious business of rearing children, and companionship through the long years involved, bring about a relation more important and more enriching to both parties than any that would exist if men had no responsibility for their children'.

It is that cooperation between husband and wife which has so far been of fundamental importance for our society. It has, in effect, redeemed the profanity and triviality of sexual relations and provided the justification for the institution of marriage. Our society will have to decide whether it wishes marriage to continue as an institution, or whether it considers that means can be evolved whereby the long arm of the State will ensure the rearing of children.

On the other hand, if a long-term view is taken of the interests of our children and their progeny, we must surely have to admit that, realistically, there is no substitute for the family as a social, economic and emotive unit, where husband and wife support each other in their different roles, whatever they may have chosen them to be, and cooperate to bring up their children in the belief that marriage is for life, that duties are as important as rights and that the unbridled assertion of one's individuality and expectations of happiness is self-defeating.

If this image were upheld by the State with the same eagerness with which it endeavours to uphold – unsuccessfully, so far – the dignity and the independence of woman, we might have a society that was preferable to the one in which we live at the moment, where our parliamentarians were chosen because of their integrity and abilities rather than through the colour of their party badges, where the law was respected through conviction rather than fear, where women were honoured because of their importance and standing rather than through liberalizing legislation; a society where violent crime, cruelty to animals and children, and sexual abuse of the grossest and most unnatural kind would be the exception rather than the rule.

NOTES

1. Ndhwana -v- Hofmeyr. Appellate Division, South Africa Supreme Court, 1937.
2. *Marriage and Morals*, London: Unwin, 1929 & 1961

APPENDIX

The American experience

It is a fact that, after Russia, the United States of America has the highest divorce rate in the world. It stands at 4.6 per 1,000, which means in practical terms, that more than 50% of marriages end up in divorce.

There is equally no doubt that the American public has throughout the years manifested its concern at the high rate of divorce. Reference has already been made in the Preface to certain statistical data and it would be somewhat beyond the scope of this work to provide a detailed history of divorce in the USA, also because a number of American writers, male and female, have made extensive studies of the problem, a number of which I have referred to or quoted throughout this study.

It may, however, be useful to briefly trace certain relevant developments in the present context. The Puritans claimed that the first divorce in the New World occurred in Massachusetts in 1639. The ground of divorce was one that is rarely used today, namely bigamy. The unfortunate wife did manage to get all the property, her husband was fined, placed in the stocks, and apparently – the final indignity, it seems – exiled to England.

The seventeenth and eighteenth centuries witnessed a certain amount of fornication and inter-racial adultery, which was probably inevitable, given the freedom that the Americans claimed for themselves, not only in political, but also in social terms. But we have to wait until 1880 for the concern about divorce to express itself. It was in that year that the National Divorce Reform League was founded, when the Commerce Department in one of its reports highlighted the fact that one in sixteen marriages was failing. This was – for the USA – a historic high. The divorce bandwagon rolled on, compounded by the problems brought about by the Second World War, and glorified in the 1960s when the sexual revolution gave it the respectability that it lacked, say, even fifty years before when, although common, divorce was still considered somewhat shameful.

The State of Nevada made history when it passed its lenient divorce laws and it began to attract couples eager to by-pass the rather more stringent requirements which prevailed in other States of the Union. In those other States, divorce could be obtained easily, but one of the parties had to prove that the other had been at fault, in terms of their conduct, either because of adultery, or insanity, or bestial conduct, and so on. Broadly speaking, the grounds of divorce through 'misconduct' of one of the parties could be equated with those prevailing in England, namely adultery, desertion, cruelty, unsoundness of mind, sodomy, bestiality, rape.

The campaign for more liberal divorce laws to give effect to new sociological views and rampant feminism had been gathering momentum over the years, and it was in 1969 that the then Governor of California, Ronald Reagan, appended his signature to the first 'no-fault' divorce laws. California set the example, Iowa followed in 1971, as did many others, despite efforts by the Catholic Church (who in 1968 introduced the Marriage Encounters Counselling Programme) and Jimmy Carter (who, in 1977, asked Congress to curb the tax advantage of 'living in sin'). The pressure by women's movements was becoming irresistible and the divorce rates kept rising.

Throughout the 1970s and 1980s, arguments were raised about the possibility of either increasing or reducing the free availability of divorce through the tax system, but one has to wait until 1987 for the first major criticism of the no-fault divorce laws. This was contained in the book *The Divorce Revolution*[1] by the Stamford University sociologist Lenore Weitzman, and was reinforced four years later by San Francisco psychologist Judith Wallerstein who, in *Second Chances*, made it quite clear that the impact of divorce on children was much more dramatic than even she had recorded a little earlier in *Surviving the Break-Up*, a fundamental text to which extensive reference is made in a Chapter 5.

The family values debate gathered a little steam in the 1990s and the targeting of no-fault divorce continued, both by politicians and by some sociologists, and 'men of the cloth'. The politicians were accused, by the more liberal-minded and by feminists, of supporting family values solely in order to feather their own caps and as electioneering posturing, the sociologists who expressed reservations about no-fault divorce were criticized for having previously supported it and priests were told that the freedom of the individual was to be paramount.

Even so, the divorce rate remained high and although the debate continues on whether the no-fault divorce laws should be repealed and, in any event, it should be made much more difficult to dissolve a marriage freely entered into, there do not seem to be any concrete signs that the general American public believes that its freedom to divorce should be fettered. According to the National Centre for Health Statistics in 1994, there were 1.2 million divorces in the United States.

Everybody believes the studies by Judith Wallerstein showing that divorce has a detrimental effect on children – but nobody is prepared to accept that the right to divorce should be sacrificed. A CBS News – *New York Times* poll in May 1995 did show that 78% of the population viewed divorce as a major cause of a 'decline in personal values among the American people' and this was thought to be a wonderful step forward, until March 1996 when two-thirds of those responding to an ABC News poll still maintained that divorce was the best option if a couple could not get along, even though there were children. In other words, in common with their British cousins, Americans realize that divorce is damaging where there are children, but are not prepared to do anything about it.

The attitude is all the more difficult to understand because it is recorded that after Michigan enacted its no-fault divorce laws in 1972 the divorce rate climbed from 6.7 per 1,000 population in 1970 to 9.7 in 1980. A later study by the University of Oklahoma showed that only three years after no-fault divorces were introduced in the early 1970s, the divorce rate increased in forty-five of the fifty American States; and so much of this evidence was accepted in Michigan when a Bill was put forward that would restore the old requirement of proving fault in cases where only one spouse is seeking to divorce. Put differently, no-fault divorce would disappear and couples could only get separated if one of them had behaved improperly. The suggested 'faults' would include desertion, drug or alcohol abuse, physical or mental abuse, infidelity or a prison sentence of three or more years.

Suggestions are still made from time to time in the USA as to what can be done to reduce the rate of divorce. Some say that before getting married, engaged couples should take part in an educational programme, others that the marriage licence fee should be increased, others still that there should be counselling before a divorce goes through (although the value of premarital counselling seems to be discounted completely), and the Quakers have perhaps adopted the most practical approach by stipulating that when a couple want to divorce, they should face members of the Congregation who would try and ask them the kind of questions that they are quite clearly incapable of facing themselves.

Coupled with the fact that there is a national campaign for same-sex marriage, that in 1993 the Hawaii Supreme Court decreed that gay marriages could be legal unless a lower Court could show a compelling State interest in banning them and with a concern that cohabitation was increasing so fast that marriage would disappear, it is clear that the Americans are concerned about family values, but cannot do much about it. Indeed, it is interesting that some gay lobbyists claim that same-sex marriages should be sanctified for the very reason that divorce statistics are so horrifying, and the divorce rate is so high. They go so far as to claim that the State, having an interest in fortifying stable relationships, should support those relationships whether they are heterosexual or homosexual.

Nevertheless, the picture is not entirely bleak. The Counsel on Families in America, sponsored by the Institute for American Values, has recently (1995) highlighted the fact that the divorce revolution has failed and that the obvious tide that is flowing against marriage should be off-set by a change in the law that would make marriages more difficult to dissolve. Indeed, in 1996 William Galston, Professor of Public Affairs at the University of Maryland, proposed a compromise. He suggested a two-tier system, one applying current law for couples who have no children, and a new one that eliminates the unilateral no-fault option for couples with dependant children, arguing that the well-being of the children should be paramount, even where it conflicts with the desires of their parents.

The conflict between libertarians and moralists is often expressed as a conflict between realism and idealism. Constance Ahrons[2] is very keen on making the point that we have to cater for human fallibility. The well-known statement by anthropologist Margaret Mead, 'I didn't have any failed marriages, I've been married three times, and each marriage was successful', keeps cropping up; but it is quite meaningless.

I would suggest that it is the proponents of absolute freedom in matters sexual who are idealists because they are chasing a dream, namely, perfection or happiness in human relationships. A cynic might argue that the mere frequency with which one changes one's sexual partners, or one seeks release from one relationship or the other, is not even idealism, but neuroticism.

One can, like some therapists, write books outlining the basic stages that most marriages go through, one may examine current sexual behaviour to see how it has evolved from the days of the caveman, one can try and give advice to couples on how to go through rough periods in their lives, and one can reach the conclusion that instead of arguing about divorce, about the rights and wrongs of the parties, we should accept it and make it as fair as possible. At the end of the day, however, there is no point in even comparing the USA with the United Kingdom, for the developments in the two countries are parallel. The Anglo-American world suffers from the same malaise.

Increasingly, in the United States activists for the repeal of the no-fault divorce legislation are trying to shift the blame from the parties themselves to therapists and clergy. The former are accused of encouraging people, who are unhappy, to divorce, rather than to face up to the problems which are causing their unhappiness, and the latter for marrying people too easily and for failing to underline the importance and the responsibilities engendered by marriage.

There is the usual polarization of views between those who maintain the sanctity of marriage and those who believe that divorce is a panacea and that if and insofar as the State felt that there were too many divorces, the fault would seem to be not in the concept of divorce, but in the fact that the parties were not educated to develop better skills in handling both marriage and divorce.

Finally, it is worth noting that it was an American psychologist, John Watson, who in 1927, predicted the end of marriage within half a century. His prediction has not yet come true, possibly because there are a number of forces and bodies fighting hard to preserve marriage. For example, in 1968 the Catholic Church started its 'marriage encounters' programme which led on to the present 'Retrouvaille' programme. Practically at the same time, the American Association for Marriage Counselling was founded, a precursor of today's American Association for Marriage and Family Therapy.

'Marriage Savers' and 'The Pairs Foundation' back up The American Association for Marriage and Family Therapy and the Family Research Council, as well as the Institute for American Values. But then, against that trend, in 1973 the Episcopal Church updated its policy so that a marriage no longer had to be annulled for a specific reason before the church would remarry a parishioner.

Nevertheless, some comfort may be derived from the fact

that according to 'Public Agenda On Line' (telephone interview March 1997) 80% of 950 American adults think that divorce is sometimes wrong, 62% of 2004 adults believe it should be made harder (March 1998) and according to CBS News of September 1997, 89% of 1051 adults interviewed over the phone decided that intercourse with someone other than one's spouse is always wrong. The finding sits rather uncomfortably with the high rate of adultery in American society.

For the record, since 1970 the number of American couples who cohabit has multiplied by a factor of three. From 1970 to 1994 the number of never-married persons doubled from 21.4 million to 44.2 million, and the number of divorced Americans quadrupled from 4.3 million to 17.4 million.

According to the Stepfamily Association of America (based on the 1990 census), 1 out of 3 Americans is now a step-parent, stepchild, a step-sibling, or some other member of a step-family; more than half of Americans today have been, are now, or will eventually be in one or more step situations, and that the most common step-families where children reside are stepfather families or combined stepfather-stepmother families. In this latter case, his children from the prior marriage typically do not reside in the step-family.

NOTES

1. Weitzman, Lenore, Free Press, 1987
2. *The Good Divorce; Keeping your family together when your marriage comes apart*, Bloomsbury, 1994

POSTSCRIPT

The hypocrisy of successive British governments when dealing with the family is nauseating and makes a mockery of natural justice at its most basic level. The most recent example (1999) is a Green Paper entitled 'Supporting Families'. The choice of wording itself would be laughable if it were not pitiable. Some of the steps the government proposes to take as outlined in this Green Paper cannot be considered as supportive of the family in any shape or form. It has been decided to abolish the Married Couple's Tax Allowance. This is clearly a blow to marriage. Coming at the same time as the ending of tax relief on divorce maintenance payments, this makes the position of the families of divorced parents not a very happy one, to say the least.

It has been calculated, for example, that the removal of the tax relief on divorce maintenance payments, which will start in April 2000, could prove expensive for some divorced fathers with teenage children, and might amount to as much as £4,000 a year per child. The former wives would also lose money because if they are not in employment and have no other income, they will cease to be entitled to claim a refund of their personal allowances, as well as those of their children, in addition to the basic rate tax which has been deducted by the father before payment was made.

On the other hand, this is good news for lawyers, because it will result in more business for them: fathers whose earnings have fallen and who can no longer afford to make maintenance payments at their previous level, will inevitably be tempted to challenge the original maintenance order on the basis that there has been a change in their financial position.

These inconsistencies of approach are mentioned for the sake of the record. It is somewhat outside the terms of reference of this book to delve too deeply into the destruction of the family caused by successive governments; it is even outside the sphere of the subject of divorce. Put differently, one could theoretically have a divorce law in circumstances where all kinds of steps are taken by the State to buttress the family. What we now have is a divorce law which is reinforced by the systematic destruction of the family.

Select Bibliography

The amount of writing on divorce, the family and related topics is enormous. Titles appear at regular intervals, as books or as papers; much can also be traced on the Internet.The output in the USA is particularly voluminous and noteworthy, especially in the 'self-help' type of publication.

ADLER, Felix, *Marriage and Divorce*, New York, McClure, Phillips & Co., 1905

AHRONS, Constance, *The Good Divorce*, Bloomsbury, 1994

ALVAREZ, Alfred *Life after Marriage: scenes from divorce*, London, Macmillan, 1982

ANDERSON, C.P., *Father: the Figure and the Force*, New York, Warner 1983

ANDERSON, Digby, (Editor) *The Loss of Virtue*, Social Affairs Unit, 1992

ANDERSON, Digby, (Editor) *This Will Hurt*, Social Affairs Unit, 1995

ANDERSON, Michael, *A History of the Western Family 1500-1914*, Penguin, 1980

ARGYLE, Michael, *The Psychology of Happiness*, Routledge, 1987

BABER, Ray Erwin, *Marriage and the Family*, 2nd edn., McGraw-Hill, 1953

BASSERMANN, Lujo, *The Oldest Profession: a History of Prostitution*, translated from the German by James Clengh. Baker, 1967

BEMENT, Katharine Davis, *Factors in the Sex Life of Twenty-two Hundred Women*, New York and London, Harper & Brothers, 1929

BENYON, Francis, *The Sex Code*, Weidenfeld & Nicolson, 1988

BERĠHES, L., *Lone Parenthood and Family Disruption*, London, Family Policy Studies Centre, 1993

BERGLER, Edmund, *Unhappy Marriage and Divorce: a study of neurotic choice of marriage partners*, with an introduction by A.A.Brill. New York, International University Press, 1946

BERGLER, Edmund, *Divorce won't help*, New York, Harper, 1948

BERNARD, Jessie, *The Future of Motherhood*, Penguin, New York, 1974

BLUM, M., *The Daycare Dilemma*, Lexington, Massachusetts Heath, 1983

BLUSTEIN, Jeffrey, *Parents and Children, the Ethics of the Family*, Oxford University Press, 1982

BOWMAN, Henry Adelbert, *Marriage for Moderns*, 3rd edn., McGraw-Hill, 1954. Previous edn., 1948

BRADSHAW, J. and MILLAR, J., *Lone-Parent Families in the UK*, London, HMSO, 1991

BRANDON, Ruth, *The New Women and the Old Men*, London, 1989 Secker & Warburg

BRIGGS, Asa, *The Age of Improvement*, London, 1959

BRYANT, Keith, *A Biography*, London, Hogarth Press, 1962

BURGESS, Ernest Watson & COTTRELL, Leonard S. jr., *Predicting Success or Failure in Marriage*, New York, Prentice Hall, 1939

CAINE, Barbara, *Victorians Feminists*, Oxford, 1992

CARR, Gwen B., *Marriage and Family in a Decade of Change*, Philadelphia, Addison Wesley, 1972

CHESSER, Eustace, *Is Marriage Necessary?*, W.H.Allen, 1974

COMFORT, Alex, *Sexual Behaviour in society*, Duckworth, 1950

DICKINSON, R.L. & BEAM, Lura , *A Thousand Marriages*, Baltimore, 1931

DOMINIAN, Jack, *Marital Breakdown*, Longman & Todd, 1968

ELLIS, Albert, *Sex without guilt*, New York, Lyle Stewart, 1958

ELLIS, Albert, *The Encyclopaedia of Sexual Behaviour*, Heinemann Medical, 1961. [Originally published, Hawthorn, 1961]

ELLIS, Havelock, *Studies in the Psychology of Sex*, Volumes 1 to 7 Philadephia, F.A. Davis Company, 1894

ELLIS, Havelock, *Man and Woman*, London, Walter Scott Publishing Company, 1914

FERRI, Elsa, *Growing Up in a One-parent Family*, Concern 20, 1976

FERRI, E., *Step Children*, Slough, NFER-Nelson, 1984

FERRIS, Paul, *Sex and the British*, Mandarin, 1994

FIELD, Frank *Losing out*, Oxford, Basil Blackwell, 1989

FLUGEL, J.C., *The Psycho-analytic study of the family*, London, Hogarth Press, 1921

FRANCOEUR, Robert, *Utopian Motherhood*, New York, Doubleday, 1970

FRIEDAN, Betty, *The Feminine Mystique*, London, Gollancz, 1963

FUKUYAMA, Francis, *The Great Disruption: Human Nature and the Reconstruction of Social Order*, Profile Books, 1999

GILDER, George, *Sexual Suicide*, London, Millington, 1974

GILDER, George, *Wealth & Poverty*, London, Buchan, 1982

GILLIS, John, *For Better or for Worse*, Oxford University Press, 1985

GLOVER, Edward, *The Psycho-pathology of Prostitution*, 2nd edn., Institute for the study and treatment of Delinquency, 1957 [Previous edn.1945]

GLOVER, Edward, *The Roots of Crime*, London, Allen & Unwin, 1960

GOODALL, Richard, *The Comfort of Sin*, Folkestone, Renaissance Books, 1995

GOODE, William J., *After Divorce*, New York, Free Press, 1956

GOODSELL, Willystine, *Problems of the Family*, New York, Appleton Century Company, 1929

GORER, Geoffrey, *Exploring England's Character*, Phillips SG, 1956

GORER, Geoffrey, *Sex and Marriage in England Today*, Nelson, 1971

GROVES, E.R., *The Marriage Crisis*, New York, Longmans, Green and co., 1928

HALL, M.P., *The Social Services in Modern England*, 1952

HARDWICK, Elisabeth, *The Simple Truth*, Virago, 1987

HARVEY, Eleanor, *The Other Woman*, London, Elm Tree Books, 1971

HASKEY, John, *Population Trends*, Vol. 91, Spring, 1998

HASTE, Cate, *Rules of Desire*, London, Chatto & Windus, 1992

HEDBITCH David and ANNING, Nick, *Porn Gold: inside the pornography business*, London, Faber, 1988

HOGHUGI, Masud, *Break-up: a map of intimate relationships*, London, Optima, 1989

HOOPER, Douglas and ROBERTS, John, *Disordered Lives – an interpersonal account*, Longmans, 1967

HUMPHRIES, Steven, *A Secret World of Sex*, London, Sidgwick Jackson, 1988

ISAACS, Susan, *The Psychological Aspects of Child Development*, Published in association with University of London Institute of Education by Evans Bros, 1949. First Published, 1935

Children and Parents: their problems and difficulties, Routledge & K.Paul, 1968. Originally published as 'Troubles of Children and Parents', Methuen, 1948

Childhood and After: Some Essays and Clinical Studies, Routeledge, 1999

ITZIN, C., *Splitting Up: Single Parent Liberation*, London, Virago, 1980

JACOBSON, Paul, *American Marriage and Divorce*, New York, Rinehart & Co., 1959

JAMES, Oliver, *Marriage and Society*, Hutchinson, 1952

JAMES, Oliver, *Britain On The Coach: Why We're Unhappier Compared With 1950 Despite Being Richer*, Century, 1997

JEHU, Derek, *Beyond Sexual Abuse: therapy with women who were childhood victims*, Wiley c., 1988

JOAD, Cyril Edwin Mitchinson, *Thrasymachus or The Future of Morals*, New York, E.P.Dutton & Co., 1925

JUNG, Carl, *The Wise Men of India*, 1944

JUNG, Carl, *Marriage as a Psychological Relationship*

KEY, Ellen, & SOFIA, Carolina *Love and Marriage*, New York and London, G.P. Putnams' sons, 1911

KIERNAN, Kathleen, *Family Change and Future Policy*, J. Rowntree Foundation, 1990

KIERNAN, K.E. and ESTAUGH, V., *Cohabitation: Extra Marital Childbearing and Social Policy*, London, Family Policy Studies Centre, 1993

KIERNAN, Kathleen, Centre of the Analysis of Social Exclusion, LSE, September, 1997

KIERNAN, K., and MUELLER, G., *The Divorced and Who Divorces?*, CASEpaper, CASE/7, Centre for Analysis of Social Exclusion, May, 1998

KINSEY et al, *The Sexual Behaviour of The Human Male*, Philadelphia, W.B. Saunders Company, 1948

KINSEY et al, *The Sexual Behaviour of The Human Female*, Philadelphia, W.B. Saunders Company, 1953

KLEMER, Richard Hudson, *Marriage and Family Relationships*, New York & London, Harper & Row, 1970

LATEY, William, 'The Tide of Divorce', Harlow, Longmans, 1970

LECKY, W.E.M., *The History of European Morals*, New York, Longmans Green, 1911

LEECH, P., *Children First*, Harmondsworth, Penguin Books, 1994

LESLIE, Gerald R., *The Family in Social Context*, New York, Oxford University Press, 1967

LOCK, Harvey J. *Predicting Adjustment in Marriage*, New York, Holt Reinhard & Winston, 1951

LUNDBERG & FARNHAM, *Modern Woman (The Lost Sex)*, New York, Harper, 1947

LYNDON, Neil, *No More Sex War (the failures of feminism)*, Sinclair Stevenson, 1992

MACE, David, *Does Sex Morality Matter?*, London, Rich & Cowan, 1943

MACE, David *Encyclopaedia of Sexual Behaviour*, New York, Hawthorn Books, 1961

MACKENZIE, Norman & Jeanne (Eds), *The Diary of Beatrice Webb*, Cambridge, Massachusetts, 1983

MALINOWSKI, B., *Sex and Repression in Savage Society*, Routledge & Kegan Paul, 1960 [Original edition 1927]

MALINOWSKI, Bronislaw, *Argonauts of Western Pacific: an account of native enterprise and adventure in the archipelagos of Melanesian New Guinea*, London, Routledge and Kegan Paul, 1978. [Originally published: London, Routledge, 1922]

MANTEGAZZA, Paolo, *Fisiologia della Donna*, Treves, Milan, 1893

MARRO, Antonio, *La Pubertà studiata nell'uomo e nella donna in rapporto all'antropologia, alla psichiatria, alla pedagogia ed alla sociologia*, Fratelli Bocca, Turin, 1897

McCORMACK, Mary, *Divorce and After: Fathers Tales*, London, McDonald Optima, 1990

McGREGOR, Oliver Rossi, *Divorce in England*, Heinemann, 1957

McRAE, S., *Cohabiting Mothers*, London, Policy Studies Institute, 1993

MILL, John Stuart, *The Subjection of Women*, Cambridge (Mass); London, M.I.T. Press, 1970. [Originally published, London: Longmans, Green, Reader and Dyer, 1869]

MILLET, Kate, *Sexual Politics*, Virago, 1985

MURRAY, Charles, *Losing Ground American Social Policy, 1959/80*, Basic Books, 1989

MURRAY, D.W., *Poor Suffering Bastards: An Anthropologist Looks at Illegitimacy*, Policy Review, No. 68, Spring 1994

NEILL, Stephen, *The Breakdown of the Family*, Oxford University Press, 1949

PHILLIPS, R., *Putting Asunder: A History of Divorce in Western Society*, New York, Cambridge University Press, 1988

POLICY STUDIES INSTITUTE REPORT – London, November 1998

PORTER & HALL, *The Facts of Life*, Yale University Press, 1995

PYM, Thomas Wentworth, *Sex and Sense*, London, Nicolson & Watson, 1938

REED, Angela, *The Challenge of Second Marriage*, London, Plume Press & Ward Lock, 1973

REED, Angela, *The Woman on the Verge of Divorce*, London, Plume Press & Ward Lock, 1974

RIESMAN, David, *The Lonely Crowd*, Yale University Press, 1950

ROYAL COMMISSION REPORT, 1850

ROYAL COMMISSION REPORT, 1949

ROYAL COMMISSION REPORT, 1951

ROYAL COMMISSION REPORT, 1957

RUBINSTIEN, Helga, (Ed.), *The Oxford Book of Marriage*, Oxford University Press, 1990

RUSSELL, Bertrand, *Marriage & Morals*, London, Unwin, 1929 & 1961

RYLE, Anthony, *Neurosis in The Ordinary Family*, London, Tavistock Publications, 1967

SACHS, Jonathan, *Faith in the Future*, Darton Longman & Todd, 1995

SANCTUARY, G. & WHITEHEAD, C., *Divorce and After*, London, Gollancz, 1970

SHORTER, Edward, *The Making of the Modern Family*, Collins, 1975

SOCIAL TRENDS 29, Office of National Statistics, 1999

SPEAK, S., CAMERON, S. & GILROY, R., *Young Single Fathers*, London, Family Policy Studies Centre, 1997

SPENDER, Dale *Women of Ideas*, Pandora, London, 1982

HALL, Stanley G., *Morals*, New York, Appleton & Co., 1920

STEPHENS, Sir James Fitzjames, *Liberty, Equity and Fraternity*, London, Smith, Elder & Co., 1873

STONE, Lawrence, *Road to Divorce*, Oxford University Press, 1990

STOTT, John Robert Walmsley, *Divorce, The Biblical Teaching*, London, Church Pastoral Aid Society, 1972

TERMAN, Louis M. et al *Psychological factors in marital Happiness*, New York, McGraw Hill Book Company, 1938

UNWIN, J.D., *Sex and Culture*, London, Oxford University Press, 1934

WADSWORTH, M.E.J., *Roots of Delinquency*, New York, Barnes & Noble, 1979

WALLERSTEIN, Judith S. & KELLY, Joan Berlin *Surviving the Break-up: how children and parents cope with divorce*, London, Gran McIntyre, 1980. [Also published: New York, Basic Books, 1980]

WALLERSTEIN, Judith S. & BLAKESLEE, Sandra, *Second Chances: Men, Women and Children a Decade After Divorce*, London, Corgi, 1990

WALLER, Willard, *The Old Love and the New; Divorce and Readjustment*, New York, H. Liveright, 1930

WEEKS, Jeffrey, *Sex, Politics, and Society*, London, Longmans, 1981

WEITZMAN, Lenore, *The Divorce Revolution*, New York, Free Press, 1987

WELLS, Herbert George, *The New Macchiavelli*, Penguin, 1966

WELLS, H.G., *An Englishman Looks at the World*, London, Cassell, 1914

WELLS, L. & RANKIN, J.H., *Families and Delinquency: Meta-analysis of the impact of Broken Homes*, Social Problems, Vol. 38, No.1, 1991

WERNER, E. & SMITH, R., *Vulnerable But Invincible*, New York, McGraw Hill, 1982

WEST, D.J., *Delinquency: Its Roots, Career and Prospects*, London, Heinemann, 1982

WESTERMARCK, E. *The History of Human Marriage*, London, Macmillan, 1922

WOLF, Sula, *Children under Stress*, London, Allen Lane, the Penguin Press, 1969

WOLFF, Virginia, *Professions for Women*, in collected essays, New York, 1967

WOODWARD, E.L., *The Age of Reform 1815-1817*, Oxford, 1938

WOLLSTONECROFT, Mary, *Vindication of Women*, London, Penguin Books, 1891

WOOTTON, Barbara, *Social Science and Social Pathology*, London, Allen & Unwin, 1959

MONTAGU, Mary Wortley, *Woman not Inferior to Man, or, a short and modest vindication of the natural right of the fair-sex to a perfect equality of power, dignity and esteem with the men by Sophia, a person of quality*, reprinted Bentham Press, London, 1975

WYNN, Margaret, *Fatherless Families*, London, Michael Joseph, 1964

ZIMMERMANN, Carle Clark & FRAMPTON, Merle E., *Family and Society; a study of the sociology of reconstruction*, New York, D. Von Nostrand company, 1935

INSTITUTE OF ECONOMIC AFFAIRS (HEALTH & WELFARE UNIT) PUBLICATIONS IN THE CHOICE IN WELFARE SERIES

DAVID, Miriam (Ed.), *The Fragmenting family: Does it matter?*

DAVIES, John (Ed.), *The Family: Is It Just Another Lifestyle choice?*

DENNIS, Norman, *Rising Crime and Dismembered Family*

HIMMELFARB, Gertrude, *The Demoralisation of Society*

LEVIN, Michael et al, *Equal Opportunities: A Feminist fallacy*

LISTER, Ruth (Ed.), *Charles Murray and the Underclass – The Developing Debate*

MORGAN, Patricia, *Farewell to the Family*

MORGAN, Patricia, *Who Needs Parents?*

MURRAY, Charles, *The Emerging British Underclass*

MURRAY, Charles, *Underclass: The Crisis Deepens*

QUEST, Caroline (Ed.), *Liberating Women . . . From Modern Feminism*

WHELAN, Robert (Ed.), *Just a Piece of Paper?*

NB. The Bibliography referred to in the above publications is extensive and exhaustive.

Index